Barack Obama and the Myt
Post-Racial America

The 2008 presidential election was celebrated around the world as a seminal moment in U.S. political and racial history. White liberals and other progressives framed the election through the prism of change, while previously acknowledged demographic changes were hastily heralded as the dawn of a "post-racial" America. However, by 2011, much of the post-election idealism had dissipated in the wake of an ongoing economic and financial crisis, escalating wars in Afghanistan and Libya, and the rise of the right-wing Tea Party movement.

By placing Obama in the historical context of U.S. race relations, this edited book interrogates the idealized and progressive view of American society advanced by much of the mainstream literature on Obama. *Barack Obama and the Myth of a Post-Racial America* takes a careful look at the historical, cultural, and political dimensions of race in the United States, using an interdisciplinary analysis that incorporates approaches from history, political science, and sociology. Each chapter addresses controversial issues such as whether Obama can be considered an *African American* president, whether his presidency actually delivered the kind of deep-rooted changes that were initially prophesized, and whether Obama has abandoned his core African American constituency in favor of projecting a race-neutral approach designed to maintain centrist support.

Through cutting edge, critically informed, and cross-disciplinary analyses, this collection directly addresses the dimensions of race in American society through the lens of Obama's election and presidency.

Mark Ledwidge, Senior Lecturer in the Department of History and American Studies, has been appointed Vacation Visiting Research Fellow at the prestigious Rothermere American Institute (RAI), University of Oxford. Dr Ledwidge is also a founding member of the Arts and Humanities Research Council Network on the Presidency of Barack Obama, and his research focuses on the relationship and impact of African Americans on U.S. foreign policy. It provides a unique insight into the effect race and ethnicity has had upon U.S. foreign policy, as well as highlighting how race has been relatively excluded from mainstream theories in international relations.

Kevern Verney is a Professor in American History and Associate Dean in the Faculty of Arts and Sciences at Edge Hill University in the United Kingdom. Together with Professor Inderjeet Parmar and Dr Mark Ledwidge he is currently a co-organizer of the Barack Obama Research Network funded by the Arts and Humanities Research Council.

Inderjeet Parmar currently teaches in the Department of International Politics at City University London, having for the previous 21 years taught at the University of Manchester. His latest book is *Foundations of the American Century: Ford, Carnegie, and Rockefeller Foundations in the Rise of American Power*. He is President of the British International Studies Association and Chair of the Obama Research Network.

Routledge Series on Identity Politics

SERIES EDITOR: Alvin B. Tillery, Jr., *Rutgers University*

Group identities have been an important part of political life in America since the founding of the republic. For most of this long history, the central challenge for activists, politicians, and scholars concerned with the quality of U.S. democracy was the struggle to bring the treatment of ethnic and racial minorities and women in line with the creedal values spelled out in the nation's charters of freedom. In the midst of many positive changes, however, glaring inequalities between groups persist. Indeed, ethnic and racial minorities remain far more likely to be undereducated, unemployed, and incarcerated than their counterparts who identify as white. Similarly, both violence and workplace discrimination against women remain rampant in U.S. society. The Routledge series on identity politics features works that seek to understand the tension between the great strides our society has made in promoting equality between groups and the residual effects of the ascriptive hierarchies in which the old order was rooted.

Barack Obama and the Myth of a Post-Racial America

Edited by
Mark Ledwidge
Kevern Verney and
Inderjeet Parmar

NEW YORK AND LONDON

First published 2014
by Routledge
711 Third Avenue, New York, NY 10017

and by Routledge
2 Park Square, Milton Park, Abingdon, Oxon OX14 4RN

*Routledge is an imprint of the Taylor & Francis Group,
an informa business*

© 2014 Taylor & Francis

Library of Congress Cataloging in Publication Data
Barack Obama and the myth of a post-racial America / edited by Mark
Ledwidge, Kevern Verney, Inderjeet Parmar.
pages cm. — (Routledge series on identity politics)
1. Obama, Barack. 2. United States—Politics and government—2009-
3. United States—Race relations—Political aspects. 4. Post-racialism—
United States. I. Ledwidge, Mark, author, editor of compilation.
II. Verney, Kevern, 1960- author, editor of compilation. III. Parmar,
Inderjeet, author, editor of compilation.
E907.B377 2013
973.932092—dc23
2013012391

ISBN: 978-0-415-81393-8 (hbk)
ISBN: 978-0-415-81394-5 (pbk)
ISBN: 978-0-203-06779-6 (ebk)

Typeset in Sabon
by Taylor & Francis Books

Printed and bound in the United States of America by Publishers Graphics,
LLC on sustainably sourced paper.

Contents

Introduction

A Dream Deferred?

Kevern Verney

The election of Barack Obama on November 4, 2008, was a key moment in the history of the United States. It attracted enormous popular and scholarly interest, not merely in America but around the world. The inspirational ideas and rhetoric of the Obama campaign generated high expectations of change. Euphoric supporters believed that his election would bring an end to the discredited, unpopular policies of the Republican administration of George W. Bush. At the same time, Obama promised to break down traditional party lines, bringing together members of both major political parties, Republicans and Democrats, in support of a new, bipartisan, political agenda.

Domestically, it was hoped that Obama could stabilize and revive an American economy beset by the nation's worst financial crisis since the 1930s. His election was also seen by some commentators as the final fulfillment of Martin Luther King's vision that individuals should be judged by the content of their character rather than the color of their skin, as King articulated so memorably in his speech at the March on Washington on August 28, 1963 at the height of the Civil Rights Movement. Charismatic, youthful in appearance, and offering the hope of a better tomorrow, Obama seemed to embody many of the characteristics associated with the martyred civil rights leader.

On the international stage, the 2009 award of the Nobel Peace Prize to the new President reinforced the hope that his administration would mark the start of a more enlightened era in American foreign relations. In particular, that American diplomacy would place greater emphasis on "soft power," the use of persuasion and positive incentives to achieve U.S. objectives, combined with more sensitivity to the views of others, as opposed to overreliance on "hard power," embodied in hardline rhetoric, the threat of sanctions, and the use of military force. Moreover, Obama's own life experience encouraged the belief that, more than any of his predecessors in the White House, he would be able to empathize with the hopes and fears of Muslim and Third World nations.

In sharp contrast to such high expectations, the political realities confronting the new President could hardly have been more discouraging. From the outset his administration faced unprecedented domestic and foreign policy challenges, including the worst national and international economic crisis since the 1930s and involvement in two costly unresolved foreign wars, in Iraq and Afghanistan. The victory of Obama notwithstanding, race remained a divisive issue in society with African Americans and other ethnic minority groups continuing to suffer acute socioeconomic deprivation, high crime levels, and racial prejudice.

It was clear that the success or failure of the Obama administration in addressing these problems would have profound implications, not just for the citizens of the United States, but also for governments and peoples around the world. In 2010 the three editors of this currrent volume took the lead role in the formation of a new international research network on the Obama presidency. Funded by the Arts and Humanities Research Council (AHRC) in the United Kingdom, the network was established to bring together scholars from a diverse range of subject areas—including economics, history, international relations, media, politics, and the social sciences—as well as journalists, government officials, and business leaders to study the political philosophy and policies of the new president as they evolved during his time in office.

Over the last three years the Obama network has organized a variety of public lectures and symposia events, as well as a schools conference. These have been hosted and supported by a range of partner institutions and organizations, to which, together with the AHRC, the editors are deeply indebted for the time, funding, and resources they contributed to make the work and aspirations of the network possible. They include the Eccles Centre at the British Library in London, the Foreign and Commonwealth Office, the Institute for the Study of the Americas (ISA), City University, London, Edge Hill University, the University of Manchester, the Rothermere American Institute at the University of Oxford, the University of Middelburg, and the University of Warwick.

A wide range of important issues were discussed. Did the election of Obama as the first African American President of the United States mark the end of race as a significant factor in U.S. political life, or was it the result of a unique set of circumstances? To what extent were the challenges confronting the Obama administration comparable to those experienced in the 1930s, and what lessons could be learnt from the policies introduced by the then Roosevelt administration to meet them? Would Obama be able to maintain his bipartisan philosophy given the controversial nature of his proposed domestic reforms? Did such initiatives, like the economic stimulus package and the "Obamacare" health provision reforms, provide effective remedies for the problems they sought to address, and what would be their long-term impact on U.S. politics and society? In international relations, did the Obama administration mark a decisive change in U.S. diplomacy, or simply the use of new rhetoric to pursue existing policies?

In the immediate aftermath of Obama's election a number of commentators hailed his victory as proof that America was now a post-racial society and as such the final chapter in the nation's long civil rights struggle. Encapsulating this mood of optimism, MSNBC news host David Gregory declared a "son of an African father, a Kenyan, and a white mother from Kansas, in a country that was stained by slavery, is now president of the United States, the ultimate color line has been crossed." Unfortunately, during Obama's first term of office a succession of high-profile race-related incidents seemed to cast doubt on this sanguine outlook.[1]

In February 2009 the publication in the *New York Post* of a cartoon with a chimpanzee signing the President's new economic stimulus package into law was widely condemned as being racially offensive and the paper was forced to issue a public apology. In July that year the so-called "Gatesgate" affair led to another media furore when the distinguished African American Professor Henry Louis Gates was arrested outside his Harvard home by a white police officer sent to investigate a reported break-in. Asked to comment on the incident by a journalist, Obama condemned the actions of the law enforcement officer as "stupid," prompting claims by some right-wing commentators, including *Fox News* host Glenn Beck, that the president was himself racially prejudiced in his views on white people. Obama retracted his statement and brought diplomatic closure to the story by holding a much publicized "beer summit" for all the parties involved at the White House.[2]

In September 2009 former President Jimmy Carter sparked new controversy by claiming that opposition to Obama's health care reforms was, in part, motivated by racism. Vigorously rebutted by political opponents and dismissed by the President himself, Carter's comments were viewed sympathetically in many African American communities. In another incident two months later internet giant Google was forced to apologize when a racist image of Michelle Obama was posted on one of its websites. In an ugly and offensive caricature, the face of the First Lady was morphed into that of a chimpanzee to resemble one of the characters from the Hollywood *Planet of the Apes* film franchise.[3]

In January 2010 U.S. Senate majority leader, Harry Reid, was forced to apologize for comments that he had made in a book that Obama had won the 2008 election because he was "light skinned" and "with no Negro dialect." The same month the discovery of a hanged effigy of Obama in Plains, Georgia, the home town of Jimmy Carter, arguably provided at least partial vindication for the former President's earlier remarks.[4]

In June 2010 Jake Knotts, a Republican state senator in neighbouring South Carolina, disrespectfully described President Obama as a "raghead" in a remark with obvious racial connotations. In July it was the U.S. State Department that became a subject of criticism when it dismissed an African American employee, Shirley Sherrod, after media reports that she had made racist comments at a dinner hosted by the nation's oldest and best-known civil rights organization, the National Association for the Advancement of Colored People (NAACP). It soon became clear that such claims were inaccurate and that video clips of her remarks on the internet had been deliberately edited to distort the views she had expressed. Sherrod was duly vindicated by being reinstated in a new job and also given a formal White House apology. The same month, in what was clearly a high-profile media period for the NAACP, at its annual convention in Kansas City the Association passed a resolution condemning what it described as "racist elements" in the grassroots Tea Party Movement that had developed in opposition to the policies of the Obama administration.[5]

In February 2012 Trayvon Martin, an unarmed African American teenager, was shot dead by George Zimmerman, a neighbourhood watch organizer in a gated housing community in Sanford, Florida. Zimmerman was initially released without charge by the police, prompting a public outcry led by prominent African American spokespeople, including Reverend Al Sharpton and Reverend Jesse Jackson. President Obama himself commented that "When I think about this boy, I think about my own kids. ... If I had a son, he would look like Trayvon." An online petition set up by Trayvon's mother collected over 2.2 million signatures calling for Zimmerman's arrest. Under intense public and media pressure the Florida authorities finally charged Zimmerman with second degree murder with a trial date set for June 2013.[6]

The essays in this collection were inspired by the first Obama network symposium held at Edge Hill University, in 2011, to consider the present-day state of U.S. race relations and the impact that Obama's presidency would have on the racial outlook and policies of the United States, both at home and abroad. They include extended versions of papers originally given at the symposium as well as additional essays specially commissioned for this volume. Their publication in 2013, coinciding with the 50th anniversary of Dr King's "I have a dream" speech, is particularly apposite. The various contributors highlight both the progress that has been made in race relations since the 1960s, and also the distance that yet remains to be traveled before the United States can truly be characterized as a post-racial society.

In Chapter 1, Mark Ledwidge assesses Obama's presidency in the context of American history and with reference to theoretical frameworks on the ideology, structures, and deployment of power in the United States. He addresses the key question of to what extent Obama, or any individual president, can meaningfully act as a catalyst for change given the wider cultural, economic, social, and political constraints operating within American society.

Carl Pedersen discusses the extent to which the 2008 election highlighted two competing visions of what it means to be American. One, rooted in a "backlash national identity" was "socially conservative, largely white and conservative Christian" with its geographical strength in "non-urban areas of the U.S." The other was progressive, more cosmopolitan in outlook and composition and strongest in metropolitan America. Looking at the issues of voter registration and health care reform, he examines the ways in which these two groups have each sought to appropriate the nation's past to present themselves as the true defenders of the American political and historical tradition.[7]

Robert Busby analyses the difficulties confronting the Republican Party in the 2008 campaign as a result of Obama's unique position as the first non-white candidate to be nominated for the presidency by either of the two main political parties. He argues that the McCain campaign never managed to develop a successful strategy for dealing with the challenges posed by Obama's African American identity. The party fatally resigned itself to the fact that it could never win over African American voters together with large sections of the non-white electorate. Moreover, in failing to develop a coherent and credible critique of Obama's candidacy, the Republicans lacked the means to effectively undermine the sense of public euphoria created by the Democrat's promises to deliver hope and change.

Focusing on the Democratic Party strongholds of the Northeast, Kevin J. McMahon challenges the claims advanced by political scientists Donald Kinder and Allison Dale-Riddle that Obama's winning margin in 2008 was significantly reduced because of racial factors. Studying the election in an historical context, he argues that it would have been difficult, if not impossible, for any Democratic challenger for the presidency to have bettered Obama's performance in the region. Moreover, he contends that the reverses suffered by the party in the Northeast in the 2010 mid-term elections rather than being a result of "racial resentment," as argued by Kinder and Dale-Riddle, can be explained by more predictable and less controversial factors—low voter turnout, the number of "swing districts" up for election, and the state of the economy.[8]

Heidi Beirich and Evelyn Schlatter consider the serious and neglected topic of the rising level of racially motivated crimes and proliferation of race hate websites during the first Obama administration. Disturbingly, they highlight the fact that the largest and oldest white supremacist website in the United States, Stormfront, reputedly saw a sixfold increase in online traffic in the immediate aftermath of election night in 2008. They point out that the number of recorded anti-black hate crimes in the United States rose from 2,658 in 2007 to 2,876 in 2008, an 8 percent increase. Obama himself was granted Secret Service protection earlier in the election campaign than any other presidential candidate because of the fear that there might be attempts on his life. After the election he received more death threats than any previous president-elect. By 2011 there were over 1,000 recognized race hate groups in the United States compared to 602 in 2000. "Committed racists," as Beirich and Schlatter chillingly observe, are "not quietly accepting their fate."[9]

Rogers Smith and Desmond King contrast the stark racial inequalities in almost all areas of present-day U.S. society—crime, employment, education, housing, health care, and income—and contrast this with the marginalization of race in the 2008 election. They explain this paradox as a result of both political ideology and necessity within the two main political parties and assess the challenges confronting Obama in addressing racial injustice and inequalities during the course of his presidency.

Kevern Verney looks at the growing concerns in the United States about rising immigration levels, most notably from Mexico. Such fears have been increasing since the early 1990s with heightened public awareness of the profound demographic changes taking place in the nation. It is now commonly recognized that by 2042, if not earlier, white Americans will for the first time in the history of the United States comprise less than 50 percent of the population. The election of Obama in 2008 and his re-election in 2012, on both occasions with a minority of the white vote, have been seen as an early indication of the political consequences of such change. Verney examines these claims and considers the views expressed by leading conservative commentators on immigration and places them in the context of similar anxieties expressed by native white Americans during the "great wave" of immigration between 1880 and 1914. He concludes that this historical experience suggests that the alarming predictions made by current advocates of tougher immigration controls, like Pat Buchanan, are overstated. In particular, they exaggerate the sense of collective identity in immigrant communities and underestimate the continuing capacity of the United States to facilitate their cultural assimilation.

Lisa García Bedolla reflects on the policies of the Obama administration towards the Latino community. Contrary to the views of some right-wing critics that he extended preferential treatment to Latino voters for electoral gain, she argues that his first term of office did not mark a significant departure from the previous George W. Bush administration. Indeed, the level of immigrant repatriations significantly increased under Obama. Looking at the four areas of public policy of greatest concern to the Latino community—education, housing, health care, and immigration—she argues that, like his recent Democratic and Republican predecessors, the new President engaged in "mariachi politics"—symbolic gestures toward Latino voters, but without any meaningful policy initiatives.[10]

Chapters 9 and 10, by Lee Marsden and Michael Krenn, respectively, examine Obama's foreign policy record. They both conclude that, in spite of widespread hope that his election would mark a new, more enlightened, era in U.S. relations with the Third World and Muslim countries, his administration, in fact, saw no significant departure from traditional policies and attitudes. This was reflected in Obama's strong pro-Israel outlook, the U.S. boycott of the United Nations World Conference against Racism, the increasing use of drone attacks in Afghanistan and Pakistan, and the failure to close the Guantánamo prison camp—despite a pre-election pledge to shut it down. Marsden attributes these failings to the nature of U.S. political institutions and the policymaking process, which perpetuate the pursuit of a foreign policy that is "institutionally racist." Krenn emphasizes Obama's personal accountability, in particular his "nearly absolute silence on the international implications of race."[11]

In a concluding postscript on the 2012 elections, Inderjeet Parmar reflects on the foreign policy prospects for Obama's second administration, arguing there is likely to be little change as, his personal life history notwithstanding, the President has fully internalized the values of the traditional foreign policy establishment. Nirmal Puwar and Sanjay Sharma continue this theme, exploring the paradox that in his background and outlook Obama is "an outsider who is simultaneously an insider" and consider the impact this had on both the 2008 and 2012 election campaigns.[12] Lee Marsden considers the impact of Mitt Romney's Mormonism on the 2012 campaign. He concludes that although 2012 did not turn out to be the "Mormon moment" it was the Republican's conservative social policies rather than his faith that contributed more to his electoral defeat.[13]

Notes

1 David Gregory quoted in J.K. White, *Barack Obama's America: How new conceptions of race, family, and religion ended the Reagan era* (Ann Arbor: University of Michigan Press, 2009), p. 213.

2 BBC News, "NY Post sorry for 'Obama' cartoon," February 20, 2009, http://news.bbc.co.uk/1/hi/world/americas/7900963.stm; BBC World Service, "Race row after arrest of professor," July 28, 2009, www.bbc.co.uk/worldservice/news/2009/07/090728_us_race_row_nh_dm.shtml.

3 BBC News, "Carter says Obama row is 'racist'," September 16, 2009, http://news.bbc.co.uk/1/hi/world/americas/8258011.stm; BBC News, "Michelle Obama racist image sparks Google apology," November 25, 2009, http://news.bbc.co.uk/1/hi/world/americas/8377922.stm.

4 BBC News, "Harry Reid apologises for 'light-skinned' Obama remarks," January 10, 2010, http://news.bbc.co.uk/1/hi/world/americas/8450402.stm; BBC News, "Effigy of Obama hanged in U.S. town," January 4, 2010, http://news.bbc.co.uk/go/pr/fr/-/1/hi/world/americas/8438852.stm.

5 Guardian.co.uk, "South Carolina's Republican mud-wrestling: 'ragheads' and affairs," June 4, 2010, www.guardian.co.uk/world/richard-adams-blog/2010/jun/04/south-carolina-republicans-ragheads; BBC News, "White House sorry for Shirley Sherrod 'racism' firing," July 21, 2010, www.bbc.co.uk/news/world-us-canada-10716237; NBC News.com, "NAACP condemns racism in Tea Party," July 14, 2010, www.nbcnews.com/id/38234502/ns/politics/.

6 BBC News, "Trayvon Martin: Obama says teenager's death a tragedy," March 23, 2010, www.bbc.co.uk/news/world-us-canada-17492445; BBC News, "Who are Trayvon Martin and George Zimmerman?," April 11, 2012, www.bbc.co.uk/news/world-us-canada-17682245; BBC News, "Change.org petition site targets UK campaigners," May 14, 2012, www.bbc.co.uk/news/technology-18033968.

7 See p. 27.

8 See p. 76.

9 See pp. 80–1, 82, 84.

10 See p. 134.

11 See pp. 148, 165.

12 See p. 191.

13 See pp. 205, 208–9.

1 Barack Obama: First African American President

Continuity or Change

Mark Ledwidge

Fearing that publicly raising racial issues will undermine the president in the eyes of white voters, African Americans appear to have struck an implicit pact with Obama. Even as we watch him go out of his way to lift up other marginalized groups (such as gay Americans) and call for policies that help everyone, we've accepted his silence on issues of particular interest to us. In exchange, we get to feel symbolic pride at having a black president and family in the White House.

Fredrick Harris

This chapter will provide critical insight and analysis pertaining to the impact of race on the Obama presidency and American political culture, while making broader claims regarding the racial dimensions of American power. It maintains that the failure to accredit racial power with a central role in shaping American history has created a conceptual blind spot that has encouraged an idealized and distorted view of American history[1] and the American creed. The chapter will also discuss the pluralist, statist, and elitist theories of American power and introduce a racial theory of American power that should be used in conjunction with the aforementioned theories. The chapter also questions the degree of change that Obama's stewardship has ushered in and evaluates whether Obama can be considered an African American president. Last, it both debunks and invalidates the assumptions that Obama's 2008 election represented the beginning of a post-racial phase of American history. Overall, the chapter will demonstrate that Euro-Americans created a racialized polity that has defined African Americans' domestic status and bequeathed to them sociopolitical and economic disadvantages that still persist today.[2] Conversely, given that Obama has defined himself as an African American,[3] it is important that we conduct an analysis of the racial status of the African American community in conjunction with the Obama presidency.

White Supremacy

The controversy concerning the existence of legacies of white supremacy has been compounded by mainstream historians (predominately Euro-American) and American intellectuals and academics who have promoted a benign, libertarian, depiction of America. In short, according to Vitalis, "white supremacy is not generally discussed either as an historical identity of the American state or an ideological commitment on which the 'interdiscipline' of international relations is founded."[4] In addition, social and political scientists have neglected to construct an accurate theoretical model of American society that foregrounds the racial dimensions of American power,[5] such that "political science theorists" (such as Dunleavy and O'Leary's *Theories of the State: politics of liberal democracy*; Birch's *Concepts and Theories of Modern Democracy*; and Marsh and Stoker's *Theory and Methods in Political Science*) omit substantive coverage of racial theories, in their analysis of American history and American political culture … which is problematic, since contemporary sociologists Omi and Winant have demonstrated the importance of racial issues.[6] Even the excellent work of C. Wright Mills fails to account for the racial dimensions of the power elite and although William Domhoff does a better job there is still room for additional research.

Theories of American Power

Most theories of American power have accorded the pluralist, statist, Marxist, and elitist models varying degrees of legitimacy. In regards to pluralism, most pluralists argue that power in the United States is diffuse and that organized groups have the potential to organize to meet their interests. It is assumed that the dispersal of sociopolitical and economic power prevents the concentration of power in any singular group.

Pluralism

Pluralism suggests that America's separation of powers and the federal system, which allows for states' rights, prevents the concentration of power in the American political system. However, the pluralist argument does not adequately account for African Americans' historical exclusion from the political system or the denial of their right to vote. Of course, the denial of the vote obviously precluded African Americans' ability to elect an African American president until the late 20th and early 21st century. Unfortunately, pluralism generally ignores the existence of racial power in America and the manner in which Euro-Americans were able to stifle African Americans' ability to compete by institutionalizing racial conventions that justified their marginalization.

Statism

This argues that the state is not inherently benevolent and neither does it provide equal protection for all social groups.[7] Given the American state's historic commitment to the protection and privileging of Euro-American interests, one would expect statists to account for the state's tendency to neglect the interests of the non-white population.[8] In addition, Euro-Americans' predominance within the state apparatus has also facilitated the adoption of policies aligned with white interests. Again, the conceptual frameworks of statism neglect to mention that in actuality the state and American politics are contested arenas and despite the "state's role in the strategic realignment of the color-line statists must also highlight the state's role in perpetuating the color-line in both foreign and domestic politics."[9]

Marxism

Marxism maintains that economics is the core facet of sociopolitical relations. Marxism suggests that class conflict, not race, is the central feature of American power. Marxists contend that capitalism is based on the exploitation of the proletariat by the bourgeoisie.[10] While exceptionalists argue against the existence of a rigid class structure in America, there is scope to argue in terms of class differentiation especially when one accounts for the huge discrepancies in terms of wealth that exist in the United States.[11]

Marxism does confer a relative degree of autonomy to the state but it also suggests that the state is beholden to the interests of the ruling class.[12] Marx also suggests that economic dominance is augmented via the ruling class's production of ideas and culture, which is predicated on "producing ideas that reinforce the status quo."[13] Marxism's insistence on the existence of a concentration of power in a particular class and the ruling class's ability to promote and pursue ideological hegemony is important; since African Americans are in some regards analogous to a subordinate class. Nonetheless African Americans' racial identity often supersedes their class status.[14] Marxism's shortcoming pertaining to its depiction of American power is its failure to indicate how Euro-American racism has fashioned a sociopolitical context where white privilege and Euro-American dominance has defined the sociopolitical status of African Americans irrespective of their economic or class status.[15]

Although somewhat less developed or less popularized by social scientists, elitism provides a plausible critique of U.S. society. Elitism suggests that a small and powerful cadre utilizes its sociopolitical, economic and institutional capacity to secure its own interests.[16]

While Mills and Domhoff have demonstrated the existence of a power elite that possesses the ability to bypass aspects of the democratic system while asserting its own interests, Mills ignores race while Domhoff has instigated an important discourse in relation to the racial identity of America's elite. More work needs to be done to apply this analysis more broadly within the social sciences and even within the humanities. In short, race's impact regarding both the identity and actions of the power elite needs to be widely acknowledged. That is, America's power elite has generally been part of the white Anglo-Saxon Protestant community (WASP).[17] In addition, the values and worldview of America's power elite may have expanded due to challenges from below in the 20th and 21st century but, Obama notwithstanding, America's elite is still overwhelmingly white and arguably still adheres to a WASP worldview.[18]

To a certain extent, the reactions to the election of Obama are indicative of the perception that the "identity of state executives affects the substance of state policies."[19] Consequently, the racial identity of the WASP elite is assumed to have provided privileges for white America and to have shaped the character of domestic and foreign policy.[20]

Controversial or not, it has been suggested that American race relations between Euro- and African Americans are comparable to a form of racialized colonialism.[21] It has been argued that the "political oppression and economic exploitation of the Black community ... stand at the heart of any form of colonialism"[22] and that African Americans have had political decisions thrust on them "by the colonial masters ... [whose] ... decisions ... [were] ... handed down directly or through a process of 'indirect rule',[23] via 'blacks who are responsive to the white leaders.'"[24]

The theory argues that Euro-American racial hegemony is a central feature of U.S. society,[25] which determines the relative power of African Americans in relation to white America.[26] The theory maintains that white racism insured its institutional control over the key decision-making apparatus in America.[27] Hence the U.S. state has been an instrument of white power, which has generally promoted and protected white interests.[28] This theory argues that African Americans have been politically and economically colonized by whites.[29] In short, the economic and political dominance of white America over blacks is assumed to constitute white colonial dominance over blacks

> on the basis of the division and separateness of the black and white American communities as well as the gross political and economic inequalities which inhere between them. We believe that the relationship of the white to the black community can be more accurately and productively described as that between an imperial nation and its economically dependent colony.[30]

Thus black interests are defined and determined by elite whites who either cajole or force blacks into accepting their dictates. This theory does account for an anticolonial challenge from African Americans whose relative success would also depend on their own actions.[31]

Of course, the presence of Obama complicates this argument; nevertheless, the recruitment and/or leadership of members of subordinate classes is an established practice of hegemonic groups. Again the relative inability of Obama to protect and promote the interests of African Americans raises key questions regarding his power to depart from America's racial conventions.[32] Essentially, the presence of African Americans in the superordinate class would correspond to penetration from below and the outward appearance of equality in order to sustain the legitimacy of what would amount to a racially stratified society. In particular, the "presence of just a few African-Americans in previously white-dominated elite positions may provide stability to the social system as a whole, thereby decreasing the likelihood of the kind of collective action that created opportunities for individual mobility in the first place."[33] Subsequently, the election of Obama may actually legitimize notions of a color-blind society without making it a reality.[34] While the racial colony paradigm challenges the liberal and pluralist depictions of U.S. society the continuities regarding the existence of a racial divide requires that social and political scientists explore, validate, or invalidate the racial colony thesis. Regardless of the existence of Obama, the tendency to ignore or deny the intractable character of U.S. race relations makes it more likely that racial conflict will continue to plague America[35] as opposed to a peaceful transition into a post-racial society with change that meets the collective interests of all Americans.

Ironically, it is the racial dimension of American power that contrasts with the historic and seemingly improbable election of the 44th president of the United States.[36] Obama's election was historic because it contravened the idea that people of African descent were not competent enough to occupy the lofty office of the presidency.[37] Hence African Americans' elation regarding Obama's election was partly inspired by their ongoing quest for sociopolitical and economic equality dating back to 1619.[38] Given the dramatic departure from the status quo, optimists and political opportunists chose to interpret Obama's inauguration as the dawn of a new era in American history in which the racial divisions of the past were seemingly being overcome.[39] Consequently, for many in the liberal establishment, and even conservatives on the right, Obama's presidency has been perceived as the fulfilment of Dr. King's dream regarding the elimination of color discrimination in the United States.[40]

Indeed, political analysts and scholars drew congratulatory comparisons between Jesse Jackson's run for the presidency and Obama's.[41] It was duly noted that while Jackson's presidential bids in 1984 and 1988 attracted white voters, Barack Obama's campaign amassed 43 percent of the white vote, which is indicative of a major change in American voting patterns.[42] The fact that Obama obtained 95 percent of the black vote and 43 percent of the white vote was indicative of both demographic changes and whites' willingness to vote for Barack Obama.[43] Whereas Jackson made overt calls for racial and social equality and the redistribution of wealth[44] that were comparable with the political values of Dr. King, Obama's candidacy utilized a post-civil rights race-neutral approach,[45] which avoided controversy and favored a cosmopolitan approach consistent with mainstream ideals, the suggestion being that aside from his "A More Perfect Union" speech Obama avoided racial issues in order to ensure his victory.[46]

One could argue that Obama adopted a centrist approach favored by Euro-Americans that was based on the observation of Anatol Lieven that even "conservative White Americans are no longer [overtly] racially exclusionary in the old sense."[47] In short, Obama's approach was not too dissimilar to that of Republicans and conservative Americans, which essentially avoids any meaningful discussion of race. The question is why? The answer is complex but is connected to the nature of American society.

The Duality of the Past

A broad survey of (American and Western) mainstream academic accounts of American society have emphasized a positive and benign interpretation of America's historic birth.[48] The formation of the American republic is celebrated as a progressive political project where the genius of European intellectuals and the pragmatism of the founders rejected the rigid class cleavages and the monarchical systems of old Europe.[49] Henceforth, the separation of powers and the federal system is credited with avoiding a tyrannical concentration of political power and redefining notions of governance while safeguarding and protecting the rights of the governed.[50]

Although it is clear that the Declaration of Independence, the American Constitution, and the Bill of Rights instituted a more expansive model of freedom, the original intent was to safeguard the interests of (elite) propertied white males. In short, America's early political history was characterized by an elitist model of freedom. However, the price of these new freedoms would be paid for by the native population and Africans. The near-extermination of Native Americans allowed the immigrant populations from Europe to take physical possession of Native American land,[51] while the brutal exploitation of African labor paved the way for America's rapid territorial expansion and her rapid economic growth.[52]

In short, the liberties extolled by the founders, along with the conceptualization of a racialized concept of manifest destiny, facilitated the American state's propagation of legally sanctioned oppression which, like freedom, became intertwined within the fabric of the American polity.[53] Despite the American state's modern interventions in defence of racial equality (especially in the 1950s and 1960s) its past is replete with centuries of sanctioned racial inequalities.[54] Nonetheless, as Desmond S. King and Rogers M. Smith have demonstrated, the American state apparatus has employed a chameleon-like approach to race where it has been both savior and oppressor,[55] although for the most part the state has remained the custodian of Euro-American interests. Thus, one acknowledges the merit in the view of both Dr. King and Malcolm X that America's (including the U.S. government's) treatment of African Americans should be seen through the dual lens of the American Dream and the American Nightmare.

Characterizing American Political Culture

Just as America ignores Abraham Lincoln's racism, Dr. King's castigation of American militarism and the imperialistic tendencies of American capitalism,[56] the racial under- and overtones of the 2008 presidential elections were frequently overlooked in favor of a self-celebratory and largely uncritical analysis.[57] The central facet of the (popularized) Obama narrative is that a so-called biracial man (of limited means), the progeny of a liberal white woman from Kansas and a black Muslim from Kenya, became the president of the United States.[58]

The implied meanings are postcard simple: one, that the Obama phenomenon could only occur in the United States; two, that the civil rights reforms of the 1960s and the elasticity of the American polity made it possible;[59] three, that America is headed towards a progressive future in which racial divisions will cease to exist.[60] As a result, Obama's victory has been fastened to the modern American Dream, which attributes color-blind politics, meritocratic principles, social mobility, and personal perseverance as the foundation of Obama's success.[61]

In short, some Euro-Americans have skilfully used the post-racial analysis to suggest that Obama's success is evidence that the collective oppression of African Americans is essentially over.[62] The logic that follows from this is that the relative status of African Americans is indicative of their individual or collective efforts to succeed, as opposed to the existence of racial barriers.[63] Nevertheless, despite the desire to weave Obama's rise into mainstream America's blinkered interpretation of the American Dream, a critical accounting of the facts questions whether American political culture and U.S. society has lived up to the meritocratic ideals extolled by American exceptionalists.[64]

A central facet of the problem is the (functional) historical amnesia that white America has strategically employed to avoid dealing with race.[65] According to Attorney General Eric Holder "in things racial ... [Americans have] ... always been and continue to be ... a nation of cowards."[66] For example, the inherent contradictions related to the original sins of the European Colonists and the Founding Fathers are generally ignored by most Euro-Americans and many African Americans in order to engage in "wholesome celebrations" such as the "4th of July," while the positive family values extolled during Thanksgiving celebrations seem somewhat hollow when one considers that by saving the Pilgrims the Native Americans ultimately sealed their own fate.[67]

American Heroes

When one considers that American icons such as Washington and Jefferson not only owned but engaged in the sexual exploitation of their *female property*, it is patently dishonest for American historians to portray them as the paragons of civic virtues.[68] The fact that Obama's narrative on the American Dream includes idealized depictions of the founding fathers is indicative of America's inability to interrogate its own racial mythology. Consider the case of Jefferson and Sally Hemings, his so-called mistress, whom he owned. "Many Western scholars have largely ignored the possibility that Thomas Jefferson may have had sexual intercourse with a 14-year-old girl. Perhaps they found it hard to believe that the same person who wrote that 'all men are created equal' not only owned enslaved Africans but actually sexually exploited at least one of them."[69]

The fact that some Americans have sought to sanitize Jefferson's actions by viewing his abuse of Sally Hemings as a romantic love affair speaks volumes.[70] Still, Robert Jensen provides the required clarity by noting: "Rape is defined as sex without consent. Slaves do not consent to their enslavement ... Jefferson owned ... [Hemings] ... Jefferson had sex with Hemings. Therefore, Jefferson raped Hemings, who under conditions of enslavement could not give meaningful consent."[71] Clearly, the contestation and politics of American history is central to contemporary discussions of race relations.

The Politics of History and Cultural Hegemony

While academic and intellectual apologists (on both left and right) deride critical accounts of their political and cultural heroes, it is evident that America's national history has been politically engineered in order to con-struct what Benedict Anderson would define as an "imagined community"[72] *designed* by a self-conscious political and cultural elite dedicated to forging a (racialized) national identity.[73] The evidence indicates that America's WASP elite adopted and propagated inaccurate historical accounts that have dis-torted America's historical and political consciousness.[74] Ultimately, the facts have been arranged to present a liberal image to promote and amplify America's soft power credentials.[75]

This falsification of America's political consciousness is reflected in Obama's failure to overtly provide an accurate analysis of America's past. It is clear, given Obama's familiarity with the critical appraisals of American power authored by Frederick Douglass, Malcolm X,[76] and the neocolonial critiques of Fanon and others of that ilk,[77] that Obama, the academic, civil rights lawyer and alleged Africanist,[78] has an acute awareness of the realities of American racism.[79] In brief, *Dreams from my Father* and even his 20-year tenure under Rev. Jeremiah Wright indicate Obama's acute understanding of America's troubled past.[80] Arguably, Obama's reliance, as a politician, on the votes and economic patronage and sponsorship from U.S. corporations, the Euro-American power elite, and white voters, has tempered and constrained his public and private discussions on race.

According to Christopher Metzler, Obama's racial identity has also forced him to prove to Euro-Americans that he is not a closet black militant or a race advocate committed to championing *real* racial equality.[81] Cer-tainly, one recognizes that Obama's pragmatic critique of the arrest of Prof. Henry Louis Gates precipitated a major outcry[82] that, at heart, reflected some Euro-Americans' discomfort regarding Obama's defence of another black man, thereby implying the existence of a racial loyalty. One sympathizes with Metzler who argues that some Euro-Americans have struck a tacit bargain with the president, and other successful African Americans, through which they can receive mainstream acceptance, only as long as they avoid reminding white America of its chequered racial past, or attempting to resolve contemporary racial inequalities by authoring action-orientated solutions.[83] Of course, critics applaud Obama's historic "A More Perfect Union" speech on U.S. race relations. The speech's (relative) candor, tone, and associated risk during the 2008 election is noteworthy indeed. Unsurprisingly given Obama's bravery and magnificent oratory, few scholars have carefully unpacked that speech and highlighted its obvious deficiencies.

"A More Perfect Union" identified the existence of racial divisions and African American anger due to the attendant disparities caused by centuries of oppression.[84] However, the allusion to African American anger is thematic and stereotypical as it points to an emotional rather than a rational characterization of African American efforts to end racial inequality in America. The speech also highlights Euro-American impatience with affirmative action, but, worryingly, Obama suggests Euro-Americans are "justified in their outrage as are those blacks who continue to experience discrimination, even though there is little evidence that whites have been harmed by affirmative action or other compensatory programs."[85] The key question is not why Obama, as a black man, is not doing more for the black community. Rather, what is he doing for the most loyal constituency of the Democratic Party, a constituency that just happens to be black, and just happens to be in need of policies that are universal as well as targeted to address longstanding inequalities?[86]

Thus one finds sympathy with Professor Cornell West's assertion that the Obama administration has helped maintain the socioeconomic and political status quo. West lost faith in Obama when he brought people with close ties to Wall Street and the financial crisis into his administration. He names the president's former economic adviser, Larry Summers, Treasury Secretary, Tim Geithner, and his budget chief, now chief of staff, Jack Lew. The Obama administration has concentrated the power of both government and the financial sector, West says, in ways that have been "good for banks and bad for common people."[87]

West's critique is particularly relevant in the 21st century. Given the huge financial inequalities between Euro- and African Americans,[88] it is the quest for economic equality that may unsettle white America the most. That is why the speech was indicative of Obama's genius, as it struck a chord with blacks by seemingly speaking truth to power and also engendering support from many whites by tacitly indicating that Euro-Americans would not have to surrender any of their white privileges through a recognition of past grievances. Simply put, the discussion regarding the racial dimensions of America's political economy is still in its infancy.[89]

Euro-America's historical amnesia is both self-induced[90] and functional, as a formal accounting (or legally sanctioned apology) of the severe sociopolitical and economic cost borne by African Americans[91] might lend additional impetus to compensatory claims that even the 40 acres and a mule edict, concurrent with the emancipation proclamation issued by Lincoln, recognized as legitimate.[92] In brief, it is impossible to provide a rational argument in favor of race-specific compensatory actions without having an accurate understanding of America's history. That is why the racially polarized cultural wars of the 1990s,[93] which were led by an African American intellectual vanguard, were fraught with heated debates over revisionist interpretations of American and African history.[94]

In brief, African American scholars sought to utilize history to explain the enormity of the race problem and to validate the need for African Americans to be awarded special consideration due to the innumerable injustices that have arrested their development in the United States.[95] In addition, African American scholars lobbied to make their interpretation of American history central to discussions of American society in order to address their historic marginalization.

Obama and the Politics of Race

The politics of race are intimately related to myriad issues related to power, both political and economic,[96] which discourages American politicians, intellectuals and academics from engaging in a systematic analysis of race.[97] These include the controversy surrounding calls for reparations on behalf of African Americans and affirmative action that require knowledge of American history to legitimize the call for the redistribution of wealth along racial lines.[98] A dispassionate analysis would reveal that white America has consistently punished, harassed, co-opted and even assassinated African American political activists in order to discourage their constructive engagement with racial matters.[99] In addition, when one recognizes that the federal government has furnished Euro-Americans with generous economic and land handouts that were denied to African Americans,[100] it is little wonder that the political establishment is reluctant to address the economic aspects of U.S. race relations. Obama is doubtless aware that any in-depth discussion or solution pertaining to the origins of the economic and political disparities between Euro- and African Americans would be political suicide.

Given the increasing diversification of the American population[101] some scholars have suggested that the black and white narrative needs updating.[102] However African Americans' continuous commitment to struggle and the unique stigma of 246 years of enslavement, 100 years of Jim Crow, and the tendency for immigrants both non-white and white to assimilate and adhere to the established racial schema, means the black–white paradigm is still central to discussions of race.[103] Nonetheless, the assumption that the Civil Rights Acts of 1964 and 1965 created a level playing field for blacks has hampered Obama's ability to pursue overt racial policies. That is, despite African Americans' overwhelming electoral support for Obama, given his racial neutrality, he has failed to (overtly) enact any policies designed to directly address the racial discrimination that exists in American society.

In addition to the erroneous belief that race is primarily about prejudice, derived from ignorance and irrational forms of hatred, this makes it difficult to combat racism especially since Obama's success can be used to bolster the post racial discourse. Ultimately, part of the problem that critical scholars of race must contend with is the confusion over the nature and function of race.

A Brief Analysis of Race

Many scholars and intellectuals discuss race without challenging unsubstantiated clichés bristling with common sense assumptions. For example, many people, including Obama, may have subtly implied that racism is on the retreat due to increases in social interactions, intermarriage, and a liberal education that emphasizes commonalities as opposed to differences.[104] In this regard, the union of Obama's parents is held up as evidence that interracial marriage is bound to decrease racism in the U.S. However, intermarriage, educational reforms, and frequent social interactions cannot and will not bridge the economic and power disparities that exist between African and Euro-Americans.

Unfortunately, too many scholars fail to define racism within a collective context whereby current sociopolitical groups are still engaged in intense struggles for power that are a continuation of unresolved conflicts from the past. The fact that race is not a valid scientific category[105] often escapes both scholars and laymen. Despite the suggestion that racism is something endemic to the human experience, the existence and practice of racism can be traced to the rise and relative power of Europe and Europeans.[106] The roots of racism are significant as racism was conceived and perpetuated within the context of conquest and the acquisition of power which is why it has played such a pivotal role in European and American history.[107] Simply put, race is a sociopolitical construct that created, rationalized, and, despite adaptations, challenges and adjustments, has maintained hierarchical power relations predicated on European or Euro-American hegemony.[108] In practice, the pursuit of power and finite resources led to the creation of race and racism that has been used to create a hierarchical color-line both at home and abroad.[109]

In short, racial ideology established and informs modes of behaviour that create the conditions to reinforce its core contentions. Irrespective of the relative existence of animus or not, racism has served as a means to secure Euro-American dominance over America's political and economic institutions.[110] The fact that 43 out of 44 presidents have been white is a direct result of systematic practices that prevented the emergence of an African American or a non-white president. Racism, however, is not a monolithic closed system as it is subject to adaptations that result from counter-offensives from below or from above. Still, in America, racism is characterized by exploitation and privilege whereby whites have been given license and a rationale that legitimizes their predominance.[111] Whereas prejudice is not limited to any specific group, racism requires the power to constrain or determine the sociopolitical and economic options available to subordinate groups.[112] Hence the defining feature of American (classical) racism has been white America's ability to facilitate or negate African Americans' interests and to legitimize said decisions within the context of American political culture. Consequently, the absence or presence of overt hatred is less significant than the ability to manage, co-opt, constrain or prevent assaults from the subordinate groups.[113]

Consequently, simplistic discussions concerning whether all whites are racist or whether blacks can engage in racist behaviour does little to change the fact that in the age of Obama, Euro-Americans still have superordinate power in the United States.[114] Despite African American agency/resistance, their occupancy of impermanent positions of power such as the presidency does not indicate the absence of racism,[115] or the reversal of the racial status quo, as the incorporation of an individual can be based on a host of factors such as merit, strategic calculations, racial realignments and temporary gains. Note that, during Reconstruction, African American politicians made great strides that were later systematically dismantled with the re-imposition of racial hegemony via the Jim Crow laws, which were validated by the Supreme Court with the compliance of the U.S. government, i.e. the WASP elite.[116]

In the same way, a host of compensatory policies such as affirmative action have been repealed and abandoned since the 1960s.[117] Evidently, progressive gains can be offset by a regressive backlash. Indeed, even the election of Obama represents change without delivering meaningful changes for the African American population. According to Rogers M. Smith and Desmond S. King, centuries of racial oppression have institutionalized the racial divide that is still perpetuated even without additional grievous or overt intent as the legacies of racial power politics are still firmly embedded in American society.[118] Significantly, I will argue later that the visible presence of Obama, and the prevalence of the color-blind theory, is being utilized to undermine African Americans' efforts to fight racial oppression.

Change We Can Believe In

On reflection, the election of President Obama does not necessarily represent "change we can believe in."[119] The 2008 election of Obama was technically a change, which chimed with the core principles of U.S. democracy. Equally, one could argue that the election of a man of African descent represents a significant change.

Still, perhaps the most dramatic aspect of the Obama phenomenon was summed up by the historian Douglas Brinkley, who described Barack

Obama as America's "first global president."[120] Here, Obama's multicultural heritage and his African and Muslim lineage prompted a wave of enthusiasm from non-whites and European progressives,[121] who identified with his intellect and his global perspective and dubbed him as the new face of America. Among people of African descent, Obama's victory was seen as a vindication of African people. Note that on June 29, 2009, the World Public Opinion.Org. announced: "Obama rockets to top of poll on global leaders." The article stated that:

> US President Barack Obama has the confidence of many publics around the world—inspiring far more confidence than any other world political leader according to a new poll of 20 nations by WorldPublicOpinion. org. A year ago, President Bush was one of the least trusted leaders in the world.[122]

Overall, the article demonstrated Obama's support from progressives and among non-white nations. In essence, Obama's engaging and diplomatic persona provided America with a renewed sense of purpose, which, according to Tariq Ali, led the global audience to hope or believe that Obama "would heal the wounds of the past."[123] One suspects that Obama's Nobel Peace Prize resulted from his international appeal and the humanitarianism associated with his persona. Still, Ali maintains that his ethnic identity notwithstanding, "Obama's presidency has been distinguished largely by the way it has continued on the course established by his recent predecessors."[124]

In a sense, scholars and political pundits alike generated false expectations that minimize the impact of institutional constraints within the executive branch, which are designed to constrain radical changes within the American political system. While Obama's election campaign exaggerated his ability to employ his own agency to promote changes, his campaign mantra has left many questioning his commitment or ability to secure real changes.[125] In actuality, neither Obama's race nor his ethnicity and cosmopolitan credentials has led to a real departure from the War on Terror or American militarism.[126] Neither has Obama sought to assail the extreme economic disparities that exist between America's rich and the American masses; instead, Obama has continued to prop up America's bankers and Wall Street in a manner not dissimilar to George Bush Jr. It seems the global president is unable to pursue real change in presidential politics.

Post-Obama Racial Politics

Many assumed that Obama's identity and his support from African Americans, Hispanics and liberal whites would allow him to promote racial equality, but according to Michael Eric Dyson: "Obama runs from race like a black man runs from a cop."[127] Professor Dyson concludes that Obama deserves a "C−" ... for his handling of black issues.[128] A roundtable of African

American leaders discussed Obama's performance and the intractable nature of U.S. racism at Tavis Smiley's "We Count Forum," held at Chicago State University on March 20, 2010.[129] The discussants included Princeton Professor Cornel West, the Nation of Islam's Minister Louis Farrakhan, Founder and CEO of Policy Link Angela Glover Blackwell, Reverend Jesse L. Jackson Sr., Georgetown Professor and author Michael Eric Dyson, college president and noted economist Julianne Malveaux, former alderman Dorothy Tillman, advertising pioneer Tom Burrell and NAACP President Ben Jealous.[130]

The roundtable praised Obama but maintained that his failure to target black issues was due to his fear of offending the sensibilities of white America. In addition, tensions between Obama and the Congressional Black Caucus on September 18, 2010, at the CBC Foundation Phoenix Awards Dinner prompted him to remark that his election "wasn't just about electing a black President." Some African Americans leaders have challenged the post-racial discourse and criticized Obama's failure to directly address race.[131]

The president's silence on African American unemployment, racial profiling, and the uneven incarceration rates of African American males is troubling, to say the least![132] Obama's dilemma was captured succinctly in his cautious attempt to address the racially divisive shooting of Trayvon Martin by George Zimmerman.[133] His recognition that his son would look like Trayvon Martin[134] was both a bold and timid attempt to weigh in on an issue that debunks the post-racial myth. One would think that, based on the voting returns, Obama would be mandated to focus on key African American issues?

Note Obama is yet to propose a civil rights or racial agenda to confront the issues he outlined in *Dreams from my Father: a story of race and inheritance* and *The Audacity of Hope: thoughts on reclaiming the American Dream*. While pre-presidential Barack was committed to racial equality,[135] it has been suggested that: "Far from giving black America greater influence in U.S. politics, Obama's ascent to the White House has signalled the decline of a politics aimed at challenging racial inequality head-on."[136] It is difficult not to conclude that electoral calculations, polls, the realities of power, his advisors, and racial conservatism have prompted his lacklustre performance.

Moreover, some African Americans have argued that Obama's frequent allusion to defending the middle class is a ploy to bolster his white support at African American expense. This is significant as Anatol Lieven argued that non-white power brokers would be deemed acceptable as long as they conformed to the cultural values of the "middle classes."[137] Obama's allusion to protecting Middle America reflects a coded message to segments of the white electorate unwilling to countenance overt efforts to address contemporary racial inequalities, the irony being that unlike Lincoln, Truman, Eisenhower, JFK, Lyndon Baines Johnson, and other U.S. presidents, Obama's racial designation inhibits his rhetoric and desire for social justice, and his efforts to reward a significant segment of his electoral base. That is,

Obama is walking a racial tightrope whereby prioritizing black interests (even for electoral purposes) would leave him vulnerable to erroneous charges of reverse racism.

Note that critics have attacked Obama whenever he outwardly comments on race e.g. for his reference to the African American holiday Kwanzaa.[138] It would seem that race is still an issue. Especially since

> Obama is the target of more than 30 potential death threats a day. ... Since Mr Obama took office, the rate of threats against the president has increased 400 percent from the 3,000 a year or so under President George W Bush.[139]

Note the bizarre and worryingly under-reported statements of Andrew Adler, the owner of local publication the *Atlanta Jewish Times*.[140] Adler's article described the urgency in protecting the Israeli people from threats such as Hamas and Hezbollah and argued that there were essentially only three options available to Israel: 1. attack Hezbollah and Hamas; 2. "order the destruction of Iran's nuclear facilities at all costs"; 3. assassinate Obama.[141] These death threats, like those issued against Jesse Jackson during his presidential campaigns, correspond to America's racial conventions where African Americans have been targeted, threatened, or killed in defence of the racial status quo.

Biracial or African-American President

According to AOL News, "when it came to the official government ... [census] ... President Barack Obama gave only one answer to the question about his ethnic background: African-American."[142] This is perplexing to some as he might be considered mixed race, biracial, or, crudely put, 50/50. However, this conundrum is rooted in America's past and contemporary racial politics. America's primary racial paradigm is still predicated on a white and black schemas where European and African Americans represent the polar opposites. During the period of enslavement the pigmentation of Africans was coupled with cultural and historical characterizations that defined enslaved Africans as sub-human chattel.[143] Consequently, within American history,

> the stigma carried by blackness is unique, and is affixed and perpetuated resolutely by the American practice of treating blackness as a monolithic identity that an individual either has or does not have on the basis of the principle that any African ancestry at all determines that one is simply black.[144]

The denigration of Africans culminated in the "one drop rule," which meant irrespective of Euro-American lineage, an enslaved person was still property and by definition remained enslaved. Hence the notion of hypodescent, where societies that regard some races of people as dominant or superior and others as subordinate or inferior. Hypodescent, that is the automatic assignment of children of a mixed union or mating between members of different socioeconomic groups or ethnic groups to the group that is considered subordinate or inferior,[145] became part and parcel of U.S. racial politics. David Hollinger states:

> Some of the slave era and Jim Crow regimes ... employ[ed] ... fractional classifications, providing that "Octoroons," "Quadroons," and "Mulattos" be separately counted and allowed distinctive rights and privileges in some jurisdictions. But this fractional approach was hard to administer, invited litigation, and blurred lines that many whites wanted kept sharp.[146]

The significance is threefold: hypodescent was based on the idea that white blood was superior and black blood was tainted; that mulattoes and mixed bloods were superior to blacks relative to their quantity of white blood; it also generated internal divisions among African Americans, what Du Bois referred to as a "double consciousness"[147] and the assumption that white blood was a mark of privilege and distinction.[148]

Conversely, whites "encouraged the belief in mixed race superiority and the association of light skin with the ideal of beauty and goodness."[149] Henceforth, African American intellectuals have argued that Obama's dual heritage has made him more acceptable to white America. Perhaps Senator. Harry Reid's comments describing Obama as a "light-skinned" African American "with no Negro dialect, unless he wanted to have one,"[150] conveys a different deep-seated message that Obama's complexion, class and cultural identity are more acceptable whereas a dark skinned African American would be considered more threatening.

Concepts such as mixed race, biracial, and multiracial are rooted in pseudoscientific categories that placed a premium on having white blood and utilized this schema to grade blacks according to their pigmentation. Nevertheless, despite these gradations, evidence of any African ancestry was associated with stigma.[151]

The political and cultural reforms of the 1960s and 1970s witnessed an assault on the pure blood thesis as the civil rights struggle and the black power ethos encouraged young Barry Obama and the so-called American Negro to embrace their African heritage.[152] Like Barack, many African Americans were moved by Alex Haley's *Roots* and *The Autobiography of Malcolm X*, and the exhortations of James Brown (I'm black and I'm proud) to undergo the same cultural and historical awakening that led Obama to Kenya and to Elmina and Cape Coast Castles in Ghana, to celebrate their triumph over the horror of the middle passage.[153] While Obama has never rejected his Euro-American heritage, he and Michelle Obama recognize that due to pigmentation, phenotype, and cultural orientation they and their daughters would be, and generally are, considered as African Americans.

To conclude, if Barack Obama is not an African American or black then neither was Frederick Douglass, Rosa Parks, Walter White, W.E.B. Du Bois, Malcolm X, nor Adam Clayton Powell Junior, all of whom had an ancestry that included Europeans, as do large numbers of the African American population who proclaim their African ancestry. In regards to race, our theoretical tool box has 18th- and 19th-century tools mixed in with 20th- and 21th-century realities. The debate continues. In the final analysis, taking into account African American voting patterns pertaining to Obama, his failure to date, understandable as it is, to address African American issues of unemployment, racial profiling, and mass incarceration, suggest his racial designation precludes him from addressing the interests of his core constituents. At best, Obama has adopted a racial conservatism that transformative white presidents such as Truman, JFK, Johnson, and at times even Nixon, were able to reject in order to pursue the national interest.

Notes

1 Leary, Joy D. *Post Traumatic Syndrome: America's legacy of enduring injury and healing* (Oakland, CA: Uptone Press, 2005), p. 73.
2 Asante, Molefi K. and Mazama, Ama, eds. *Obama: political frontiers and racial agency* (London: Sage Publications, 2012).
3 King, Desmond S. and Smith, Rogers M. *Still a House Divided: race and politics in Obama's America* (Oxford: Princeton University Press, 2011). Sugrue, Thomas J. *Not even Past: Barack Obama and the burden of race* (Princeton, NJ: Princeton University Press, 2010), p. 3.
4 Long, David and Schmidt, Brian C., eds. *Imperialism and Internationalism in the Discipline of International Relations* (New York: State University of New York, 2005), p. 160.
5 Ledwidge, Mark. *Race and U.S. Foreign Policy: the African-American foreign affairs network* (London: Routledge, 2011).
6 Ibid., p. 22.
7 Miliband, Ralph. *The State in Capitalist Society* (Gwent: Merlin Press, 2009), p. 4. In this regard, King's analysis of the state's poor employment record (during the period studied) in relation to African Americans highlights the government's failure to protect the political and economic welfare of blacks within state institutions and without. According to King: "the U.S. Administration constituted a powerful institution upholding arrangements privileging Whites and discriminating against Blacks. In the eight decades before 1964, the Federal government used its power and authority to support segregated race relations. Historically, the segregation of Black American citizens in the federal bureaucracy is a major but neglected aspect of the U.S. federal government, with implications for both the position of these citizens in the United States and the character of the state." King, Desmond S. *Separate and Unequal: black Americans and the US federal government* (Oxford: Clarendon Press 1995), p. vii.
8 Ledwidge. *Race and U.S.*
9 Ledwidge, Mark, Miller, Linda B., and Parmar, Inderjeet, eds. *New Directions in US Foreign Policy* (New York: Routledge, 2009); King, Desmond S. "The racial bureaucracy: African-Americans and the federal government in the era of

segregated race relations," *Governance: An International Journal of Policy and Administration* (1999): 12, 4, 345.

10 Lively, Jack and Reeve, Andrew, eds. *Modern Political Theory from Hobbes to Marx: key debates* (London: Routledge, 1991), p. 284; Dunleavy, Patrick and O'Leary, Brendan. *Theories of the State: politics of liberal democracy* (London: Macmillan, 1987), p. 206.

11 Clark, Tom, Putnam, Robert D., and Fieldhouse, Edward. *The Age of Obama* (Manchester: Manchester University Press, 2010).

12 Dunleavy and O'Leary. *Theories of the State.*

13 Ledwidge. *Race and U.S.*

14 Karenga, Maulana. *Introduction to Black Studies* (Los Angeles: University of Sankore, 2002).

15 Ibid.

16 Cox, Michael and Parmar, Inderjeet, eds. *Soft Power and US Foreign Policy: theoretical, historical and contemporary perspectives* (London: Routledge, 2010).

17 Ledwidge et al. *New Directions.*

18 Vucetic, Srdjan. *The Anglosphere: a genealogy of a racialised identity in inter national relations* (Stanford, CA: Stanford University Press, 2011), p. 132.

19 Christie, K., ed. *United States Foreign Policy and National Identity in the Twenty-First Century* (London: Routledge, 2008).

20 Ledwidge, Mark. "American power and the racial dimensions of US foreign policy," *International Politics* (2011): 48, 308–25.

21 Ledwidge. *Race and U.S.*

22 Karenga. *Introduction to Black*, p. 422.

23 Hamilton, Charles V. and Ture, Kwame. *Black Power: the politics of liberation* (New York: Vintage Books, 1992), p. 6.

24 Ibid., p. 10.

25 Wellman, David T. *Portraits of White Racism* (New York: Cambridge University Press, 1977), p. 35.

26 Omi, Michael and Winant, Howard. *Racial Formation in the United States from the 1960s to 1990s* (London: Routledge, 1994), p. 65.

27 Hamilton and Ture. *Black Power*, p. 6. King. *Separate and Unequal*, p. 80. The fact that 'Until the middle of the twentieth century Black Americans were employed in relatively few numbers by the Federal government' is indicative of white hegemony within and over the state.

28 Omi and Winant. *Racial Formation*, p. 81; Wilson, Amos. *Blueprint for Black Power: a moral, political and economic imperative for the twenty-first century* (New York: Afrikan World Infosystems, 1998), p. 141; King. *Separate and unequal*, p. 12.

29 Hacker, Andrew. *Two Nations: black and white, separate, hostile, unequal* (New York: Macmillan, 1992), p. 15.

30 Wilson. *Blueprint for Black*, p. 249.

31 Ledwidge. *Race and U.S.*, p. 20.

32 Jones, Angela. *The Modern African American Political Thought Reader: from David Walker to Barack Obama* (London: Routledge, 2013), p. 421.

33 Zweigenhaft, Richard and Domhoff, G. William. *Blacks in the White Elite: will the progress continue?* (New York: Rowman & Littlefield, 2003), p. 11.

34 Clayton, Dewey M. *The Presidential Campaign of Barack Obama: a critical analysis of a racially transcendent strategy* (London: Routledge 2010), p. 38.

35 Scott-Smith, Giles, ed. *Obama, US politics, and Transatlantic Relations: change or continuity?* (Brussels: P.I.E. Peter Lang, 2012).

36 Asante and Mazama. *Obama: political*, p. 11.

37 Ibid., p. 215.

38 Glasrud, Bruce A. and Wintz, Cary D. *African Americans and the Presidency: the road to the White House* (Abingdon, UK: Routledge, 2010).
39 Sugrue. *Not Even*, p. 1.
40 Scott-Smith. *Obama, US*, p. 39.
41 Glasrud and Wintz. *African Americans*.
42 See Marsden. Chapter 9 this volume.
43 Ibid.
44 Glasrud and Wintz. *African Americans*.
45 Jacobs, Lawrence R. and King, Desmond S. *Obama at the Crossroads: politics, markets, and the battle for America's future* (Oxford: Oxford University Press, 2012), p. 153.
46 King and Smith. *Still a House.*
47 Christie, Kenneth, ed. *United States Foreign Policy and National Identity in the Twenty-first Century* (London: Routledge, 2008), p. xiv.
48 Lipset, Seymour M. *American Exceptionalism: a double-edged sword.* (London: W. W. Norton & Company, 1997), p. 113.
49 Lipset. *American Exceptionalism.*
50 Nelson, Michael. *The Presidency and the Political System* (Washington, DC: CQ Press, 2009), p. 11.
51 Brown, Dee. *Bury my Heart at Wounded Knee* (London: Vintage, 1991); New comb, Stephen T. *Pagans in the Promised Land* (Golden, CO: Fulcrum Publishing, 2008).
52 Clarke, John H. *Christopher Columbus and the African Holocaust: slavery and the rise of European capitalism* (New York: A & B Publishers Group, 1998).
53 McCarthy, Thomas. *Race, Empire and the Idea of Human Development* (Cambridge: Cambridge University Press, 2009), p. 72.
54 King. *Separate and Unequal*; Wilson. *Blueprint for Black*; Ledwidge. "American power," pp. 308–25.
55 King and Smith. *Still a House.*
56 Kirk, John A. *Martin Luther King Jr.: profiles in power* (Harlow: Pearson Education, 2005).
57 Ledwidge, Mark. "Race, African-Americans and US foreign policy," in Ledwidge et al. *New Directions*, p. 153.
58 Glasrud and Wintz. *African Americans*, p. 208.
59 Kloppenberg, James T. *Reading Obama: dreams, hope, and the American political tradition* (Oxford: Princeton University Press, 2011), p. x.
60 Clayton. *The Presidential Campaign*, p. 4.
61 Clayton. *The Presidential Campaign.*
62 Asante and Mazama. *Obama: political*, p. 4.
63 Corsi, Jerome R. *The Obama Nation: leftist politics and the cult of personality* (New York: Pocket Star Books, 2008).
64 Lipset. *American Exceptionalism.*
65 McCarthy. *Race, Empire*, p. 107.
66 "Holder: U.S. a 'nation of cowards' on race discussions," *CNN Politics*, accessed August 21, 2012, http://articles.cnn.com/2009-02-18/politics/holder.race .relations_1_holder-affirmative-action-black-history-month?_s=PM:POLITICS
67 Yette, Samuel F. *The Choice: the issue of black survival in America* (Silver Spring, MD: Cottage Books, 1971), p. 81.
68 Breitman, George, ed. *By Any Means Necessary: speeches, interviews and a letter by Malcolm X* (London: Pathfinder Press, 1987).
69 Asante, Molefi K. and Hall, Ronald E. *Rooming in the Master's House: power and privilege in the rise of black conservatism* (Boulder, CO: Paradigm, 2011), p. 55.
70 Jensen, Robert. *The Heart of Whiteness: confronting race, racism and white privilege* (San Francisco: City Light Books, 2005), p. 43.

71   Ibid., p. 42.
72   Anderson, Benedict. *Imagined Communities* (London: Verso, 1991).
73   Hobsbawm, Eric. *Nations and Nationalism Since 1780: programme, myth, rea lity* (Cambridge: Cambridge University Press, 1995).
74   Robinson, Cedric J. *Black Marxism: the making of the black radical* (London: University of North Carolina Press, 2000), p. 186.
75   Clark et al. *The Age*, p. 4.
76   Kloppenberg. *Reading Obama*, p. 13.
77   Ledwidge. "American power," pp. 308–25.
78   Corsi. *The Obama Nation*, p. 186.
79   Kloppenberg. *Reading Obama*.
80   Corsi. *The Obama Nation*, p. 191.
81   Asante and Mazama. *Obama: political*, p. 160.
82   Sugrue. *Not Even*, p. 3.
83   Asante and Mazama. *Obama: political*, p. 160.
84   Sugrue. *Not Even*, p. 119.
85   Ibid., p. 121.
86   "Still waiting for our first black president," *Washington Post*, accessed August 20, 2012, www.washingtonpost.com/opinions/still-waiting-for-our-first-black -president/2012/06/01/gJQARsT16U_story_2.html
87   "Lunch with the FT: Cornel West," *Financial Times*, accessed August 20, 2012, www.ft.com/cms/s/2/73e4af2a-9f41–11e1-a455–00144feabdc0.html?ftcamp=pu-blished_links/rss/life-arts/feed//product&ftcamp=crm/email/2012519/nbe/ArtsLei-sure/product#axzz1vJc3Itua
88   Muhammad, Dedrick. "40 years later: the unrealized American dream," *Insti tute for Policy Studies* (April 2008); Jacobs and King. *Obama at the Crossroads*.
89   Muhammad. "40 years".
90   Jensen. *The Heart*.
91   Karenga. *Introduction to Black*; McCarthy. *Race, Empire*.
92   Cohen, Irving S. and Logan, Rayford W. *The American Negro: old world back-ground and new world experience* (Boston, MA: Houghton-Mifflin Company, 1970).
93   Schlesinger, Jr., A.M. *The Disuniting of America: reflections on a multicultural society* (London: W.W. Norton & Company, 1998); Carruthers, Jacob. *Intellectual Warfare* (Chicago: Third World Press, 1999).
94   Carruthers. *Intellectual Warfare*, p. 128; Lefkowitz, M. *Not Out of Africa* (New York: Basic Books, 1997), p. xii.
95   Karenga. *Introduction to Black*; Clarke, John H. *Malcolm X: the man and his times* (Trenton, NJ: Africa World Press, 1992).
96   Oliver, Melvin L. and Shapiro, Thomas. *Black Wealth/White Wealth: a per spective on racial inequality* (London: Routledge, 1995).
97   Alexander, Michelle. *The New Jim Crow* (New York: New Press, 2011), p. 238.
98   Karenga. *Introduction to Black*.
99   Clegg III, Claude Andrew. *An Original Man: the life and times of Elijah Muhammad* (New York: St. Martin's Press, 1997); Hill, Robert A. *The FBI's RACON: racial conditions in the United States during World War II* (Boston, MA: Northeastern University Press, 1995); O'Reilly, Kenneth. "*Racial Mat-ters": the FBI's secret file on black America, 1960–1972* (London: Free Press, 1991); Kornweibel, Theodore J.R. "*Seeing Red": federal campaigns against black militancy, 1919–1925* (Bloomington: Indiana University Press, 1998); Evanzz, Karl. *The Judas Factor: the plot to kill Malcolm X* (New York: Thunder's Mouth Press, 1992).
100 King and Smith. *Still a House*; Oliver and Shapiro. *Black Wealth*; Muhammad, "40 years".

101 Clayton. *The Presidential Campaign*, p. 47.
102 Vucetic. *The Anglosphere*, p. 133.
103 McCarthy. *Race, Empire*, p. 97.
104 Vucetic. *The Anglosphere*.
105 Painter, Nell I. *The History of White People* (New York: W.W. Norton & Company, 2010).
106 Rodney, Walter. *How Europe Undeveloped Africa* (Washington, DC: Howard University Press, 1981); Jones, Branwen G. *Decolonizing International Relations* (New York: Rowan & Littlefield, 2006); Vucetic. *The Anglosphere*.
107 McCarthy. *Race, Empire*, p. 24.
108 Ledwidge. *Race and U.S.*
109 Ibid.
110 Clayton. *The Presidential Campaign*.
111 Omi and Winant. *Racial Formation*.
112 Ibid.
113 Wellman. *Portraits of White*.
114 Vucetic. *The Anglosphere*, p. 133.
115 Asante, Molefi K. *African American History: a journey of liberation* (May wood, IL: People's Publishing Group, Inc., 1995), p. 264.
116 Dye, Thomas R. *Understanding Public Policy* (New York: Prentice Hall, 2002), p. 216.
117 Alexander. *The New Jim Crow*.
118 Jacobs and King. *Obama at the Crossroads*, p. 154.
119 Scott-Smith. *Obama, US*.
120 "Obama, Biden attend post inaugural national prayer service," *USA Today*, accessed August 15, 2012, www.usatoday.com/news/opinion/columnist/raasch /2009-04-07-newpolitics _N.htm.
121 Scott-Smith. *Obama, US*, p. 44.
122 "Obama rockets to top of poll on global leaders," *World Public Opinion*, accessed August 20, 2012, www.worldpublicopinion.org/pipa/articles/ views_on_ countriesregions_bt/618.php?nid=&id=&pnt=618&lb=btvoc&gclid=CILXO -ZlaYCFY9O4QodWj79Xw
123 Ali, Tariq. *The Obama Syndrome: surrender at home, war abroad* (London: Verso, 2009).
124 Ibid.
125 Jacobs and King. *Obama at the Crossroads*, p. 3.
126 Parmar, Inderjeet. *Foundations of the American Century: the Ford Carnegie, and Rockefeller Foundations and the rise of American power* (New York: Columbia University Press, 2011).
127 "Michael Eric Dyson: Obama runs from race like blacks from cops," *News One for Black America*, accessed August 28, 2012, http://newsone.com/nation /newsonestaff2/michael-eric-dyson-obama-black-unemployment/comment-page-2/
128 "Michael Eric Dyson".
129 "Tavis Smiley hosts live symposium on Chicago southside to discuss black agenda," *Chicago Now*, accessed August 10, 2012, www.chicagonow.com /blogs/ndigo-chi-society/2010/03/tavis-smiley-hosts-live-symposium-on-chicago -southside-to-discuss-black-agenda)
130 "Tavis Smiley hosts".
131 Jacobs and King. *Obama at the Crossroads*.
132 Alexander. *The New Jim Crow*.
133 "Trayvon Martin: Barack Obama says America should do some 'soul search ing'," *Daily Telegraph*, accessed August 10, 2012, www.telegraph.co.uk/news /worldnews/northamerica/usa/9163216/Trayvon-Martin-Barack-Obama-says -America-should-do-some-soul-searching.html

134   Ibid.
135   Obama, Barack. *The Audacity of Hope: thoughts on reclaiming the American dream* (New York: Three Rivers Press, 2006), p. 243.
136   "Still waiting".
137   Christie. *United States*, p. xiv.
138   "Obama celebrates fictitious holiday, urging black racial unity," Fellowship of the Minds: Conservatives Who Love America, accessed August 20, 2012, http://fellowshipofminds.wordpress.com/2012/01/01/obama-celebrates-fictitious-holiday-urging-black-racial-unity/
139   "Barack Obama faces 30 death threats a day, stretching US Secret Service," *Daily Telegraph*, accessed August 20, 2012, www.telegraph.co.uk/news/world news/northamerica/usa/barackobama/5967942/Barack-Obama-faces-30-death-threats-a-day-stretching-US-Secret-Service.html
140   "Andrew Adler, '*Atlanta Jewish Times*' publisher, apologizes for Obama assassination comments," Huffington Post, accessed August 20, 2012, www.huffingtonpost.com/2012/01/20/andrew-adler-atlanta-jewish-times-obama-assassination_n_1219720.html
141   "Andrew Adler".
142   "Obama's census choice: simply African-American," *Huffington Post*, accessed August 20, 2012, www.aolnews.com/2010/04/03/obamas-census-choice-simply-african-american/
143   Leary. *Post Traumatic*.
144   Hollinger, David A. "Amalgamation and hypodescent," Department of History, University of California, accessed August 20, 2012, http://history.berkeley.edu /faculty/Hollinger/articles/ amalgamation_and_hypodescent
145   "Amalgamation and hypodescent".
146   Ibid.
147   Lewis, David L. *W.E.B. Du Bois: the fight for equality and the American century 1919–1963* (New York: Henry Holt & Company, 2000).
148   Asante and Hall. *Rooming in the Master's House*.
149   Asante and Hall. *Rooming in the Master's House*, p. 30.
150   "Obama: Reid 'always … on right side of history'," Capitol Hill on *NBC News.com*, accessed August 20, 2012, www.msnbc.msn.com/id/34783136/ns/politics-capitol_hill/t/obama-reid-always-right-side-history/#.UCfZf51lTYg
151   Asante and Hall. *Rooming in the Master's House*.
152   Ledwidge. "American power," pp. 308–25.
153   Ibid.

Bibliography

Alexander, Michelle. *The New Jim Crow* (New York: New Press, 2011).
Ali, Tariq. *The Obama Syndrome: surrender at home, war abroad* (London: Verso, 2009).
Anderson, Benedict. *Imagined Communities* (London: Verso, 1992).
Asante, Molefi K. *African American History: a journey of liberation* (Maywood, IL: People's Publishing Group, Inc., 1995).
Asante, Molefi K. and Mazama, Ama, eds. *Obama: political frontiers and racial agency* (London: Sage Publications, 2012).
Birch, Anthony H. *Concepts and Theories of Modern Democracy* (Abingdon UK: Routledge, 2007).
Breitman, George, ed. *By Any Means Necessary: speeches, interviews and a letter by Malcolm X* (London: Pathfinder Press, 1987).

Brown, Dee. *Bury my Heart at Wounded Knee* (London: Vintage, 1991).

Carruthers, Jacob. *Intellectual Warfare* (Chicago: Third World Press, 1999).

Chowdhry, Geeta and Nair, Sheila, eds. *Power, Postcolonialism and International Relations: reading race, gender and class* (London: Routledge, 2004).

Christie, Kenneth, ed. *United States Foreign Policy and National Identity in the Twenty-First Century* (London: Routledge, 2008).

Clark, Tom, Putman, Robert D., and Fieldhouse, Edward. *The Age of Obama* (Manchester: Manchester University Press, 2010).

Clarke, John H. *Christopher Columbus and the African Holocaust: slavery and the rise of European capitalism* (New York: A & B Publishers Group, 1998).

Clarke, John H. *Malcolm X: the man and his times* (Trenton, NJ: Africa World Press, 1992).

Clayton, Dewey M. *The Presidential Campaign of Barack Obama: a critical analysis of a racially transcendent strategy* (London: Routledge, 2010).

Clegg III, Claude Andrew. *An Original Man: the life and times of Elijah Muhammad* (New York: St. Martin's Press, 1997).

Cohen, Irving S. and Logan, Rayford W. *The American Negro: old world background and new world experience* (Boston, MA: Houghton-Mifflin Company, 1970).

Corsi, Jerome R. *The Obama Nation: leftist politics and the cult of personality* (New York: Pocket Star Books, 2008).

Cox, Michael and Parmar, Inderjeet, eds. *Soft Power and US Foreign Policy: theoretical, historical and contemporary perspectives* (London: Routledge, 2010).

Domhoff, G. William and Zweigenhaft, Richard L. *Blacks in the White Elite: will the progress continue?* (Oxford: Rowman & Littlefield Publishers, 2003).

Dunleavy, Patrick and O'Leary, Brendan. *Theories of the State: politics of liberal democracy* (London; Macmillan, 1987).

Evanzz, Karl. *The Judas Factor: the plot to kill Malcolm X* (New York: Thunder's Mouth Press, 1992).

Falk, Avner. *The Riddle of Barack Obama: a psychobiography* (Oxford: Praeger, 2010).

Glasrud, Bruce A. and Wintz, Cary D. *African Americans and the Presidency: the road to the White House* (Abingdon UK: Routledge, 2010).

Hacker, Andrew. *Two Nations: black and white, separate, hostile, unequal* (New York: Macmillan, 1992).

Hamilton, Charles. V. and Ture, Kwame. *Black Power: the politics of liberation* (New York: Vintage Books, 1992).

Hill, Robert A. *The FBI's RACON: racial conditions in the United States during World War II* (Boston, MA: Northeastern University Press, 1995).

Hobsbawm, Eric. *Nations and Nationalism Since 1780: programme, myth, reality* (Cambridge: Cambridge University Press, 1995).

Hodge, Roger D. *The Mendacity of Hope: Barack Obama and the betrayal of American liberalism* (New York: HarperCollins Publishers, 2010).

Jacobs, Lawrence R. and King, Desmond S. *Obama at the Crossroads: politics, markets, and the battle for America's future* (Oxford: Oxford University Press, 2012).

Jensen, Robert. *The Heart of Whiteness: confronting race, racism and white privilege.* (San Francisco: City Light Books, 2005).

Jones, Angela. *The Modern African American Political Thought Reader: from David Walker to Barack Obama* (London: Routledge, 2013).

Jones, Branwen G. *Decolonizing International Relations* (New York: Rowan & Littlefield, 2006).

Karenga, Maulana. *Introduction to Black Studies* (Los Angeles: University of Sankore, 2002).

King, Desmond S. *Separate and Unequal: black Americans and the US federal gov ernment* (Oxford: Clarendon Press 1995).

King, Desmond S. and Smith, Rogers M. *Still a House Divided: race and politics in Obama's America* (Oxford: Princeton University Press, 2011).

Kirk, John A. *Martin Luther King Jr.: profiles in power* (Harlow, UK: Pearson Educa tion, 2005).

Kloppenberg, James T. *Reading Obama: dreams, hope, and the American political tradition* (Oxford: Princeton University Press, 2011).

Kornweibel, Theodore J.R. *"Seeing Red": federal campaigns against black militancy, 1919–1925* (Bloomington: Indiana University Press, 1998).

Leary, Joy D. *Post Traumatic Syndrome: America's legacy of enduring injury and healing* (Oakland, CA: Uptone Press, 2005).

Ledwidge, Mark. *Race and U.S. Foreign Policy: the African-American foreign affairs network* (London: Routledge, 2011).

Ledwidge, Mark, Miller, Linda B., and Parmar, Inderjeet, eds. *New Directions in US Foreign Policy* (New York: Routledge, 2009).

Lefkowitz, Mary. *Not Out of Africa* (New York: Basic Books, 1997).

Lewis, David L. *W.E.B. Du Bois: the fight for equality and the American century 1919–1963* (New York: Henry Holt & Company, 2000).

Lipset, Seymour M. *American Exceptionalism: a double-edged sword* (London: W.W. Norton & Company, 1997).

Lively, Jack and Reeve, Andrew, eds. *Modern Political Theory from Hobbes to Marx: key debates* (London: Routledge, 1991).

Long, David and Schmidt, Brian C. *Imperialism and Internationalism in the Discipline of International Relations* (New York: State University of New York, 2005).

McCarthy, Thomas. *Race, Empire and the Idea of Human Development* (Cambridge: Cambridge University Press, 2009).

Marsh, David and Stoker, Gerry. *Theory and Methods in Political Science* (Basingstoke, UK: Palgrave Macmillan, 2010).

Miliband, Ralph. *The State in Capitalist Society* (Gwent: Merlin Press, 2009).

Newcomb, Stephen T. *Pagans in the Promised Land* (Golden, CO: Fulcrum Publishing, 2008).

Obama, Barack. *The Audacity of Hope: thoughts on reclaiming the American dream* (New York: Three Rivers Press, 2006).

Oliver, Melvin L. and Shapiro, Thomas M. *Black Wealth/White Wealth: a perspective on racial inequality* (London: Routledge, 1995).

Omi, Michael and Winant, Howard. *Racial Formation in the United States from the 1960s to 1990s* (London: Routledge, 1994).

O'Reilly, Kenneth. *"Racial Matters": the FBI's secret file on black America, 1960–1972* (London: Free Press, 1991).

Painter, Nell I. *The History of White People* (New York: W.W. Norton & Company, 2010).

Parmar, Inderjeet. *Foundations of the American Century: the Ford Carnegie, and Rockefeller Foundations and the rise of American power* (New York: Columbia University Press, 2011).

Robinson, Cedric J. *Black Marxism: the making of the black radical tradition* (London: North Carolina Press, 2000).

Rodney, Walter. *How Europe Underdeveloped Africa* (Washington, DC: Howard University Press, 1981).

Schlesinger, Jr., Arthur M. *The Disuniting of America: reflections on a multicultural society* (London: W.W. Norton & Company, 1998).

Scott-Smith, Giles, ed. *Obama, US politics, and Transatlantic Relations: change or continuity?* (Brussels: P.I.E. Peter Lang, 2012).

Sugrue, Thomas J. *Not Even Past: Barack Obama and the burden of race* (Princeton, NJ: Princeton University Press, 2010).

Vucetic, Srdjan. *The Anglosphere: a genealogy of a racialized identity in international relations* (Stanford, CA: Stanford University Press, 2011).

Wellman, David T. *Portraits of White Racism* (New York: Cambridge University Press, 1977).

Wilson, Amos. *Blueprint for Black Power: a moral, political and economic imperative for the twenty-first century* (New York: Afrikan World Infosystems, 1998).

Yette, Samuel F. *The Choice: the issue of black survival in America* (Silver Spring, MD: Cottage Books, 1971).

Chapters in books

Ledwidge, Mark. "Race, African-Americans and US foreign policy," in Ledwidge, Mark, Miller, Linda B., and Parmar, Inderjeet, eds. *New Directions in US Foreign Policy*. (New York: Routledge, 2009), pp. 150–69.

Articles

King, Desmond S. "The racial bureaucracy: African-Americans and the federal government in the era of segregated race relations," *Governance: An International Journal of Policy and Administration* (1999): 12, 4, 345–77.

Ledwidge, Mark. "American power and the racial dimensions of US foreign policy," *International Politics* (2011): 48, 308–25.

Muhammad, Dedrick. "40 years later: the unrealized American dream," *Institute for Policy Studies* (April 2008): 3–18.

Websites

Capitol Hill on *NBCNews.com*. "Obama: Reid 'always … on right side of history'," accessed August 20, 2012. www.msnbc.msn.com/id/ 34783136/ns/politics-capitol _hill/t/obama-reid-always-right-side-history/#.UCfZf51lTYg

Chicago Now. "Tavis Smiley hosts live symposium on Chicago southside to discuss black agenda," accessed August 10, 2012. www.chicagonow.com/blogs/ndigo-chi -society/2010/03/tavis-smiley-hosts-live-symposium-on-chicago-southside-to-discuss -black-agenda)

CNN Politics. "Holder: U.S. a 'nation of cowards' on race discussions," accessed August 21,2012. http://articles.cnn.com/2009-02-18/politics/holder.race.relations_1_holder-affir mative-action-black-history-month?_s=PM:POLITICS

Daily Telegraph. "Barack Obama faces 30 death threats a day, stretching US Secret Service," accessed August 20, 2012. www.telegraph.co.uk/news/worldnews/north

america/usa/barackobama/5967942/Barack-Obama-faces-30-death-threats-a-day
-stretching-US-Secret-Service.html

Daily Telegraph. "Trayvon Martin: Barack Obama says America should do some
'soul searching'," accessed August 10, 2012. www.telegraph.co.uk/news/worldnews
/northamerica/usa/9163216/Trayvon-Martin-Barack-Obama-says-America-should
-do-some-soul-searching.html

Department of History, University of California. "Amalgamation and hypodescent,"
accessed August 20, 2012. http://history.berkeley.edu/faculty/Hollinger/articles
/amalgamation_and_hypodescent

Fellowship of the Minds: Conservatives Who Love America. "Obama celebrates fictitious
holiday, urging black racial unity," accessed August 20, 2012. http://fellowshipof
minds.wordpress.com/2012/01/01/obama-celebrates-fictitious-holiday-urging-black
-racial-unity/

Financial Times. "Lunch with the FT: Cornel West," accessed August 20, 2012.
www.ft.com/cms/s/2/73e4af2a-9f41–11e1-a455–00144feabdc0.html?ftcamp=pu
blished_links/rss/life-arts/feed//product&ftcamp=crm/email/2012519/nbe/ArtsLei
sure/product#axzz1vJc3Itua

Huffington Post. "Andrew Adler, '*Atlanta Jewish Times*' publisher, apologizes for
Obama assassination comments," accessed August 20, 2012. www.huffingtonpost
.com/2012/01/20/andrew-adler-atlanta-jewish-times-obama-assassination_n_1219720.
html

Huffington Post. "Obama's census choice: simply African-American," accessed
August 20, 2012. http://www.aolnews.com/2010/04/03/obamas-census-choice-simply-
african-american/

News One for Black America. "Michael Eric Dyson: Obama runs from race like
blacks from cops," accessed August 28, 2012. http://newsone.com/nation/news
onestaff2/michael-eric-dyson-obama-black-unemployment/comment-page-2/

USA Today. "Obama, Biden attend post inaugural national prayer service," accessed
August 15, 2012. www.usatoday.com/news/opinion/columnist/raasch/2009-04-07
-newpolitics_N.htm

Washington Post. "Still waiting for our first black president," accessed August 20,
2012. www.washingtonpost.com/opinions/still-waiting-for-our-first-black-president
/2012/06/01/gJQARsT16U_story_2.html

World Public Opinion. "Obama rockets to top of poll on global leaders," accessed August
20, 2012. www.worldpublicopinion.org/pipa/articles/views_on_countriesregions_bt
/618.php?nid=&id=&pnt=618&lb=btvoc&gclid=CILXO-ZlaYCFY9O4QodWj
79Xw

2 The Obama Dilemma

Confronting Race in the 21st Century

Carl Pedersen

If presidential elections are quadrennial plebiscites of national identity, then the election of 2008 revealed a nation deeply divided. Two versions of what it means to be American in the 21st century were articulated as an integral part of the rhetorical strategy of the presidential campaign of 2008. One is a backlash national identity that emerged in the wake of the civil rights movement, changes in immigration law, and the rise of identity politics in the 1960s and 70s. It is socially conservative, largely white and conservative Christian, and finds its strength in nonurban areas of the U.S. It defines national identity in terms of Samuel Huntington's nostalgic, neo-nativist, and narrow view of an Anglo-Protestant culture. The other, often derided as elitist, is an emergent national identity for the 21st century. It is progressive, includes African Americans and new minorities with a sizeable component of non-Christians, and is strongest in metropolitan areas of the U.S. This national identity is more cosmopolitan and transnational in nature.[1]

The paradox of the election of 2008 and its aftermath is that the former, despite shrinking numbers, dominates political discourse, while the latter, demographically on the ascendant, finds itself stigmatized as being outside the mainstream.

In 1915 D.W. Griffith's epic of the antebellum, the Civil War, and Reconstruction eras, *The Birth of a Nation*, premiered in movie theaters across the U.S. The timing of the film was poignant. It coincided with the 50th anniversary of the surrender of the South at a courthouse in Appomattox, Virginia. The film, however, was bent on turning military defeat into social and cultural victory. The onerous establishment of black rule in the South depicted in the film had turned the orderly southern world upside down. It was payback time for the former slaves. Griffith offers scenes of whites out for a stroll on the sidewalks of the southern towns forced to step aside for the new black rulers during the new social order of the Reconstruction era where African American voter fraud is rampant.[2]

Griffith's dark vision of a white supremacist world turned upside down has a long reach. In interviews conducted in York, Pennsylvania, by National Public Radio in October 2008, one respondent expressed the view that an Obama victory would mean "payback time" for African Americans. She told the interviewers:

> I don't want to sound racist, and I'm not racist. But I feel if we put Obama in the White House, there will be chaos. I feel a lot of black people are going to feel it's payback time. And I made the statement, I said, 'You know, at one time the black man had to step off the sidewalk when a white person came down the sidewalk.' And I feel it's going to be somewhat reversed. I really feel it's going to get somewhat nasty.[3]

The notion that whites would have to cede public space to African Americans under an Obama administration was eerily reminiscent of Griffith's film. The second half of the film was devoted to the institution of black rule in the South, with the Ku Klux Klan coming to the rescue of the oppressed "Southland." Ben Cameron and his sister Flora are leaving their house, but are prevented from going past their gate by a group of black soldiers.

Silas Lynch, the protégé of Radical Republican Austin Stoneman (modeled on Congressman Thaddeus Stevens from the Reconstruction era), and described as the "mulatto leader of the blacks" confronts the couple by saying: "This sidewalk belongs to us as much as it does to you, 'Colonel' Cameron."[4]

The Birth of a Nation was, of course, based on Thomas Dixon's novel *The Clansman* and was infused with the ideology of the Lost Cause/Reconstruction historiography of the Dunning school at Columbia University. Black rule represented chaos over the antebellum order of the Southland, imposed by a hostile federal government.

In Griffith's narrative, however, the freed slaves, prodded by their nefarious northern accomplices, were singularly unfit to rule. Lascivious and endemically lazy, the only legislation of note that the South Carolina legislature could muster up energy to pass was one that permitted intermarriage between blacks and whites. To underscore his point, Griffith had black legislators, their bulging eyes full of lust, ogle the flowers of southern womanhood assembled in the galleries, awaiting the outcome with trepidation. In the film's rousing climax, order was restored when the Ku Klux Klan rode to the rescue of the hapless female population.

Griffith's choice of South Carolina was inspired. The Gadsden flag with the defiant moniker "Don't tread on me," a favorite at Tea Party rallies, was designed there. South Carolina was the first state to secede from the union and the site of the start of the Civil War. The fact that a white respondent in Pennsylvania could imagine a "payback" scenario in terms reminiscent of the discourse of Griffith's film speaks volumes about the state of race relations in what is now called the Age of Obama.

Just as with Reconstruction, the period of racial equality and justice in the 1960s was brief. A little over a year after LBJ had signed the Voting Rights Act and delivered a speech that ended with "we shall overcome," the midterm elections of 1966 marked the beginnings of a backlash against civil rights that was to be consolidated with the implementation of the southern strategy proposed by Kevin Phillips in 1968. The same year that the Kerner Commission Report concluded that "Our nation is moving toward two societies, one black, one white—separate and unequal," the Republican law and order candidate Richard Nixon and the neo-segregationist governor of Alabama, George Wallace, received 57 percent of the vote.[5]

In his second book, *The Audacity of Hope*, Obama noted that there were commentators who had interpreted the line in his 2004 Convention speech:

> There is not a black America and a white America and Latino America and Asian America—there's the United States of America" to mean that the U.S had already achieved a post-racial politics and a color-blind society. Obama sought to correct that impression by underscoring the salience of race while proposing ways to get beyond it. Thinking about race was like looking at a split screen, he argued, "to maintain in our sights the kind of America that we want while looking squarely at America as it is, to acknowledge the sins of our past and the challenges of the present without becoming trapped in cynicism or despair.[6]

Obama used two events in 2005 to illustrate his point. While attending the funeral of Rosa Parks, he reflected on how her single act of civil disobedience, refusing to give up her seat on a bus in Montgomery, Alabama, to a white passenger, sparked the civil rights movement. In a ceremony infused with memories of the segregated South in 1955 and thoughts of the improvement in race relations in the half-century that followed, Obama could not help but think of another event that unfolded only two months before. Hurricane Katrina had exposed the legacy of racial injustice and poverty that still plagued the U.S., but hope for "a transformative moment had ... quickly died away." Honoring the memory of Rosa Parks would necessitate more than the symbolic gestures of stamps and statues.[7]

Obama devoted much of the chapter on race in *The Audacity of Hope* to finding ways of bridging the racial divide by reconciling the political divide between conservative and liberal thought on race relations, acknowledging that African Americans, as liberals believed, were burdened by the legacy of racism, but also, as conservatives argued, bore responsibility for improving their own condition.

In 2004 the comedian Bill Cosby had angered many in the African American community when, speaking at an NAACP event to commemorate the 50th anniversary of the landmark Supreme Court decision on *Brown vs. Board of Education*, he launched into a rambling diatribe against parents who refused to take responsibility for their children and blamed crime and chronic black unemployment exclusively on systemic racism.[8] Later in the campaign, Obama would himself be criticized by the Reverend Jesse Jackson for making similar remarks in a Father's Day speech, in some off-color remarks Jackson made off-camera on the Fox network. Unlike Cosby, however, Obama attempted to strike a balance between urging parental responsibility and recognizing the burdens of history.[9]

The same sentiments informed Obama's speech on race. In responding to the controversy over his personal relationship with his Chicago church minister Jeremiah Wright, Obama chose to place it in the larger context of the history of race relations in the U.S. that went to the heart of American national identity. He acknowledged the gaps in understanding between white and black Americans while at the same time reminding his audience of the long struggle for racial justice. He used the idea of forming a more perfect union, enshrined in the first line of the U.S. Constitution, to resolve the inherent contradiction between the "stain" of slavery and the cause of freedom, both contained in the Constitution, in terms of a constant struggle over time. Obama's characterization of the Constitution as stained by slavery is anathema to the conservative movement. During the 2010 hearings for Elena Kagan, Obama's nominee for the Supreme Court, Republican senators criticized the first African American Supreme Court Justice, Thurgood Marshall (whom Kagan clerked for) for calling the Constitution "defective" because of the slavery issue.

According to Obama, the tension between current racial prejudices and the desire for racial reconciliation could be explained in these terms as well. As the son of a black Kenyan and a white Kansan who had chosen to be part of the African American community, Obama was in a unique position to understand the motivations behind the racial divide in the U.S. from both sides. He spoke of black anger as well as white resentment in an attempt to come to grips with the flawed reasoning that sustained the gap between races. He acknowledged the legacy of slavery and racial injustice that still affected African Americans while arguing that blaming it alone would ultimately stifle any chance for change.

Indeed, what Obama characterized as Wright's "profound mistake" was not that he spoke out against racism, but that "he spoke as if our society was static; as if no progress has been made." It was precisely this ahistorical way of looking at race that had led to a "racial stalemate." He linked the need to confront the issue of race with his own message for change and called for an end to the politics of cynicism (perhaps an implicit jab at the race baiting of the Republicans) and the need to address the problems that confronted all Americans, regardless of race or ethnic background.[10]

The speech was not only an appeal to Americans to live up to the creed of *e pluribus unum* but an attempt to see the promise of the U.S. not as a static set of ideals, but as a continuing effort toward creating a more perfect union. As a member of a new generation of black politicians with no personal memory of the civil rights movement, Obama has had to overcome the skepticism that many of the older generation of leaders voiced about the viability of his candidacy.

Less than a month after he announced that he would run for president, Obama attempted to persuade the older generation of African Americans of the viability of his candidacy. In a speech at Brown Chapel A.M.E Church commemorating the Voting Rights march in Selma, Obama paid tribute to the civil rights generation: "I'm here because somebody marched. I'm here because you all sacrificed for me. I stand on the shoulders of giants. I thank the Moses generation; but we've got to remember, now, that Joshua still had a job to do."[11]

Quoting Robert F. Kennedy, who observed that the civil rights movement sent "ripples of hope all around the world," he deftly interwove his father's desire to come to the U.S. with the message of racial justice. Looking to the future, he talked at length about the unfinished business the Joshua generation needed to accomplish.[12] For most conservatives, however, the job was done with the signing of the Civil Rights and Voting Rights Acts.

As president, Obama confronts the same dilemmas that other young leaders such as Deval Patrick, the Governor of Massachusetts, and Cory Booker, the Mayor of Newark, New Jersey, are dealing with at the state and local level. A Pew Research Center survey published at the end of 2007 found a values gap between middle class and poor blacks as well as a general attitude of pessimism about the state of black progress.[13]

The argument here is that President Obama, closely watched for signs of parochialism or racial resentment, would have less maneuvering room to champion spending on the urban poor, say, or to challenge racial injustice.[14]

Unlike the civil rights movement, the systemic forms of racism that impede African American progress today, such as lack of employment opportunities in major metropolitan areas, discrimination in housing, and inequities in the criminal justice system, are largely hidden from public view and rarely enter the public debate.[15] However, any attempt from Obama to address these problems head-on would likely encounter accusations of undue favoritism toward African Americans.

Many young black leaders come from the growing black middle class and are highly educated. As state and local leaders, however, they confront cities and districts with high rates of black poverty. Unlike in the civil rights era, no legal barriers exist to prevent black progress. Yet inequities between blacks and whites persist. The new generation of black politicians is clearly aware of these disparities but has to walk a fine line in order not to be perceived as pandering to the African American community. Furthermore, while President Obama will clearly serve as a role model to young blacks, his success can erode the already fragile support for affirmative action programs. Paradoxically, the first African American president may well find it difficult to fight against racial injustice or champion programs to help improve the plight of the urban poor.

Despite these possible problems, Obama is unwavering in his belief that transformative change is not only possible, but necessary. In his victory speech in Grant Park, Chicago, on November 4, he offered a poignant example of how the arc of history is bent toward justice. He told the story of Ann Nixon Cooper, who at 106 years old, was born the year after the African American leader and educator Booker T. Washington visited the White House, and the year before W.E.B. Du Bois penned the prophetic words in *The Souls of Black Folk*. Cooper, Obama reminded the jubilant crowd that had gathered to celebrate his election as the 44th President of the

United States, "was born just a generation past slavery; a time when there were no cars on the road or planes in the sky; when someone like her couldn't vote for two reasons—because she was a woman and because of the color of her skin."[16]

Obama cited a litany of the momentous transformations during the 20th century brought about by war, social movements, and science to drive home his point that the U.S. is not, as Wright would have it, irrevocably racist and the American people not forever susceptible to coded racism, as the Republicans might like to think. Ann Nixon Cooper's freedom to vote is part of a larger story of the meaning of freedom. If freedom is central to American national identity, the story of Ann Nixon Cooper, which recalls that of Ernest Gaines's fictional character of Jane Pittman, is testament to the fact that freedom is not a fixed category but has been subject to changing definitions as a result of debates and struggles.[17]

The 21st-century *Birth of a Nation* is perhaps not quite as blatant as Griffith's film, but the sense that the U.S. has been taken over persists not only among a vocal minority, but also within the ranks of the Republican Party. The so-called "birther" movement contends that Obama was born in Kenya and therefore is an illegitimate president. In a poll taken by CNN/Opinion Research Corporation on Obama's 49th birthday, August 4, 2010, more than one-quarter of all Americans still harbored doubts about Obama's citizenship. Eleven percent of those polled stated categorically their belief that Obama was not born in the U.S., while another 16 percent responded that he was "probably not" born in the country. Obama's place of birth is not the only issue among conservatives. Businessman and host of *Celebrity Apprentice* Donald Trump revived the "birther" issue during his brief flirtation with running for President in the spring of 2011 and as late as October 2011 presidential candidate Governor Rick Perry of Texas persisted in casting doubt on Obama's birthplace. In a recent article in *Forbes*, Dinesh D'Souza accused Obama of inheriting an anticolonial mindset from his father, a view echoed by former Speaker of the House and Republican presidential candidate Newt Gingrich.[18]

A brief glance at some of the conservative political discourse in recent decades brings a sense of *déjà vu*, an amalgam of antebellum, Civil War, and Jim Crow-era themes. Several prominent Republican politicians, including Rick Perry, have openly talked about secession from the union as a protest against what conservatives see as a federal government takeover of the U.S.

In 1980 Ronald Reagan chose to begin his presidential campaign in Neshoba, Mississippi, where three civil rights workers were murdered in 1964. Reagan used the occasion to proclaim his allegiance to the principle of states' rights, a rallying cry of segregationist forces since Strom Thurmond's "Dixiecrat" movement in 1948. In the 21st century the call for states' rights comes from the so-called "tenthers" (adherents of states' rights who have the 10th Amendment to the Constitution as their guiding light) and the Tea Party movement, whose ubiquitous use of the Gadsden flag has been recast fromresistance to the British colonizing power to the tyranny of the federal government.

In August 2010 Senator Lindsay Graham (R-SC) recommended rescinding the birthright citizenship clause of the 14th Amendment. As Garrett Epps observed in his study of the amendment, it "has, over time, changed almost every detail of our national life. Scholars have called it 'the second Constitution.' [It produced] 'a more perfect union' than the old one."[19] During the debate over the amendment, President Andrew Johnson weighed in with this argument:

> This provision comprehends the Chinese of the Pacific States, Indians sub-ject to taxation, the people called Gipsies (sic), as well as the entire race designated as blacks, people of color, negroes, mulattoes, and persons of African blood. Is it sound policy to make our entire colored population and all other excepted classes citizens of the United States?[20]

In his speech on race, Obama advanced the view that history is unfolding and social, economic, and political progress can suffer setbacks as well as victories. Even though he is fond of amending Martin Luther King's refrain the "arc of justice" to the the "arc of history bends toward justice," he is, of course, fully aware of the role that human agency plays in advancing justice. Not so for many conservative historians (from Gertrude Himmelfarb to Lynn Cheney to the current darling of conservatives, David Barton). History is almost frozen in time, punctuated by the efforts of American heroes to represent goals already set in stone.

By acknowledging that the birth of the U.S. had been tainted by the scourge of slavery, Obama was drawing on decades of academic work on early America. As early as 1975 the historian Edmund Morgan observed in his seminal work *American Slavery, American Freedom* that in order to understand the paradox of early U.S. history, the coexistence of slavery and freedom, Virginia would be the place to begin.[21]

Virginia, it would seem, would also be the place to elide slavery from American memory, if it were left to the newly elected Republican governor, Bob McDonnell. In the state that was home to the Confederate capital, Richmond, and the CSA's most famous general, Robert E. Lee, in the 1860s, but which elected the first African American governor, Douglas Wilder, in 1990 and which voted Democratic in a presidential election for the first time since LBJ in 1964, McDonnell reintroduced Confederate History Month, with no mention of slavery because, as he put it, he wanted only to focus on the "significant" issues of 1861–65.

McDonnell's view of Confederate history conforms to that of a number of reenactment groups and organizations such as the League of the South, the Council of Conservative Citizens and the Sons of Confederate Veterans.[22] The historical amnesia seems almost willful, an attempt, to paraphrase Griffith, to expunge U.S. history of those whose presence in America "planted the first seeds of disunion."[23] It is hardly surprising that a school board that suggested placing the inaugural address of Jefferson Davis, first and only president of the Confederacy, alongside that of Abraham Lincoln, should be based in Texas, where Rick Perry only recently talked openly of secession from the Union.

Obama's view of history is clearly at odds with that of most conservatives in the U.S. The history wars are an important component of the politics of backlash, rooted as they are in changes in historical interpretation during the decade conservatives love to hate, the 1960s. As a weapon against what many conservatives see as a conscious attempt by a left-wing academy to undermine American exceptionalism by looking at U.S. history from the bottom up, curriculum proposals have become a battleground. Conservatives mounted sustained attacks against the National Standards during the Clinton years and heartily approve of the more recent proposals for amending textbooks in U.S. history put forward by the Texas school board.

In September 2009 former President Jimmy Carter offered an explanation for the resistance to what many perceive as black rule in the 21st century. "I think an overwhelming portion of the intensely demonstrated animosity toward President Barack Obama is based on the fact that he is a black man, that he's African American."[24]

One way of assessing the validity of Carter's statement is to look at three issues that have racial dimensions: health care reform, voter registration, and the incident that became known as "Gatesgate." Like Griffith's epic, we see in these three issues the purported arrogance of African Americans, their propensity for fraud in order to gain power, and their forcing through legislation that favors minorities and disadvantages whites. Health care, voting rights, and racial justice have long been supported by progressive ideology and opposed by reactionary ideology.

During the 2008 presidential campaign, several groups with no direct affiliation with the Obama campaign became involved in voter registration drives. Perhaps the most prominent was the grassroots organization Association of Community Organizations for Reform Now (ACORN). ACORN was formed in 1970 and, according to its website, "'is the nation's largest grassroots community organization of low- and moderate-income people with over 400,000 member families organized into more than 1,200 neighborhood chapters in 110 cities across the country."[25] ACORN first garnered national attention for its work in helping to rebuild the devastated 9th Ward in New Orleans in the wake of Hurricane Katrina.

In the course of the 2008 campaign ACORN launched voter registration drives in primarily poor neighborhoods across the country. The overzealousness of some recruits caused the organization to come under fire from the McCain campaign and conservative talk radio. There had been several instances where enthusiastic volunteers, in their eagerness to submit long lists of voters, had filled out registration cards with names such as Mickey Mouse. ACORN regretted these isolated glitches, but pointed out that the names would have been rejected at the polling booth anyway, and there was consequently no justification for John McCain to charge in October 2008 that ACORN "is now on the verge of maybe perpetrating one of the greatest frauds in voter history in this country, maybe destroying the fabric of democracy."[26]

Project Vote, an affiliate of ACORN, had been at the forefront of the registration drives. Since Obama had been head of the local Project Vote office in Chicago in 1992, Republicans sought to link ACORN directly to the Obama campaign. However, Project Vote was an independent grass-roots organization during the time Obama worked for it in Chicago. So persistent were the rumors of Obama's affiliation with ACORN that the campaign website set up to respond to false accusations, "Fight the smears," posted a page devoted to refuting right-wing claims about ACORN.[27]

In October 2008, at the height of the campaign, a full 78 percent of the negative attacks on ACORN were devoted to "voter fraud." A report published in September, 2009 found:

> The attacks on ACORN originated with business groups and political groups that opposed ACORN's organizing work around living wages, predatory lending, and registration of low-income and minority voter. These groups created frames to discredit ACORN that were utilized by conservative "opinion entrepreneurs" within the conservative "echo chamber"—publications, TV and radio talk shows, blogs and websites, think tanks, and columnists—to test, refine, and circulate narrative frames about ACORN. These conservative "opinion entrepreneurs" were successful in injecting their perspective on ACORN into the mainstream media.[28]

So successful was the conservative narrative that Congress voted to cut off funding for ACORN in September 2009. Beset by the lethal combination of negative press and funding difficulties, ACORN filed for bankruptcy in March 2010. As James Atlas argues in his comprehensive study of ACORN, without grassroots organizations such as ACORN, it will be difficult for Obama to achieve his ambitious agenda.[29]

Recent Republican efforts to curtail voting rights for minorities and the poor show that the ACORN episode was not an aberration, but rather emblematic of current Republican attitudes. The Brennan Center for Justice has presented overwhelming evidence that 19 laws and two executive actions passed in 14 states with Republican governors and legislatures can result in restricting the right to vote for more than 5 million eligible voters and that there is "substantial evidence that these laws will make it more difficult for minorities than whites to vote."[30] Little wonder that veteran Civil Rights activist and current Congressman from Georgia John Lewis has characterized these laws as nothing less than "a poll tax by another name."

In July 2009 Obama held a press conference intended to promote his health care reform. However, it was the last question that attracted the most attention, even though it had nothing to do with health care. Obama was asked what he thought of the arrest of Harvard professor, Henry Louis Gates, Jr.

Gates had been arrested at his house in Cambridge, Massachusetts, after the police had received a phone call suggesting that a burglary was in progress. Gates had tried to force his jammed front door open and was in his house when the police arrived. He was handcuffed but later released. The arresting officer, Sergeant James Crowley, was white. Gates was an African American.

At the press conference, Obama, obliquely referring to the existence of racial profiling among law enforcement, said the Cambridge police had acted "stupidly" in arresting Gates. He went on to say that racial profiling in the U.S. was an indisputable fact. In a discussion on *Fox News*, the popular right-wing host Glenn Beck expressed his view that Obama's comment revealed "a guy who has a deep-seated hatred for white people or the white culture."[31]

In characterizing the arrest as an example of racial profiling, Obama was hardly being controversial. A number of reports have uncovered instances of racial profiling across the U.S. Just a month before the incident involving Gates, The American Civil Liberties Union published a wide-ranging report on *The Persistence of Racial and Ethnic Profiling in the United States*. According to the report, racial minorities suffered from unfair victimization by authorities "while they work, drive, shop, pray, travel, and stand on the street."[32]

But something else was at work in the conservative response to Obama's remarks. In the eyes of many conservatives, Obama had revealed himself to be a racial partisan, instinctively taking the side of African Americans against whites. The much-heralded "beer summit" between Obama, Vice President Joe Biden, Gates, and Crowley did little to resolve these divisions. As Charles Ogletree concluded in his study of the case, the arrest of Gates "proves ... that America has not achieved its goal of being a post-racial society."[33]

As the ACLU report showed, the persistence of racial profiling has contributed to the over-representation of minorities in the nation's prisons. Disparities in sentencing and incarceration between black and white are, according to Michelle Alexander, a new form of Jim Crow, since former nonviolent felons suffer from disenfranchisement and legal discrimination in housing.[34]

In February 2010 radio talk show personality Rush Limbaugh characterized Obama's health care reform bill as something more insidious. "This is a civil rights bill, this is reparations," intoned Limbaugh, after saying that Obama's policies amount to nothing less than returning the wealth of the U.S. to its rightful owners.[35]

In the 1940s opposition to President Harry S. Truman's proposal for national health care from southern politicians was rooted in the fear that it would mean integrating hospitals. The backlash against the civil rights movement in the late 1960s and early 1970s was in large part based on the perception that the Johnson administration was favoring the interests of African Americans over the white population.

Demonstrations against "Obamacare" and what are regarded as Obama's redistributive tax policies featuring posters of him as a socialist and/or communist (the two political ideologies seem interchangeable on the right) conflate the fact that the president is African American and the perception that the civil rights movement was influenced by communism, and that national health care constitutes alms for the undeserving poor (read minorities). As Carol Polsgrove points out:

> As the great lid of McCarthyism settled over postwar America, advocates of racial change were so frequently labeled communist that it is hard not to believe that resistance to racial change accounted for much of the energy behind the domestic assault on communism.[36]

In his speech dedicating the monument to Martin Luther King in Washington, DC, in October 2011, President Obama reminded his audience that King "was vilified by many, denounced as a rabble rouser and an agitator, a communist and a radical."[37]

A 2010 survey of the Tea Party movement reveals how these sentiments fuel opposition to Obama. According to a CBS News/*New York Times* poll published in April, the overwhelming majority of Tea Party supporters are white (89 percent versus 77 percent of the population as a whole). They make up about 18 percent of the electorate and over half (54 percent) vote Republican. A sizeable majority regard themselves as conservative (34 percent somewhat conservative, 39 percent very conservative).

On the question of racial attitudes, the responses are revealing, to say the least. Fifty-two percent of Tea Party respondents believe that "too much [has] been made of the problems facing black people" even though only 25 percent replied that the Obama administration favored blacks over whites. However, the figure among all respondents was a paltry 11 percent.[38]

The weekend of August 28–29, 2010 can serve as a fitting illustration of the challenge Obama faces in attempting to form a more perfect union. On the 47th anniversary of the March on Washington for Jobs and Freedom, conservative *Fox News* commentator Glenn Beck held a rally on the steps of the Lincoln Memorial that he called Restoring Honor. One of the aims of the rally was, in his words, to "reclaim the civil rights movement." According to this version of history, full and equal rights for African Americans were obtained in 1964/65 and Martin Luther King Jr.'s "dream" of judging all by the "content of their character" had been achieved. Persistent calls for affirmative action and the rise of identity politics in the 1970s had turned the dream into a sectarian nightmare. Like Obama, Beck cast himself as someone standing on the shoulders of the leaders of the civil rights movement. Unlike Obama, Beck's connection to the civil rights movement is virtually non-existent.

The legacy of Martin Luther King Jr. has been narrowed considerably since his death in 1968. Most Americans only know the "I have a dream" speech (especially the phrase "content of their character"). The Martin Luther King of 1968, who spoke for economic justice and against militarism in Vietnam, has been airbrushed from history. So insidious is this selective memory that Michael Eric Dyson has proposed a 10-year moratorium on reading or listening to the speech.[39]

Almost a half-century after King's final campaign on behalf of sanitation workers in Memphis, African Americans suffer disproportionately from economic inequality. The most recent report by the organization United for a Fair Economy (UFE), *State of the Dream 2011: austerity for whom?* explores the devastating effects of economic inequality on the African American community and "builds on [Martin Luther] King's call for economic equality in a 'second phase' of the Black Freedom Movement."[40] The statistics make for depressing reading:

- The official unemployment rate is 15.8 percent among blacks and 13 percent among Latinos as of December 2010. The white unemployment rate is 8.5 percent.
- While blacks gained five cents to each white dollar of median family income from 1947 to 1977, they gained only one cent in the 32 years since.
- Blacks earn 57 cents and Latinos earn 59 cents to each dollar of white median family income. The corresponding figures for median household income are 60 cents and 70 cents.[41]

Recommendations include an active role for the federal government in implementing "a 'Marshall Plan for the United States' or 'Works Progress Administration for the 21st Century'."[42]

August 29, 2010 marked the fifth anniversary of Hurricane Katrina. Spike Lee released a four-hour documentary, *If God is Willing and da Creek Don't Rise*, on the current state of New Orleans. Many displaced African Americans have still not returned to the city. Low-cost housing has been demolished in favor of gentrification. Hospitals and schools serving low-income residents have not been re-opened. Another HBO production, *Treme*, is both homage and dirge, chronicling the struggle for survival after the hurricane. For many in New Orleans, the dream has, in the words of poet Langston Hughes, been deferred, and the sores allowed to fester.[43]

The "birther" movement, the secessionists, the "tenthers," those advocating revising the 14th Amendment, the history revisionists and the Tea Party movement, the accusations leveled against ACORN, Obama's response to "Gatesgate," and the perception that health care reform favors African American and other minorities all highlight the dilemma facing the first African American president. Obama, who clearly views history in terms of incremental progress constantly in danger of setbacks, is constrained politically by those who view his presidency in terms of illegitimacy, voter fraud, unjust persecution of African American by white authorities, and undue favoritism toward African Americans and other minorities in the form of government handouts.

Obama's task is further compounded by the fact that Democratic politicians like Bill and Hillary Clinton were not above race baiting during the 2008 campaign. Bill Clinton, in comments following the South Carolina primary, sought to link Obama with the more controversial Jesse Jackson. Hillary Clinton made overt appeals to white working-class Americans in her effort to overcome Obama's lead in the primaries.

Furthermore, according to Houston Baker, many high-profile black intellectuals (including Gates) have betrayed Martin Luther King's legacy by, like many of their white counterparts, focusing on the "Dream" speech instead of his emphasis on economic justice and a domestic Marshall Plan. King saw the Civil Rights and Voting Rights Acts as a beginning, not an end. He was, as Baker puts it, a "political radical" who was "on the path to Black Power."[44]

For his part, Obama has made no secret of his intellectual influences. His political activism may have started in the anti-apartheid movement in the 1980s, but the man who came of age after the civil rights movement was well versed in its accomplishments. He spoke of the first volume of Taylor Branch's magisterial study of Martin Luther King and the civil rights movement, *Parting the Waters*, as "my story." In his autobiography, he recounts how his mother introduced him to books on the civil rights movement.[45] At Occidental College, he studied neocolonialism and Franz Fanon.[46] At the University of Chicago, he taught a seminar on current issues in racism and the law that included discussions of discriminatory sentencing, welfare policy, and reparations and a course on individual rights that dealt with issues such as equal protection and voting rights. The packet of readings covered the history of Reconstruction, Jim Crow, and the civil rights movement, excerpts from Booker T. Washington, W.E.B. Du Bois, Martin Luther King, and Malcolm X, as well as debates over slavery and affirmative action.[47]

Obama's deep knowledge of African American history and contemporary racial issues and his political activism as a community organizer in a major U.S. city could have laid the groundwork for a comprehensive transformation of not only the discourse of race, but of public policy. However, Obama's efforts at reconciliation and racial justice face obstacles because, and not in spite of, his being an African American. He can quietly establish an Office of Urban Affairs in order to "develop an effective strategy for urban America" but has been criticized for giving it too little power, no doubt from fear of opposition from the right.[48] By the same token, in August 2010, Obama signed into law the Fair Sentencing Act, reducing disparities in penalties for crack and powder cocaine, which could in the long term alleviate the mass incarceration resulting from Reagan's War on Drugs that is waged primarily in poor communities of color.

Demographic developments in the U.S. point in one direction—toward a majority–minority nation by mid-century. But the political reality of the first decades of the 21st century points in two directions, which have everything to do with the future of U.S. national identity. Americans can choose to accept what Obama in his inaugural address characterized as the strength of their "patchwork heritage" and work toward a society in which race no longer has salience. Or, as many on the right of the political spectrum believe, Americans have a patriotic obligation to take their country back by opposing Obama's race-based form of socialism by any means necessary. The irony of the present situation is that a president who first gained national prominence with his vision of One America as a more perfect union presides over a United States that is still a house divided.

Notes

1   See Pedersen, Carl. *Obama's America* (Edinburgh: Edinburgh University Press, 2009).
2   See the script of *Birth of a Nation* in Lang, Robert, ed. *The Birth of a Nation: D. W. Griffith, director* (New Brunswick, NJ: Rutgers University Press, 1994), pp. 43–161.
3   Inskeep, Steve and Norris, Michele. "York voters express post-election hopes, fears," National Public Radio, *All Things Considered* (24 October 2008), www.npr.org/ templates/story/story.php?storyId = 96187966
4   Lang. *The Birth*, p. 99.
5   Report of the National Advisory Commission on Civil Disorders (Washington: U.S. Government Printing Office, 1968).
6   Obama, Barack. *The Audacity of Hope: thoughts on reclaiming the American dream* (New York: Crown, 2006), p. 233.
7   Obama. *The Audacity of Hope*, p. 230.
8   Cosby, Bill. "Address at the NAACP" on the 50th Anniversary of *Brown v. Board of Education*, www.americanrhetoric.com/speeches/billcosby pound cakespeech.htm
9   For two sides of the debate on black responsibility, see Dyson, Michael Eric. *Is Bill Cosby Right? Or has the black middle class lost its mind?* (New York: Basic Civitas, 2006); Williams, Juan. *Enough: the phony leaders, dead-end move-ments, and culture of failure that are undermining black America—and what we can do about it* (New York: Three Rivers Press, 2007).
10 Obama, Barack. "A more perfect union," March 18, 2008, http://my.barack -obama.com/page/content/hisownwords
11 Obama, Barack. "Remarks at Selma Voting Rights Commemoration," March 4, 2007, www.barackobama.com/2007/03/04/selma_voting_rights_march _comm.php
12 Ibid.
13 Pew Research Center. "Blacks see growing values gap between poor and middle class," November 13, 2007, http://pewsocialtrends.org/pubs/700/black -public-opinion
14 Bai, op.cit.
15 Wilson, William Julius. *More Than Just Race: being black and poor in the inner city* (New York: Norton, 2009).
16 Obama, Barack. "Victory speech," November 4, 2008, *Huffington Post*, www. huffingtonpost.com/2008/11/04/obama-victory-speech_n_141194.html

17   Gaines, Ernest. *The Autobiography of Miss Jane Pittman* (New York: Bantam, 1982).

18   D'Souza, Dinesh. "How Obama thinks," *Forbes* (September 27, 2010), www. forbes.com/forbes/2010/0927/politics-socialism-capitalism-private-enterprises-obama-business-problem.html

19   Epps, Garrett. *Democracy Reborn: the fourteenth Amendment and the fight for equal rights in post-Civil War America* (New York: Henry Holt, 2006), p. 11.

20   Johnson, Andrew. Quoted in Epps. *Democracy Reborn.*

21   Morgan, Edmund. *American Slavery, American Freedom* (New York: Norton, 1995).

22   See the Southern Poverty Law Center, www.splcenter.org/get-informed/intelligence-files/ideology/neo-confederate

23   Griffith. *BN* 44.

24   MacAskill, Ewan. "Jimmy Carter: animosity toward Obama is due to racism," *Guardian*, September 16, 2009, www.guardian.co.uk/world/2009/sep/16/jimmy-carter-racism-barack-obama

25   See acorn.org.

26   Rood, Justin. "McCain ACORN fears overblown," *ABC News: the blotter from Brian Ross*, October 16, 2008, http://abcnews.go.com/Blotter/story?id=6049529

27   See the Obama website. "Fight the smears," www.fightthesmears.com/articles/20/acornrumor

28   Martin, Christopher R. and Dreier, Peter. "Executive summary," *Manipulating the Public Agenda: why ACORN was in the news, and what the news got wrong*, September 2009, www.uni.edu/martinc/acornstudy.html

29   Atlas, James. *Seeds of Change: the story of ACORN, America's most controversial antipoverty community organizing group* (Nashville, TN: Vanderbilt University Press, 2010), p. 257.

30   The Brennan Center for Justice, *Voting Law Changes in 2012*, http://brennan.3cdn.net/d16bab3d00e5a82413_66m6y5xpw.pdf

31   "*Fox News* host: Obama is a 'racist'," *Huffington Post*, July 28, 2009, www.huffingtonpost.com/2009/07/28/fox-host-glenn-beck-obama_n_246310.html

32   The American Civil Liberties Union, *The Persistence of Racial and Ethnic Profiling in the United States*, June 2009, www.aclu.org/files/pdfs/humanrights/cerd_final report.pdf#page=13

33   Ogletree, Charles. *The Presumption of Guilt: the arrest of Henry Louis Gates, Jr. and race, class, and crime in America* (New York: Palgrave Macmillan, 2010), p. 115. Ogletree includes interviews with 100 African American men who have been illegally arrested.

34   Alexander, Michelle. *The New Jim Crow: mass incarceration in the age of colorblindness* (New York: New Press, 2009).

35   "Limbaugh criticizes health care reform as a 'civil rights bill' and 'reparations'," *Media Matters*, February 22, 2010, http://mediamatters.org/mmtv/201002220021

36   Polsgrove, Carol. *Divided Minds: intellectuals and the civil rights movement* (New York: Norton, 2001), p. 74.

37   Remarks by the President at the Martin Luther King, Jr. memorial dedication, October 16, 2011, www.whitehouse.gov/the-press-office/2011/10/16/remarks-president-martin-luther-king-jr-memorial-dedication

38   Zernike, Kate. *Boiling Mad: inside tea party America* (New York: Times Books, 2010), p. 211.

39   Dyson, Michael Eric. *I May Not Get There With You: the true Martin Luther King, Jr.* (New York: Free Press, 2000), p. 15.

40   United for a Fair Economy, *State of the Dream 2011: austerity for whom?*, www.faireconomy.org/files/State_of_the_Dream_2011.pdf

41   United for a Fair Economy, p. v.
42   United for a Fair Economy, p. 25.
43   Hughes, Langston. "A dream deferred," in *Montage of a Dream Deferred* (New York: Henry Holt & Co., 1951).
44   Baker, Jr., Houston A. *Betrayal: how black intellectuals have abandoned the ideals of the civil rights era* (New York: Columbia University Press, 2008), pp. 41, 36.
45   Obama, Barack. *Dreams from my Father: a story of race and inheritance* (New York: Three Rivers Press, 1995), p. 50.
46   Ibid., p. 100.
47   Remnick, David. *The Bridge: the life and rise of Barack Obama* (New York: Knopf, 2010), pp. 262–63.
48   Executive Order. Establishment of the White House Office of Urban Affairs, February 19, 2009, www.whitehouse.gov/the_press_office/Executive-Order-Establishment-of-the-White-House-Office-of-Urban-Affairs/. Dayo Olopade,"What happened to the Office of Urban Policy?" *The Root*, April 27, 2009, www.theroot.com/views/what-happened-office-urban-policy

3 Republican Mavericks

The Anti-Obama Impulse in the 2008 Election

Robert Busby

The historic election of Barack Obama in 2008 ignited a celebration over the ascendancy of an individual of African American descent to the White House. As an overarching theme this received significant coverage, as did the individual candidacy of Obama and his opposition to the Republican Party, its political legacy, and its economic management. The Republican Party, in addressing the challenge of Obama through 2008, faced challenges distinctive to this particular election. Its candidate, John McCain, had to attack the Obama candidacy without appearing to create blatant offense on grounds of race, or being seen to use queries over Obama's past as a political weapon through which to look for electoral advantage. That the Republican party was unlikely to gain any significant proportion of votes from ethnic minority groups made this particular challenge less, rather than more, difficult. McCain had no real expectation of entertaining votes from this demographic group and as a consequence had little need to campaign at length in seeking to accommodate the African American constituency, or to allocate party finance towards a futile goal. As a consequence the nature of the relationship between the Republican Party, Obama, and the minority voter was one that had an added and somewhat complex dimension. The Republican Party had its own electoral mandate, targeted traditionally supportive demographic groups intended to fulfill a winning electoral coalition, and received significant media coverage for both its presidential and vice presidential candidates.

The outcome of the 2008 election rested on issues such as electoral demographic composition, political culture, popular interpretations of Obama, and the plight of the incumbent party in the White House. This chapter considers the strategy of the Republican Party in addressing the challenges posed by Barack Obama. These strategies entertained familiar and well-practiced tactics that were imbued with a conservative spirit, designed to appeal to a traditional Republican vote and shore up the electoral coalitions that had proved successful on prior occasions and had proved to appeal to swing voters in 2004. In parallel, there existed an offensive strategy that stressed selected attributes of Obama's past associations, and queried the grounds on which race as a distinctive element might be introduced into the election. The variable of race was one that was significant during the election.

There were expectations that race factors counted against Obama as potentially the first African American president and these might deter white voters from rallying to the Democrat cause. In conjunction with this, there existed an understanding that some might actually vote for him on the grounds that he might be the first African American president and would make history as a consequence. Within the overall remit of the debate subgroups emerged, especially in relation to older voters, who in particular expressed anxiety about the possible election of a black president (Redlawsk, Tolbert, and Franko 2010).

Theoretical discussion about the meaning of the election of an African American president to the Republican Party and what it reveals about the contemporary politics of race is widespread and divergent in its interpretations and conclusions. Commentators such as Edge believed that the election of Obama did not represent a marked change in the beliefs of Republican voters or white voters and that understandings of race and politics were changed in terms of perception rather than reality (Edge 2010). Underlying partisan divisions on race remained intact both before and after the election. Harris and Davidson considered that there were pronounced alterations in the electoral landscape. They asserted that: "The far right has been broadly rebuffed, the neoconservative war hawks displaced, and the diehard advocates of neoliberal economics are in thorough disarray" (Harris and Davidson 2009). In a more constructive tone, Ford, Johnson and Maxwell considered that partisan politics had been altered by Obama's campaign and his victory. They contended that there were more widespread issues relating to the demographic construct, and that Obama had forged a new dynamic in American politics. They asserted:

> by taking advantage of a politically correct atmosphere that no longer tolerates the blatant race-baiting characterized by the Southern Dixiecrats or the Republican Southern strategy campaigns of the 20th century, Obama built a coalition of White voters, comprising Democrats, Independents, and some crossover Republicans.
>
> (Ford, Johnson, and Maxwell 2010)

Prevailing research has pinpointed race and race-based attitudes as having a role to play in determining party identity and affiliation, through periods of realignment and consolidation in the modern era, with the Republican Party being associated with an Anglo affiliation and the Democrats accommodating racial minorities (Philpot 2007).The activities of the parties in campaign activity and rhetoric has entrenched this racial division and added to it, further to embed the ongoing historical trends (Hutchings and Valentino 2004). The election of 2008 proved to be a barometer not only of the Obama candidacy, but also of the position of the GOP in American politics, and of its position in pulling together meaningful electoral coalitions in a demographically changing contemporary America.

In the first instance, McCain's task of forging a Republican coalition hinged on an appreciation of the nature of the American electorate in 2008.

However, a dissection of the voting bloc, taken in conjunction with voter mobilization and turnout, highlights the enhanced prospects for Obama as a consequence of demographic change. The 2008 election was the most diverse in terms of ethnicity of all American presidential elections. The number of potential voters from ethnic minority groups was the largest, the turnout of ethnic minority groups was the largest, and the share of the potential vote by white voters was the lowest in history (Lopez and Taylor 2009). The variation in voter turnout and the composition of the vote in 2008 witnessed notable voter mobilization in younger ethnic groupings and among African American women. There were also significant statistical variations in the changes population growth brought on the nature of the electorate. While the increase in voter eligibility increased among the general populace by 4.6 percent, "the increase in the Hispanic populace was from 16.1 million in 2004 to 19.5 million in 2008, or 21.4%" (Lopez and Taylor 2009). The year 2008 witnessed a disproportionate increase in the participation of minority voting groups as opposed to the participation of white voters, whose involvement increased only marginally. While changes in voting eligibility and turnout give valuable information about the changing demographics of the American electorate, the dispersal of votes gives some indication of the template on which the election was based and the nature of the campaign strategies that were employed by the Republican and Democrat camps respectively. Minority groups were increasingly significant in creating a winning position. Yet in the modern era the GOP had struggled to incorporate minority groups into its winning coalitions to any significant degree. There are, however, dissenting voices about the notion of turnout and its transference into an Obama victory. Osborn, McClurg, and Knoll argue that while turnout was a factor, Obama's ability to change the minds of voters to support his cause was a contributory element (Osborn, McClurg, and Knoll 2010). This suggests that not only were those who were mobilized persuaded of Obama's stance, but other issues, such as disillusionment with the Republican cause, the power of advertising, and the unique nature of the Obama candidacy may have had an impact in forging Obama's electoral coalition.

There were discernible differences in the turnout of majority and minority groups and who they voted for in 2008. The evidence suggests that the impact of these votes both reflected the campaign strategies employed by the political parties and shaped the outcome of the race. Ninety-five percent of black voters voted for Obama, alongside 67 percent of Latino voters and 62 percent of Asian voters. Reflecting an undercurrent of race-based statistical evidence, the white vote favored McCain by 55 percent to 43 percent. The Joint Center for Political and Economic Studies found evidence to suggest that the already weak identification of black Republicans with the party had declined by 60 percent since the 2004 election (Sositis 2008). McCain's candidacy for the GOP was considered to entertain the lowest ever rating from African Americans for a first time nominee in a presidential election, with the support of 22.8 percent of black respondents. On virtually every count of the African American vote, there were record low figures for the McCain candidacy, or pronounced changes from the support afforded Bush and the Republican Party since the 2004 election. Only 4 percent of black voters considered themselves Republicans, in contrast to 10 percent in 2004 (Sositis 2008). To a large degree, the positioning of the Republican Party here is instructive. It had very little to lose if it alienated the African American vote as it had so little of it in the first instance. Attacking Obama on the grounds of his playing to narrow demographic constituencies on account of his background and past associations, or that he might make history for the African American community, were, in theory at least, all viable components in the Republican armory as the Republican Party was one that largely did not appeal to the African American voting bloc.

Conflicts and contrasts existed within the Republican fold over whether Obama, on account of his political mandate, offered a viable alternative to a Republican ticket that was both difficult to identify ideologically, and appeared to sporadically veer to the right and offer little to those who were dispossessed or suffering most from the pitfalls of the economic downturn. Among the senior echelons of the Republican Party, there existed a conflict of interests over what Obama offered as an alternative to the GOP, particularly to those individuals who were of African American heritage. In media circles and in the political sphere, the attraction of Obama was evident from early in the election cycle, allowing the dissemination of doubt within the Republican Party as to its contemporary resonance and its position in the political debate regarding the economy. The most senior individual who voiced doubt about whether he might retain Republican allegiances was Colin Powell, former Secretary of State. He argued: "I will vote for the individual I think that brings the best set of tools to the problems of 21st century America and the 21st century world regardless of party, regardless of anything else other than the most qualified candidate" (USA Today 2008). While Powell's considerations left a little to the imagination, creating muted public doubt about the Republican ticket, others were more forceful in addressing the attraction of an African American candidate to the black vote, and particularly the African American Republican voter. Writer Joseph C. Phillips began to call himself an Obamacan—an Obama Republican. Other black Republicans were, however, more hesitant in addressing race as a prime consideration in voting choice. Michael Steele, former lieutenant governor of Maryland, believed that Obama would not, on account of his demographic background, necessarily solve the plight of sections of the black community in America and that ideological considerations and party affiliation weighed more heavily than the creation of an historic or watershed moment in American politics (USA Today 2008).

A core reason for the lack of faith of high-profile black Republicans, both those involved in the 2008 race and those who had been prominent in the party in previous times, was the simple lack of racial diversity within the Republican Party in 2008. Racial disparity between the parties, in advance of the head-to-head race in the fall of 2008, highlighted the underlying challenge to Republican leaders of both providing an attractive base for those who were new or mobilized voters in the race, and of persuading disaffected swing voters that the Republican party was an inclusive and multiethnic organization. The Republican Party had, in 2008, no African Americans in either the House of Representatives or the Senate, providing little in the way of iconic leadership or a natural counterpoint to the appeal of Obama. At the Republican convention in St. Paul further evidence suggested a disparity between the parties with respect to the appeal to the minority vote. At the Democrat convention in Denver 1,087 delegates were black, constituting approximately one-quarter of the total delegate attendance. In St. Paul there were 36 delegates of an African American background, which amounted to less than 2 percent of the total delegate attendance (Nasaw 2008). The year 2008 witnessed problems further afield for the Republican Party, its lack of political resonance and diversity being identified as limited not only to the convention hall. The Joint Center for Political and Economic Studies identified only seven black Republican nominees for political office running in 2008, testament to a deeper problem for the Republicans in cultivating grassroots membership or generating figures in politics who might broaden the appeal of the party, even on a superficial level (Nasaw 2008). Evidently an issue therefore that affected the ability of the Republican ticket to attract African Americans to mobilize to its cause was a self-reinforcing perception that the party was not one that harbored, or had harbored, any meaningful or deep affiliation with the African American community, and the outcome of this was a dearth of African American candidates or delegates, further enforcing and hardening this view.

This particular issue and dilemma for the Republican Party was not new and has been reinforced in a range of studies evaluating race, party affiliation, and the likelihood of voters perceiving the parties as being, in part, representations of demographics in America. Political scientist Peter Wielhouwer asserted that: "African Americans continue to be the most cohesive and loyal component of the Democratic Party's deteriorating New Deal coalition" (Wielhouwer 2000). Ideological partisanship may therefore be an element in an explanation of the role of the Republican Party in approaching both African American voters and in not fielding a demographically diverse range of candidates. Edge conversely asserts that: "The lack of outreach to people of color over the last few decades has finally begun to affect Republicans at the polls, where they are increasingly seen as clinging to a narrowing White con stituency" (Edge 2010). Thereafter it is plausible that there is a race component that has engrained itself into the political process and there are not necessarily negative or racially motivated components to the Republican Party, its candidates, voters, or agenda. In a detailed evaluation of the role of race as a predictor of vote preference Greenwald identified a "blend" of ideological beliefs and racial attitudes (Greenwald et al. 2009). Highton posited a range of observations concerning the role of race and its effects on voter interpretations of political candidates. He asserted in 2004 that the "leading hypothesis contends that white voters prefer white candidates to black ones, thereby placing severe limits on the likelihood of black candidate success" (Highton 2004). However, variables emerge suggesting that race, and percep- tions of race factors are not simply underpinned by discrimination. African American candidates were less likely to be present in races and this pre- sented a statistical outcome that was not necessarily the product of voter dis- crimination. Preferences of party elites and issues of disparity in wealth appeared to influence the appeal of candidates present in political races, alongside the dis- persal of African American political office holders (Highton 2004). The pre- sence of Obama in the 2008 election, on a national platform, eradicated several of the variables that might have provided an explanation of the prior failure of a candidate of African American origin from running for office and being successful in that aim. In part, it may well have been that until 2008 no credible candidate in a position of political moderation had been in a posi- tion to advance themselves as worthy of serious consideration, thereby providing an appeal to swing voters. However, some African American commentators argued that the Republican Party had simply continued with an ineffective strategy of trying to lure the black vote, and it was a strategy that had failed to work in the past, and continued to fail in the contemporary era (Sowell 2008).

Conventionally in presidential elections, parties entertain a significant hold over those disposed towards the party cause and the core realm of the fight and interplay between the parties revolves around endeavors to enter- tain independents and swing voters. Occasionally, new electoral coalitions can be forged, however, that mitigate against the conventional split between the two parties. In 1980 Reagan created a new coalition of Reagan Demo- crats, which changed the foundations of electoral politics in that decade. In 2008 there existed similar questions about whether Obama could alter the viewpoints of demographic sections of the voting block and prise voters away from a Republican stance to embrace his Democrat platform and its message of "hope and change." Colin Powell's decision to endorse the candi- dacy of Obama prompted queries within the African American community, and among political pundits, as to whether the African American vote might abandon the Republican Party altogether, and whether the statistical change this might bring in the overall vote would give Obama a significant advantage in key states. This was an important issue. In 2004 the African American vote in Ohio, for example, had increased for the Republican Party from 9 percent to 16 percent, albeit that Kerry took 88 percent of the Afri- can American vote in a national context (Guelzo 2010). Media reports identified the dilemma facing African American Republican voters, and whether they might desert the party they favored ideologically. Ron Christie, a former special assistant to President George W. Bush argued that, for all the attraction of voting for Obama and his endorsement by Powell: "I'm not voting for a race, I'm voting for an individual" (NPR 2008). Conversely, Kevin Ross, who had voted for McCain in the Republican primary process, felt that there were tensions between loyalties to the Republican Party that conflicted, in this particular instance, with loyalty to his race (NPR 2008).

He aimed to vote for Obama in order to provide an example to his children that race barriers in the United States had been broken down.

The election result witnessed popular and media declarations that issues of racial politics had been overcome with the election of Obama and there had been a "national catharsis" (Nagourney 2008). This was not lost on the Republican Party or its candidate. McCain understood the historic symbolism of the time and the national endorsement of his opponent in his concession address. He stated:

> This is a historic election, and I recognize the significance it has for African Americans and for the special pride that must be theirs tonight. We both realize that we have come a long way from the injustices that once stained our nation's reputation.
>
> (Nagourney 2008)

In the aftermath of the election results, there was continued doubt about the role that Republican strategy played in either healing or exacerbating race agenda politics. Inferences that white voters, particularly those of a working-class disposition, were disposed against Obama on account of his color were prominent on a consistent basis. There had been fear that in states including Ohio and Pennsylvania, there were potential problems for Obama's candidacy on account of the demographic construct and its impact on the vote. Senator Bob Casey (D-Pa) argued: "I always thought there was a potential prejudice factor in the state. I hope this means we washed that away" (Nagourney 2008).

There were overt allegations concerning action taken to try to limit African American participation in the election, and opponents of the Republican ticket planted the blame firmly at the door of the Republican Party, as had been done in Florida in 2000 with respect to disbarred African American voters. *Newsweek* identified the use of a 2008 Supreme Court decision, *Crawford vs. Marion County Indiana Election Board*, as a catalyst by which voters could be prevented from participation in the election on the grounds that driving licenses would be required to demonstrate eligibility, or as an alternative prospective voters would have to take the time to acquire a nondriver photo identification. The stated Republican aim appeared to be to reduce issues relating to voting fraud. *Newsweek* contended that the issue of race was linked to partisan affiliation, not one founded on racism per se:

> The motive here is political, not racial. Republicans aren't bigots like the Jim Crow segregationists. But they know that increased turnout in poor, black, neighborhoods is good for Democrats. In that sense the effort to suppress voting still amounts to the practical equivalent of racism.
>
> (*Newsweek* 2008)

As a counterpoint, however, there are associated issues suggesting that the interplay between the parties and the strategies invoked to try and gain electoral advantage were not implemented only by the Republicans. In Ohio, for example, a key state in the Electoral College race and a state predicted as a barometer of the likely outcome of the election, the opportunity existed for voters to register to vote and cast an absentee ballot at the same time. This was thought to give a pronounced advantage to Obama, particularly in attracting young voters in colleges and universities (Newsweek 2008). Thirty-six of the 50 states offered voters the chance to vote early in the election, with estimates that there might be as much as 30 percent of the total electorate choosing to vote before November 4. This was considered to be favorable to Democrat interests because of anticipated challenges to voter eligibility and the effect that this might have on turnout (MacAskill 2008).

Republican polling, particularly that taken late in the race, suggested that there were legitimate concerns about how the election race would play out, given the influence of the Obama candidacy on the increasingly important African American vote. *Wall Street Journal* published an internal Republican memo that pointed out aspects of strength and weakness in the Republican campaign, and pinpointed areas for strategic review. With respect to the issue of the Republican Party and race in the election, it gave a warning about the predicted weakness of African American voter mobilization behind the Republican Party and argued that the predictions of a Democrat surge in this demographic were real and largely decided. The memo stated:

> In most polls, McCain is losing these African American voters by margins like 97% to 1%. This means when you see Senator Obama's number in a survey, it already reflects his significant and full support among African American voters. Functionally, this means the only undecided/refuse to respond voters are white and Latino.
>
> (Levin 2008)

This assists in explaining why the Republican Party could maintain strong claims against both Obama's policies and character and cast him as a person who was not fully in tune with American society. In large part, in advance of the vote in November, Republican strategists had already given up on mobilizing the African American community to its cause. In the aftermath of the campaign, Schmidt dismissed the strategy criticisms concerning the Republican associations with African American voters, claiming that the issues were not related to strategy within a single election:

> Routinely African American voters have cast over 90 percent of their vote for Democratic candidates in presidential elections, and the Republican Party needs to make it a generation's work to reach out into the black community and to connect on issues that African Americans care about and to build upon its credibility.
>
> (Cox 2008)

The strategy that underpinned McCain's attempt to challenge Obama for the presidency was initially balanced, subject to constraints on its geographic appeal and financial grounds, and on occasion overtly barbed in its attempts to portray Obama as either inexperienced or naive—or both. Efforts to address the issues advanced by Obama and to counteract his appeal were present from the spring of election year onwards, far in advance of his winning the Democrat nomination. John Quelch, a professor at Harvard Business School, identified the routes through which Hillary Clinton's campaign had sought to counter Obama's popularity and how negative ads were used in conjunction with positive brand images of Clinton. The means through which early attacks on Obama were made were "fear appeal," relating to Obama's lack of experience, "guilt-by-association," relating to a friendship between Obama and his former pastor, "roll-your-own" attacks, which highlighted contradictions in Obama's argument, and "policy comparison" advertisements, which drew issues of contention to the fore (Quelch 2008). In the early part of the race between Obama and McCain, the same features that had appeared during the Obama–Clinton primary contests reappeared. Sullivan identified the problem for Obama: "He allowed McCain to portray him as an inexperienced, celebrity narcissist, constructing a cult of personality on a welter of insubstantial rhetoric" (Sullivan 2008). That the essence of the anti-Obama campaigns, from Democrat and Republican perspectives, revolved around largely the same themes suggests not a distinctively Republican manifestation of policy attack, but simply an endorsement of the identification of weaknesses in the Obama candidacy, with elements surfacing steadily and repeatedly throughout the year.

Negative advertising had a familiar role to play in the campaign, located in its commonplace position of creating fear and distrust about the future if the opposition candidate were to be elected. Research undertaken by Nielsen Media Research, evaluating campaign advertising from June 3 to September 7, found that McCain's campaign ran 76,238 negative ad placements, in comparison with 75,246 negative ads from Obama. The broadcast presentations were concentrated in battleground states (Begley 2008). Across the duration of the campaign McCain's ads became increasingly negative, testament to him being behind in the polls, supplemented by an overarching strategy towards Obama of turning his positive attributes into negative ones. Additionally opinion polls suggested that the advertisements advanced by McCain's campaign were significantly "nastier" than those advanced by Obama. However, caution has to be exercised. Opinion polls indicating this perception may have been influenced by prior partisan leanings. Elite party figures within the Republican Party were concerned by the onset of negative advertising, and the attritional role it might play in countering Obama's poll standing. Political strategist Karl Rove contended: "Both campaigns are making a mistake, and that is they are taking whatever their attacks are and going one step too far. They don't need to attack each other in this way" (Yen 2008). Republican advertisements addressed Obama's comments regarding small town America and his claim that residents in Pennsylvania were "bitter people" who "cling to guns and religion" in expressing their annoyance at the economy and prevailing political scenario (Peston 2008).

Criticism exchanged in adverts became increasingly personal as the campaign progressed, including an Obama comment about "lipstick on a pig," an indirect reference to Sarah Palin, and television commercials with age-based inferences suggesting that McCain could not send emails or use a computer. Exploiting Rove's doubt about the tone of the campaign, spokesman Tommy Vietor stated: "In case anyone was still wondering whether John McCain is running the sleaziest, most dishonest campaign in history, today Karl Rove, the man who held the previous record said McCain's ads have gone too far" (Yen 2008). Across the duration of the campaign both sides addressed negative advertising prominently and, according to Darrell West of the Brookings Institution, the negativity was a feature of the race at an earlier stage than expected "because you have nasty ads, misleading campaign appeals, statements being taken out of context" (Newshour 2008). Indeed, even in the nomination process, there was evidence of record spending on advertising, supplementing a higher rate of advertising negativity to that found in the period from 1972 through 2008 (West 2008).

Republican criticism of Obama followed quite a similar line to that entertained by his Democrat opponents in the primary process earlyin the year. Issues and concerns related to race were frequently brought to the fore by both camps in a process of strike and counterstrike The evolution of contention on race-based issues emerged in a convoluted format.When Obama made comments on race as a feature of modern America, the McCain team argued that Obama was making his race a feature of the campaign. Alternately, when McCain made comments regarding race, he was accused of bringing unnecessary issues into his campaign. McCain frequently claimed that Obama was making race and race politics an issue in the campaign and was fostering rather than downplaying racial considerations as a factor in the election, and, in turn, this proved to be harmful to the Republican Party's endeavor to be inclusive and unifying. A focal point was the outcome of varying perceptions about comments made by Obama concerning his own appearance. Obama had stated: "What they're going to try to do is make you scared of me. You know, he's not patriotic enough, he's got a funny name, you know, he doesn't look like all those other presidents on the dollar bill." Obama's team did not view this as an issue designed to inflame a race-based discussion, yet McCain's team believed that it inferred a covert race-based agenda. McCain stated in July in Wisconsin: "I'm disappointed that Senator Obama would say the things he's saying" (Associated Press 2008). McCain's campaign manager at that time, Rick Davis, gave a more blunt assessment: "Barack Obama has played the race card, and he's played it from the bottom of the deck. It's divisive, negative, shameful and wrong" (Associated Press 2008). Joe Trippi, chief strategist for Democrat contender John Edwards, stated that:

> Obama opened the door and they drove straight through it. They clearly think they will get some benefit, because whenever race comes

up it is bad for Obama. It risks making him appear to be the 'black' candidate when he is more than that.

(Spillius 2010)

Obama aspired to defuse the potential line of attack that might arise. His spokesman downplayed the issue of race in the election. He argued: "Barack Obama in no way believes that the McCain campaign is using race as an issue" (Associated Press 2008). Additional commentary by Obama suggested that he was very much aware that demographic considerations were important factors. He made race related comments in locations such as Berlin and Missouri on account of his race and his name, for example: "It's a leap, electing a 46-year-old black guy named Barack Obama" (Associated Press 2008). Again this presented the McCain camp with a challenge of either ignoring the theme, or addressing it and thus appearing to suggest that race was a component that might affect voter preference.

Obama's major address on race, its relevance to modern America, and how it was received by Republicans, provides an insight into the dilemmas facing the contemporary Republican Party organization in incorporating race into an inclusive election strategy. Writing in *PS*, political scientist Patricia Lee Sykes asserted that the nature and presentation of Obama's address on race created a new dimension in American politics: "The public has tended to view Obama as a genuine unifier, not a divider, and Republicans and Democrats alike applauded his subsequent speech on race" (Sykes 2008). Obama's main election address on race was entitled "A More Perfect Union" and was delivered in Philadelphia in March 2008. Its objectives were to address the issue of race in modern American and at the same time dispel some of the criticism and indeed myths about his campaign on the grounds of a race-based pretext. This involved both advancing his own interpretations of race and its relevance to his own background, and unpicking the controversy caused by the firebrand sermons of Reverend Wright. A primary aim appeared to be to dispel race as a simple variable in the selection of a presidential candidate or a president. This served not to present an American society that was wholly unified, but, rather, one that was interwoven with a variety of divergent experiences regarding race and ethnic demographics, and how these experiences related to contemporary policy issues. Obama stated:

> We can pounce upon some gaffe by a Hillary supporter as evidence that she's playing the race card, or we can speculate on whether white men will all flock to John McCain in the general election regardless of his policies. We can do that. But if we do, I can tell you that in the next election, we'll be talking about some other distraction.
>
> (Huffington Post 2008)

Within the overall remit of the campaign, there were several pronounced episodes that suggested that there existed an undercurrent of race-based politics that threatened to come to the surface and potentially tarnish the reputation of one or both of the campaigns. In large part, there were matters raised beyond the scope of the direct control of Obama or McCain involving a range of issues on a local scale disseminated via the internet and new media devices. In the later stage of the campaign, there were signs that McCain had adopted a defensive strategy in trying to redress charges that the Republican campaign exacerbated divisive race relations. John Lewis, a Democrat congressman from Atlanta and a veteran civil rights activist, claimed in a partisan attack that the Republicans were "sowing the seeds of hatred and division" (Pilkington 2008). Sarah Palin, in particular, was thought to have a more confrontational approach in addressing Obama on personal issues as well as considerations of policy. Her self-anointed position as a pit bull in the campaign allowed her a more flexible remit to respond to Obama. She accused Obama of "palling around with terrorists" and argued that he was "not a man who sees America the way you and I see America" (Pilkington 2008). However, it is clear that the comments made by Palin required a narrow and specific interpretation to perceive them to accord to a racial mandate, and her addressing of Obama in a personal capacity was countered, by Obama and in the media, with reference to her appearance, policy understanding, and political credibility.

There were areas of controversy in which Obama's past associations were exploited. Depending on political partisanship and interpretation, these were either legitimate areas of investigation or were unwarranted intrusions into Obama's past and were areas that had little or no meaning to the election and the issues that faced America. The focal point of division about race and Obama's personal life was his past friendship with Jeremiah A. Wright Jr. Obama entitled his second book *The audacity of hope* after one of Wright's sermons. Wright had married the Obamas and baptized their children. Obama's predicament was that Wright had issued a number of statements, picked up by the media and the Republican Party, which suggested that race, and an understanding of its impact, were pivotal considerations in the election. The underlying concerns initially surfaced when divisions appeared between Obama aides and Wright, there being suggestions that white campaign aides would not understand how to present issues to the African American community. By the spring of 2008 Wright had been distanced from the campaign because of the media furore over his commentary (Powell and Kantor 2008). The nature of the presidential campaign and lack of centralized control was evident in the first instance in this area. An independent group, the National Republican Trust PAC, aired television ads in swing states such as Virginia, which raised Jeremiah Wright, and Obama's prior associations with him as issues for consideration in the election (Silva 2008). McCain's initial campaign strategy had been to avoid the Wright issue, although it was to be an issue that Palin would raise as the campaign drew to a close. Politico considered the Wright issue, and its race-based subtext to have worked to the benefit of Obama and to have created a scenario that was unconventional. It thought that Obama "has benefited from the idea that negative attacks, that in a normal campaign would be commonplace, in this year would carry an out-of-bounds racial subtext. That's why Obama's long association with the Rev. Jeremiah Wright was basically a nonissue in the general election" (Harris and VandeHei 2008).

An additional component and issue with respect to Wright was the variable of religion in the election and how it impacted the vote. The Republican Party made greater play of the influence of religious beliefs on its ideology, which were prominent with Reagan, and more recently with Bush Jr. and his faith-based reform. While religious issues are a factor in the formation of voting blocks and in the dissemination of social and moral values, the religious lure of the Republican Party for African Americans appears to have been limited. In part, this is explained by policy issues that were considered to be inappropriate to the needs and interests of minority communities, such as the Republican position on welfare provision and affirmative action. In addition, while Palin's rhetoric and emotive use of her personal values and lifestyle may have created a factor appearing to suggest that biblical literal interpretation may have served to attract an array of socially religious groups, the religious attributes appeared to have had a limited appeal in bridging racial divides. McDaniel and Ellison asserted: "The appeals to traditional values by Republican activists and candidates—on abortion, gay rights, and other 'pro-family' issues, as well as the role of faith in the public sphere—have not yet won over even these Evangelical Latinos. Among African Americans, there has been virtually no movement whatsoever among biblical literalists towards the Republican party" (McDaniel and Ellison 2008).

Religion was also used during the campaign by dissident elements of the Republican Party to create the impression that Barack Obama was downplaying his religious affiliation and might be a Muslim as opposed to his stated faith of Christianity. In June 2008, early in the national campaign, an individual involved in the famous Willie Horton campaign ad of 1988, Floyd Brown, released a web advertisement through his National Campaign Fund PAC, suggesting that Barack Obama was being deceitful in covering up a Muslim background (Stein 2008). The material was not endorsed by McCain's official campaign, yet its presence engendered a dynamic to the campaign where the web acted as an unregulated agent replete with satire, speculation and assumption. There were frequent assertions about Obama's faith through the duration of the campaign, including visual portrayals on the web, unsanctioned by the McCain team, of Obama in stereotypical Islamic dress. The focal point of this discussion was the cover page of the *New Yorker*, which depicted Obama in Islamic dress, in an Oval Office with a portrait of Osama Bin Laden on the wall and an American flag alight in the fireplace. This created a storm of protest about the role of satire in the election and the misportrayal of Obama's background in such a mainstream media production, on the grounds that it might legitimize the interpretations of Obama that had been circulating online. McCain condemned the cover, asserting that he would understand if

Obama found the depiction offensive (Lawrence 2008). Obama's campaign staff were similarly dismissive. Obama spokesman Bill Burton stated:

> The New Yorker may think, as one of their staff explained to us, that their cover is a satirical lampoon of the caricature Sen. Obama's right-wing critics have tried to create. But most readers will see it as tasteless and offensive. And we agree.
>
> (Allen 2008)

Some Conservative writers considered there to be more room for maneuver on the part of Obama on account of the publication. Philip Klein of *The American Spectator* wrote: "The cartoon is intended to make fun of conservatives as ignorant racists, and essentially marginalize any criticism of Obama as moronic" (Lawrence 2008). Poll evidence in July of 2008 suggested that the undercurrent of speculation about Obama had some resonance. In a *Newsweek* poll, 12 percent of voters incorrectly believed Obama was a Muslim and more than one-quarter thought that he had been brought up in a Muslim household (Miller 2008).

There were changes in the structure and nature of the McCain campaign on account of a revised strategy and the introduction into the campaign team of experienced Republican strategist Steve Schmidt. Schmidt was important in the initiation of a campaign against Obama designed to cast the Senator as inexperienced and vacuous (Issenberg 2008). Across the summer of the election period attention was directed towards Obama's integrity, personal attributes, and the underlying rationale for his running to be President. Mark Rozell from George Mason University considered that the underlying strategy was to "build a picture" across the election period about the character of Obama. He stated: "These things are always orchestrated. I have no doubt there has been a running conversation within Republican circles about what the theme should be in going after Obama and how that theme could be reinforced" (Shear 2008). Schmidt, a disciple of Karl Rove and once called "human artillery," was instrumental in pursuing a more aggressive stance against Obama and in seeking to alter poll statistics that were going against McCain in early August 2008. Schmidt was pivotal in sanctioning a negative advert against Obama comparing him to Britney Spears and Paris Hilton, suggesting that Obama's international tours and public appearances were tantamount to the welcome afforded pop stars and celebrities. The advert declared: "He's the biggest celebrity in the world, but is he ready to lead?" (Draper 2008) In part, this was a blunt demonstration of Schmidt's underlying objective of turning any perceived positive reactions that Obama might entertain into negative perceptions and interpretations (Spillius 2010). While Obama maintained a pronounced and pervasive web presence, and utilized the internet to great effect, particularly in the Democrat primaries, Schmidt was considered to be beneficial to the Republican understanding of the news media environment. A notable element in this context was a pronounced attack on Obama's convention appearance in an outdoor arena. The Republicans portrayed the Democrat choice as pretentious, egotistical, and self-centered, in contrast to the emergent Republican theme of Country First.The Republican news releases entitled the setting the "Temple of Obama," a tag that was broadcast widely on conventional news media and on blogs (Rutenberg and Nagourney 2008). Attacks,therefore, were not merely constricted to issues of policy or demographicsensibilities. Rather, Obama was confronted on a multitude of fronts, from his character to his cultivation of popular support on grounds of his personality as opposed to his political experience or standing. The Democrat strategists considered the attacks on Obama, across the duration of the campaign to be counterproductive and asserted that the Republican Party was embroiled in a political tactic of which the American people were bored. Spokesman Bill Burton argued that: "It's our view that's exactly the politics that the American people are sick and tired of. The only ideas they have to promote are the failed ones for the last eight years" (Shear 2008).

There were problems for the McCain team in presenting a message across the duration of the campaign that reached its target vote and thereafter resonated with voters and served to mobilize them. McCain, in attempting to distance himself from the Bush presidency and the political fallout if he adopted a stereotypical Republican ticket, cast himself as a Maverick candidate. This appeared to be politically expedient at the time. However, in the prelude to the national vote, in poll data gathered at the end of October, PEW research suggested that 47 percent of voters thought that, even by this pivotal moment in the presentation of the McCain campaign, McCain would continue to follow the policy line advocated and implemented by President Bush (PEW Research Center 2008). While allegations about serving special interests are commonplace in elections, in this instance, there was a greater perception that McCain would favor the wealthy if elected, as opposed to those who thought that Obama would do "too much for blacks" (PEW Research Center 2008). This evidence suggests that the issue of race took a minor role in shaping the considerations of voters, it being a minor variable in the middle of a deep economic recession. A further plausible explanation for the success of Obama and the problems encountered by the McCain camp was the way that this was manifested in political advertising during the campaign. While the impact of advertising as a single variable is low, it nevertheless earmarked a notable difference between the political campaigns. Political scientists Michael M. Franz and Travis N. Ridout perceived that "a consistent message about Obama from the Obama campaign was more effective than an inconsistent message coming from multiple sources about McCain" (Franz and Ridout 2010). The University of Kansas scholar Robert C. Rowland considered that McCain was constrained in his options during the campaign and the Maverick tag was one which served to mask a conservative voting record (Rowland 2010). He was caught in a double bind of appealing to bedrock party support, while seeking to address issues of policy that would distance him from

Bush and his legacy. This presented a scenario where the incorporation of Palin was a logical and necessary step. It helped shore up, morally and socially, the Republican right and there was an increasing disposition of both Republican candidates to base their campaign rhetoric on personal narratives as opposed to policy-based resolutions to national problems. Rowland dissected McCain's convention acceptance address and identified that: "The core of the speech was McCain's presentation of himself as a maverick. Early in the speech, the focus is on McCain and Palin as mavericks" (Rowland 2010). Yet McCain created a policy realm in which he looked to be a traditional conservative, flanked by an individual in the form of Palin who had the credentials of a conventional Republican right-wing candidate. Although she was presented to appeal to swing voters and lower class white women in the first instance, the demographic voting block she finally mobilized was that of the traditional Republican right, appealing primarily to older wealthy socially conservative individuals. The dilemma that faced McCain and Palin was that a campaign based on an ill-defined notion of entertaining Maverick credentials lacked the policy depth needed to suggest a viable alternative to the ongoing economic recession of the time. Obama held a pronounced advantage in this realm. His policy articulation offered a viable alternative to the conservative message. His personal embodiment of the American dream offered a sense of optimism, fused with his message of change, and efforts to portray him as unqualified or illegitimate as a candidate created the type of tension that worked against rather than for the McCain candidacy.

Palin had a distinctive role to play in fermenting the anti-Obama impulse in the election, in part, because she could exercise her own interpretation of the Obama candidacy and, in part, because she had more latitude in doing so, not being the primary candidate on the ticket. In the aftermath of her poor television performance in interviews, and her competent performance in the sole televised vice presidential debate, Palin announced that it was "time to take the gloves off" (Orr 2010). Palin articulated a range of charges against Obama, which served to fuel further heated confrontations between the respective campaign camps. She contended: "Our opponent is someone who sees America it seems as being so imperfect that he's palling around with terrorists who would target their own country" (Orr 2010). She cited the *New York Times* and claimed Obama had a supporter, Bill Ayers, who was founding member of the Weather Underground, a group labeled by the FBI as a terror organization. Ayers had supported Obama in fundraising in 1995. The Obama camp responded by asserting that Obama had been 8 years old when the Weather Underground was formed and that Obama was not close to Ayers. Indeed, the issue had been raised previously as a point of contention in the Democrat primaries. At that time Obama had given a forthright answer:

> This is a guy who lives in my neighbourhood. The notion that some-
> how as a consequence of me knowing somebody who engaged in

detestable acts 40 years ago—when I was 8 years old—somehow reflects on me and my values doesn't make much sense.

(CNN 2008)

Palin dissented and continued to press on the Ayers association, but was challenged that her criticism of Obama had a "racially tinged subtext that McCain may come to regret" (Associated Press 2008). Palin provided a focal point for an aggressive strategy in the final period of the head to head campaign. Greg Strimple, a McCain strategist, was reported in the Associated Press as promising "a very aggressive last 30 days" (Associated Press 2008). Palin's position was important as she was increasingly seen as the main draw on the Republican ticket, entertained disproportionate media coverage in comparison to her running mate and rivals, including Obama, and attracted large vocal crowds to her rallies. Poll evidence suggested that the allegations about inappropriate contacts and friendships had only a limited bearing on the impression of the Obama candidacy. *Newsweek* polled respondents about the reasons why some might consider not voting for Obama in the 2008 election (Newsweek 2008). The primary concerns revolved predictably around tax and economic concerns. The personal themes had some resonance but were largely dismissed by voters as minor considerations:

> Please tell me if this is a major concern that might keep you from voting for Obama, a minor concern, or not a concern?
>
> Obama might share the views of Jeremiah Wright, his former pastor on race.
>
> | Major concern | Minor concern | Not a concern | Unsure |
> |---|---|---|---|
> | 27% | 19% | 50% | 4% |
>
> Obama's association with former 1960s radical Bill Ayers raises doubts about his character.
>
> | Major concern | Minor concern | Not a concern | Unsure |
> |---|---|---|---|
> | 24% | 18% | 54% | 3% |

The Obama campaign team responded promptly to the array of accusations and allegations, seeking to correct errors and create an interpretation of the McCain camp as imbued with negativity. Obama's vice presidential running mate Joe Biden led the immediate counter-offensive to Palin's assertions about terror associations. He rebuked her remarks and condemned the repeated use of Obama's middle name, Hussein, to try to create cultural separation in the mind of the voter. Biden asserted that

> you can't call yourself a maverick when all you've ever been is a sidekick. Every single false charge of baseless accusation is an attempt to get you to stop paying attention to what's really going on in this country. Beyond the attacks, what's John McCain really offering?

(Corsaro 2008)

Biden raised survey data to indicate that McCain's ads were increasingly negative and outweighed the Obama negative advertising by a considerable margin. Underpinning each respective campaign, through to the end of the election race, were tactics designed to portray the other as besmirching the integrity of the opposing side, while, at the same time, asserting lofty positions of dignity and principle with respect to their own conduct. Early in the election Republican strategist Karl Rove had considered Obama's stance on avoiding mudslinging in the campaign to be a predictably strategic and shrewd move. Obama had declared, even in the early running against Hillary Clinton, that he was the only candidate who was telling the truth. Rove interpreted his actions as: "I don't think Sen. Obama has avoided negativity, he has simply suggested he'll run a positive campaign and then with a very deft scalpel cut up his opponents" (Rove 2008).

Beyond the immediacy of the direct quotations and argument from the elite sections of the campaign teams there was criticism of Obama via the internet, which became a largely unregulated and decentralized forum for bitter and unsubstantiated allegations. Use of nonprofit donations to campaigns aided in creating a realm in which information was published on the web, with little opportunity for the public to discern the difference between fact and fiction. This was done by organizations as much as individual agitators and added a further dimension to the type and nature of information disseminated during the campaign. Building on allegations about friendship between Obama and Jeremiah Wright, a political committee called Freedom's Defense Fund ran television ads that accentuated the depth of the relationship (Scherer 2008). Writing in *Time Magazine*, journalist Michael Scherer observed: "Tough attacks, misinformation and anonymous smears are multiplying as both campaigns surrender some control of the conversation to outside groups and dirty trickster with deep pockets and technological know-how" (Scherer 2008). The lack of central control gave opportunity to those who wished to portray images from standpoints across the political spectrum that were detrimental to the policies and the characters of the candidates. This included material that would not have been sanctioned or deemed appropriate to mainstream political groups. Naturally these deviations were seized on by the mainstream media to signal the undercurrents of ageism, racism, or the negative accentuation of individual candidate attributes. Underpinning the web-based communications was the ability of both candidates to raise money over the web and to maintain a pronounced web presence. McCain was thought to lag behind Obama in web-based communication, largely based on levels of participation on social networking sites and his ability to connect to his Republican base via this avenue (Schifferes 2008).

Conclusion

The evidence from the 2008 campaign suggests that the Republican campaign struggled throughout to identify a strategy to persuade voters to rally to its cause and to create a meaningful voter coalition that might provide election victory. That Obama was an African American presented a challenge for the Republican Party in the spring to summer of election year. The GOP had not had had prior success in capturing a significant proportion of the minority vote in America, and the appearance of Obama created demographic changes as it mobilized new voting communities to turn out and bolster the Democrat cause. Polling statistics, the Republican election strategy and the election outcomes suggest a GOP campaign to persuade African American or minority groups to mobilize was not entertained as a serious or central strategic consideration through the campaign. As a consequence, Obama's campaign was able to solidify an African American vote in a pronounced and concerted fashion.

It is clear that the Republican Party did not target African American voters as a distinctive demographic group or seek to make a pronounced effort to alter its appeal to that group in the interim period between 2004 and 2008. The undercurrent of racial tension, while accentuated by media elements and addressed periodically by the Obama camp, appeared to be muted in its nature and not sanctioned or pursued aggressively by the McCain team in a centralized capacity. Rhetorical sparring suggested that there were racial undertones to the campaign, but these appeared to be forthcoming largely in response to the actions of agents outside the immediacy of the official campaign structure. The utilization of images and characterizations that explored Obama's background, life story, and racial profile made for a campaign that tested popular understandings of contemporary America for both political camps.

While the exploitation of Obama's prior associations and personal background were of importance in the contest of credibility over the use of negative advertising, there appears to be little to differentiate the opposing camps in terms of the negativity of how they portrayed one another and sought to gain electoral advantage. Although statistical measurement was carried out extensively during the campaign, the plethora of unsanctioned advertisements, use of the web to spread gossip and rumor, and the underlying partisanship suggested that this particular campaign was one that was fragmented in nature and open to accusation and counter-accusation about the tone, content, and appropriateness of personal allegations. The raising of issues related to Obama's past associations appeared to have some resonance among voters, but proved insufficient to create a cleavage in his vote coalition. Concentration in the McCain camp became more focused on Obama as an individual in later stages of the campaign. It arose, in part, on the grounds that character and personal charisma was perceived by the Obama camp to be one of the strengths of the Democrat campaign, and with Schmidt's understanding that positives could be construed as negatives the concentration on Obama's personal attributes was unsurprising.

The anti-Obama impulse in the election represented a viable strategy designed to address a range of issues where strategists considered that Obama had a contextual advantage in raising money and mobilizing support. The legacy of the

Bush brand, the undercurrent of economic disrepair, and the unique nature of the Obama candidacy created a backdrop to a campaign in which the Republicans waged a defensive strategy from the outset, largely shoring up a Republican base to ensure that the party stayed true to its roots and appealed to a traditional conservative base. Racial divisions in the contemporary era appeared to be unaffected by Obama's campaign and election to the presidency. Indeed, his presence and the mobilization of the African American voter to his cause appeared to further endorse the Democratic Party as the party of choice for the minority vote. That the GOP appeared to vacate the fight for the minority vote gives further testament to an American electoral realm where the presence of Obama has underscored an ongoing disparity between the parties and the fight for demographic sections of American society.

Bibliography

Allen, Mike. "Obama slams New Yorker portrayal," *Politico*, July 13, 2008, www. politico.com (accessed November 21, 2010).

Associated Press. "McCain, Obama go old-school in political jabs," MSNBC, July 31, 2008, www.msnbc.msn.com (accessed November 20, 2010).

Associated Press. "Palin defends Obama terrorist comment," MSNBC.com, October 5, 2008, www.msnbc.msn.com (accessed November 12, 2010).

Begley, Sharon. "Ready, aim, fire!," *Newsweek*, October 11, 2008, www.newsweek.com (accessed October 23, 2010).

CNN. "Fact check: is Obama palling around with terrorists?," CNN Politics, October 5, 2008, www.politicalticker.blogs.cnn.com (accessed November 12, 2010).

Corsaro, Ryan. "Biden calls 'veiled' McCain attacks 'outrageous', mocks Palin," CBS News, October 8, 2008, www.cbsnews.com (accessed October 25, 2010).

Cox, Ana Marie. "McCain campaign autopsy," *Daily Beast*, November 7, 2008, www.thedailybeast.com (accessed November 18, 2010).

Draper, Robert. "The making (and remaking) of McCain," *New York Times*, October 26, 2008, www.nytimes.com (accessed November 28, 2010).

Edge, Thomas. "Southern strategy 2.0: conservatives, white voters, and the election of Barack Obama," *Journal of Black Studies* (2010): 40, 426–44.

Ford, Pearl K., Johnson, Tekla A., and Maxwell, Angie. "'Yes we can' or 'yes we did?': prospective and retrospective change in the Obama presidency," *Journal of Black Studies* (2010): 40, 462–83.

Franz, Michael M. and Ridout, Travis N. "Political advertising and persuasion in the 2004 and 2008 presidential elections," *American Politics Research* (2010): 38, 2, 303–29.

Greenwald, Anthony G., Tucker Smith, Colin, Bar-Anan, Yoav, and Nosek, Brian A. "Implicit race attitudes predicted vote in the 2008 U.S. presidential election," *Analyses of Social Issues and Public Policy* (2009): 9, 1, 241–53.

Guelzo, Allen C. "Election 2010 surprise: rise of black Republicans," *Christian Science Monitor*, September 3, 2010, www.CSMonitor.com (accessed October 12, 2010).

Harris, Jerry and Davidson, Carl. "Obama: the new contours of power," *Race & Class* (2009): 50, 1–19.

Harris, John F. and VandeHei, Jim. "Why McCain is getting hosed in the press," *Politico*, October 28, 2008, http://dyn.politico.com (accessed November 19, 2010).

Highton, Benjamin. "White voters and African American candidates for Congress," *Political Behavior* (2004): 26, 1, 1–25.

Huffington Post. "Obama race speech," *Huffington Post*, March 18, 2008, www.huffingtonpost.com (accessed October 12, 2010).

Hutchings, Vincent L. and Valentino, Nicholas A. "The centrality of race in American politics," *Annual Review of Political Science* (2004): 7, 383–408.

Issenberg, Sasha. "Strategy shift boosts McCain," *Boston Globe*, August 22, 2008, www.boston.com (accessed November 20, 2010).

Lawrence, Jill. "Mag satire panned; depicts Obamas as Muslim terrorists," *USA Today*, July 15, 2008, www.usatoday.com (accessed November 24, 2010).

Levin, Yuval. "Internal polling," *National Review Online*, October 29, 2008, www.nationalreview.com (accessed December 1, 2010).

Lopez, Mark Hugo and Taylor, Paul. "Dissecting the 2008 electorate: most diverse in U.S. history," PEW Research Center for the People and the Press, April 30, 2009, www.people-press.org/ (accessed July 21, 2010).

MacAskill, Ewen. "Groundhog Day election forces rival teams to alter strategy,", *Guardian*, September 13, 2008, www.guardian.co.uk (accessed November 21, 2010).

McDaniel, Eric L. and Ellison, Christopher G. "God's party? Race, religion, and partisanship over time," *Political Research Quarterly* (2008): 61, 2, 180–91.

Miller, Lisa. "Finding his faith," *Newsweek*, July 12, 2008, www.newsweek.com (accessed November 20, 2010).

Nagourney, Adam. "Obama elected president as racial barrier falls," *New York Times*, November 5, 2008, www.nytimes.com (accessed August 12, 2010).

Nasaw, Daniel. "African Americans lacking in Republican delegation," *Guardian*, September 4, 2008, www.guardian.co.uk (accessed September 14, 2010).

Newshour, Brookings Institution/PBS. "Examining the negative 2008 Presidential campaign ads," Brookings Institution, August 7, 2008, www.brookings.edu (accessed November 1, 2010).

Newsweek. "Jim Crawford republicans," *Newsweek*, September 11, 2008, www.newsweek.com/ (accessed September 21, 2010).

Newsweek. "Newsweek poll," *Newsweek*, October 22, 2008, www.newsweek.com (accessed November 12, 2010).

NPR. "Two black Republicans, divided on Obama," October 21, 2008, www.npr.org (accessed November 5, 2010).

Orr, Jimmy. "Palin: Obama 'palling around with terrorists'," *Christian Science Monitor*, October 5, 2010, www.csmonitor.com (accessed October 21, 2010).

Osborn, Tracy, McClurg, Scott D., and Knoll, Benjamin. "Voter mobilization and the Obama victory," *American Politics Research* (2010): 38, 2, 211–32.

Peston, Mark. "Republicans use Obama as the bad guy in negative ads," CNN Politics, May 4, 2008, www.articles.cnn.com (accessed November 21, 2010).

PEW Research Center. "Obama leads by 19 among those who have already voted: McCain support continues downward spiral," PEW Research Center For the People and The Press, October 28, 2008, www.people-press.orgsb (accessed November 14, 2010).

Philpot, Tasha S. *Race, Republicans, and the Return to the Party of Lincoln* (Ann Arbor: University of Michigan Press, 2007).

Pilkington, Ed. "McCain tones down campaign as critics say tactics incite hatred," *Guardian*, October 13, 2008, www.guardian.co.uk (accessed September 25, 2010).

Powell, Michael and Kantor, Jodi. "A strained Wright–Obama bond finally snaps," *New York Times*, May 1, 2008, www.nytimes.com (accessed November 20, 2010).

Quelch, John. "How negative advertising works (and when it doesn't)," *Harvard Business Review*, May 12, 2008, http://blogs.hbr.org (accessed November 2, 2010).

Redlawsk, David P., Tolbert, Caroline J., and Franko, William. "Voters, emotions, and race in 2008: Obama as the first black president," *Political Research Quarterly*, August 4, 2010, http://prq.sagepub.com/content/early/2010/08/17/1065912910373554 (accessed August 21, 2010).

Rove, Karl. "Election 2008: Karl Rove on election strategy," *Washington Post*, May 7, 2008, www.washingtonpost.com (accessed October 21, 2010).

Rowland, Robert C. "The fierce urgency of now: Barack Obama and the 2008 presidential election," *American Behavioral Scientist* (2010): 54, 3, 203–21.

Rutenberg, Jim and Nagourney, Adam. "An adviser molds a tighter, more aggressive McCain campaign," *New York Times*, September 7, 2008, www.nytimes.com (accessed November 20, 2010).

Scherer, Michael. "Smear wars: welcome to negative ad season," *Time*, September 25, 2008, www.time.com (accessed October 21, 2010).

Schifferes, Steve. "Internet key to Obama victories," BBC News, May 28, 2008, www.bbc.co.uk (accessed October 25, 2010).

Shear, Michael D. "GOP sharpens attacks on Obama," *Washington Post*, June 30, 2008, www.washingtonpost.com (accessed November 20, 2010).

Silva, Mark. "Jeremiah Wright: Obama attack-ad fodder," *The Swamp*, November 2, 2008, www.swamppolitics.com (accessed November 20, 2010).

Sositis, David A. "National opinion poll," Joint Center for Political and Economic Studies, October 21, 2008, www.jointcenter.org/ (accessed November 20, 2010).

Sowell, Thomas. "In black and white," *National Review Online*, April 11, 2008, www.nationalreview.com (accessed December 12, 2010).

Spillius, Alex. "John McCain's 'bullet' leads the assault on Barack Obama," *Daily Telegraph*, August 1, 2010, www.telegraph.co.uk (accessed November 7, 2010).

Stein, Sam. "GOP operative releases Obama Muslim ad," *Huffington Post*, June 11, 2008, www.huffingtonpost.com (accessed November 7, 2010).

Sullivan, Andrew. "Wily Obama beats McCain on strategy," *The Times*, November 15, 2008, www.timesonline.co.uk (accessed September 18, 2010).

Sykes, Patricia Lee. "Gender in the 2008 presidential election: two types of time collide," *PS: Political Science and Politics* (2008): October, 761–64.

USA Today. "Black Republicans consider voting for Obama," *USA Today*, June 14, 2008, www.usatoday.com (accessed September 21, 2010).

West, Darrel M. "A report on the 2008 presidential nomination ads: ads more negative than previous years," Brookings Institution, July 2, 2008, www.brookings.edu (accessed October 23, 2010).

Wielhouwer, Peter W. "Releasing the fetters: parties and the mobilization of the African-American electorate," *Journal of Politics* (2000): 62, 1, 206–22.

Yen, Hope. "Republicans fault both campaigns for negative ads," *Real Clear Politics*, September 14, 2008, www.realclearpolitics.com (accessed November 4, 2010).

4   Obama in the Northeast

Race and Electoral Politics in America's Bluest Region

Kevin J. McMahon

In America's bluest region, Barack Obama and the Democratic Party performed exceptionally well on Election Day 2008. Not only did Obama win 11 of the region's 12 states (and the District of Columbia) by margins unseen since Lyndon Baines Johnson's historic 1964 landslide victory over conservative Republican Barry Goldwater, the Democratic Party also gained seven House seats and one Senate seat. In doing so, it expanded on its 2006 gains, when it captured 11 House seats and two Senate seats from the GOP.[1] On election day 2010, however, the news from the northeast was not so good for the Democrats. Republicans picked up 15 House seats and one Senate seat. What explains such a dramatic shift in the most ideologically liberal and politically Democratic region in the nation? In this chapter, by focusing on the Democratic successes of 2006 and 2008 and its failures of 2010, I consider this question. And as with the other essays in this volume, I do so with special attention to the role of race in these two elections.

Obama Soars in the Democratic Blue Northeast

To be sure, Democratic presidential candidates have performed quite well in the northeast since 1992. Since that election year, the Democratic nominee has won at least 10 of the region's 12 states and the District of Columbia. But even with this track record, Senator Barack Obama easily outperformed his three most recent predecessors. In fact, Obama captured seven of the region's 12 states with more than 60 percent of the vote. Comparatively, the previous three Democratic nominees had won a total of four states with that percentage of the vote: Bill Clinton won one (in 1996), Al Gore two, and John Kerry one. Obama's closest win was in the once solidly red state of New Hampshire. But even there, he sailed to an easy victory, winning by just under 10 percent. To be sure, unlike Bill Clinton in both 1992 and 1996, Obama did not win every state in the region. As New Hampshire has trended in the Democratic direction, West Virginia—which is a bit of an odd fit for the region—has gone the other way. And, in turn, like Gore and Kerry, Obama lost the Mountain State. In fact, it wasn't even close as Republican nominee John McCain bested him by 12 percentage points.

Even with the loss of West Virginia, Obama's success in the northeast defied earlier predictions, made most prominently by Hillary Clinton during the Democratic nomination process, that he would struggle in this section of the nation. Notably, Clinton pointed to Obama's race as a potential drawback, suggesting that the region's culturally conservative white voters—so-called Reagan Democrats—might have difficulty voting for a black man for president.[2] And her success in the region during the primary season seemingly provided evidence to support her claim. In particular, Senator Clinton won seven of the northeast's 13 election contests (12 primaries and one caucus), including its four largest states. In all, Clinton won states that were set to award 92 electoral votes in November while Obama won states that would award just 30. Of course, Clinton was not alone in suggesting concern about Obama's ability to attract white voters in a general election race against Senator McCain. In a comment that attracted a great deal of attention, Pennsylvania Representative John Murtha said that Obama's appeal in his state would be limited by his race, telling the *Pittsburgh Post-Gazette*: "There is no question that western Pennsylvania is a racist area." He continued by saying that the area was no longer as "redneck" as it used to be, but he still believed there are "folks that have a problem voting for someone because they are black."[3]

Race and Obama's 2008 Victory: The Possibility of a Landslide in Historical Perspective

But did this actually happen? Did Obama's race diminish his support among white voters either nationally, or, more specifically, in the northeast? In a provocative new book, political scientists Donald Kinder and Allison Dale-Riddle argue in striking terms that race mattered considerably in the size of Obama's margin of victory. As they write: "had the 2008 Democratic nominee been white, he (or she) would have received slightly more than 60 percent of the vote."[4] They arrive at this claim by using a method that "takes into account both the votes won by Obama by virtue of his race among African Americans and votes he lost by virtue of his race among white Americans." It shows "by virtue of his race Obama gained votes among African Americans (2.2 percent) and lost votes among white Americans (10.2 percent)." This means, according to their analysis, "if Obama had been white he would have received 60.7 percent of the vote." They then use a second method—based on "a small number of plausible models of presidential election outcomes"—that yields a slightly lower total for the Democratic nominee, but nevertheless suggests "given the conditions at the time of the 2008 election, Obama should have won 58.1 percent of the vote." They add: "The gap between the vote Obama won and the vote he was 'entitled to'—a gap estimated here to be about 5 percentage points—we attribute to race."[5] Kinder and Dale-Riddle have significantly advanced the discussion of the importance of race in the 2008 presidential election by adding a level of statistical sophistication, and by carefully—even bravely—offering a specific figure for analysis.

However, the 60 percent figure—or even something close to that—requires closer scrutiny. Here, I consider the plausibility of any presidential nominee attaining 60 percent of the popular vote from an historical perspective. And, put simply, such a result would have been an historical anomaly. Consider this: in the 47 presidential elections since 1824—when the popular vote was first tabulated—the victorious candidate has received more than 60 percent of the vote exactly four times (8.5 percent). On three of those four occasions, incumbent presidents running near the height of their popularity and/or facing opponents widely regarded as representing the extreme wings of their own party reached that high mark. Specifically, in 1936, Democrat Franklin Roosevelt, running on the progress his administration made in reviving the economy during his first term, trounced Republican Alf Landon by capturing 60.8 percent of the vote. In 1964 Lyndon Johnson won the presidency in his own right by winning 61.1 percent of the vote, the highest percentage in the history of presidential elections. He did so against a candidate, Republican candidate Barry Goldwater, who celebrated his extremism. And in 1972 Richard Nixon sailed to an easy victory, winning 60.7 percent of the vote and 49 of the 50 states. Like LBJ, Nixon faced a candidate in Democrat George McGovern who was considered by many to represent the left wing of the Democratic Party. These two most recent cases, then, were clearly "choice elections," pitting incumbent presidents thought to be representing the center of the political world facing an "outlier" on the right and then the left.[6] In 1936 Alf Landon did not necessarily represent the extreme wing of the GOP, but the party itself—in part through its support of a Supreme Court that had recently constitutionally invalidated FDR's first New Deal—had sought to sharply distinguish itself from the party in power, thereby offering voters a clear choice as well.[7]

Of course, in 2008 there was no incumbent in the race; no president with skyrocketing approval numbers ready to tout all he had done for the nation during his first term in office. Moreover, in 2008 the Republican nominee did not seek to appeal to the extreme wing of his party en route to winning the GOP nomination. Rather, Senator McCain sought to define himself as a center-right candidate—even moderate on some issues—who had displayed political courage in the past by standing up to more conservative members of his own party. Given these aspects of the race, it is uncertain whether these three contests serve as useful comparisons to the 2008 race.

Indeed, only on one occasion in the history of presidential elections has a non-incumbent presidential candidate received more than 60 percent of the popular vote (just 2.1 percent of the time). That occurred in 1920 when Republican Warren Harding captured 60.3 percent in his landslide victory over Democrat James Cox. In that election year, as Woodrow Wilson's presidency came to a close, his Democratic Party was deeply unpopular.

More importantly, with the Democrats down, scores of American women, due to the passage of the 19th Amendment, cast their vote for the first time. In all, the total number of votes cast increased by 44.4 percent from 1916 to 1920.[8] This is a very important point since scholars have consistently emphasized the importance of mobilization as opposed to conversion in assessing previous critical elections.[9] There was no such expansion in the 2008 electorate. In fact, despite predictions that it would be far higher, the total vote only increased by 7.5 percent. Notably, in 2000, the last time two non-incumbents contended for the presidency, the total vote increased by 9.5 percent.[10] So, given the rarity of candidate's reaching the 60 percent mark in American history, is it plausible that the 2008 Democratic nominee would have received over 60 percent of the vote if he or she were white?

Let us consider another piece of evidence: the nature of the Democratic Party and the historical performance of its candidates at the presidential level. Before Barack Obama captured 52.9 percent of the vote in 2008, only three other non-incumbent Democratic nominees received over 50 percent since the Democrats and Republicans emerged as the nation's two major political parties just over a century and a half ago. In contrast, non-incumbent Republicans have had a much easier time reaching this level of support, realizing it nine times during this period of time. It is unclear exactly why non-incumbent Democrats have such difficulty attaining the support of a majority of American voters. Many would likely point to the nature of its coalition, once rooted in the South and its many restrictions on voting before the implementation of the legislative and constitutional successes of the Civil Rights Movement. Others might point to the nature of the party itself, recalling Will Rogers's oft repeated line: "I don't belong to any organized political party. I'm a Democrat." Whatever the reason, the simple fact is that it has been difficult for a non-incumbent Democrat to attain 50 percent of the popular vote. Moreover, two of the three Democrats who did reach this mark, Samuel Tilden in the disputed election of 1876 and Jimmy Carter 100 years later, barely did so, with 50.9 and 50.1 percent, respectively. And due to the Compromise of 1877, Tilden—with one less electoral vote than his opponent Rutherford B. Hayes—never became president. Carter's victory came soon after the Watergate scandal forced Republican Richard Nixon from the presidency and against an opponent whose approval ratings plummeted after granting Nixon a full pardon. The third non-incumbent Democrat to exceed the 50 percent mark was Franklin D. Roosevelt in 1932.

The election of 1932 is seemingly an important comparison election for Kinder and Dale-Riddle. After all, in making their case for why Barack Obama's race mattered as much as they suggest they argue that 2008 was ripe for a landslide at the presidential level. As they write:

> Cast your mind back to the fall of 2008 and recall how closely the stars were aligned for a Democratic victory. A clear majority of Americans had come to the conclusion that the war in Iraq was a mistake.

President Bush's approval ratings had sunk to a level not seen since Richard Nixon's on the eve of his resignation. The economy was teetering on the edge of a depression and the American people knew it. In a word, the news was terrible—terrible for the country, and in electoral terms, devastating for the Republicans.[11]

No doubt, these are very good points. But of course, in 1932, the economic situation was far direr. New Deal historian William Leuchtenburg's words paint the picture of the economic situation during that fateful year:

> In the three years of Herbert Hoover's presidency, the bottom had dropped out of the stock market and industrial production had been cut more than half. At the beginning of the summer, *Iron Age* reported that steel plants were operating at a sickening 12 percent of capacity with "an almost complete lack" of signs of a turn for the better. In three years, industrial construction has slumped from $949 million to an unbelievable $74 million. ... By 1932, the unemployed numbered upward of thirteen million. Many lived in the primitive conditions of a preindustrial society stricken by famine. ... At least a million, perhaps as many as two million were wandering the country in a fruitless quest for work or adventure or just a sense of movement. ... On the outskirts of town or in empty lots in the big cities, homeless men threw together makeshift shacks of boxes and scrap metal. St. Louis had the largest "Hooverville," a settlement of more than a thousand souls, but there was scarcely a city that did not harbor at least one.[12]

With collections of homeless men living in shantytowns named after him and unemployment hovering around 25 percent—not to mention underemployment—Hoover, to say the least, stood little chance of reelection. But even with the economy in such a state of despair, in his landslide victory over Hoover Democratic presidential nominee Franklin Roosevelt was unable to break the 60 percent mark. His percentage total was 57.4 percent.[13]

So, leaving aside party for the moment, the elections of 1920 and 1932 are seemingly the most historically relevant comparisons to Kinder and Dale-Riddle's argument for Obama surpassing or nearing 60 percent in 2008. Not surprisingly, these years were not only good for the victorious presidential candidate but for his party as well. In 1920 Republicans built on gains made in previous elections to substantially increase their representation in Congress from 1912, the year the opposition party's nominee won the presidency. In the House and Senate, the GOP increased their numbers by 125 percent and 34 percent, respectively. A similar comparison for the Democrats between 1920, when they lost the presidency, and 1932 shows an even better performance on the part of the victorious party. Specifically, Democrats increased their numbers by 139 percent in the House and 60 percent in the Senate. A comparison between 2000 and 2008, however, shows no similar gain. To be sure, the Democratic increase was substantial, especially in the Senate, where its numbers increased by 30 percent.[14] In the House, their improvement in the eight years from losing the presidency in 2000 to gaining it back in 2008 was 21 percent. And while these gains were enough for the Democrats to win back both houses of Congress after the 2006 elections, they pale in comparison to the Republican gains of 1920 and the Democratic gains of 1932, especially in the House of Representatives.

Before moving on, let us consider one more historical case: the 1928 election of Republican Herbert Hoover. The 1928 election is the only other where a non-incumbent presidential candidate nearly reached the 60 percent mark. En route to trouncing the first Catholic nominee of a major party, Democrat Alfred E. Smith, Hoover won 58.2 percent the popular vote. But it might be more appropriate to place Hoover's victory alongside those of incumbent presidents since he was replacing an incumbent president in Calvin Coolidge who chose not to run again after only serving for just over five years. In other words, Hoover did not take the White House back for his party as Harding in 1920, FDR in 1932, and Obama in 2008. Moreover, much like the 1920 election, the total vote increased dramatically (by 26.5 percent) in 1928, suggesting that Hoover's landslide victory was attained through mobilization rather than conversion.[15] As noted earlier, given the comparatively small increase in the total vote, such a result was not possible in 2008.

So what does this mean for Kinder and Dale-Riddle's bold claim about the 2008 presidential contest? The point is a simple one. History has shown that it is exceedingly difficult for a non-incumbent presidential candidate to win in a landslide. Indeed, from the perspective of the Democratic Party, Kinder and Dale-Riddle are not simply suggesting a result that would have been an historical rarity. It would have been historically unique.

Race and Gender in 2008

History aside, another striking feature of Kinder and Dale-Riddle's analysis is their inclusion of two words in one of the sentences quoted earlier, namely "or she." Put simply, by including these words, they suggest that if Hillary Clinton, Barack Obama's main rival for the Democratic nomination in 2008, had won that battle she would have received over 60 percent of the vote. Of course, Clinton would have been making history herself as the first female presidential nominee for a major party, but Kinder and Dale-Riddle do not believe gender would have played nearly the role as race did in the 2008 general election results. They write, as

> Barack Obama's run for the Democratic presidential nomination challenged Americans' racial assumptions and expectations ... Hillary Clinton's campaign challenged assumptionsand expectations about gender. And yet ... while race shows up at every turn in 2008, gender is, for the most part, missing in action.[16]

But let us consider some polling that was done in the first part of 2008, when both candidates had reasonable expectations of becoming the Democratic nominee. In 41 public opinion polls—taken from just after theIowa caucus in early January to early April 2008—that posed questions pitting John McCain against Hillary Clinton and Barack Obama in hypothetical general match-ups, Obama performed better on average than Clinton by 3.39 percentage points.[17] Specifically, these polls showed McCain *losing* to Obama by 2.17 points on average while *beating* Clinton by 1.22 points. To be sure, these polls were taken well before the economic crisis of fall 2008, and the averaging of them is far less sophisticated than Kinder and Dale-Riddle's methods.Nevertheless, the results are striking. After all, according to Kinder and Dale-Riddle, Clinton would have defeated McCain by approximately 22 percentage points. But of these 41 polls, the best Clinton performed against McCain was a 5 percentage point victory. Moreover, while only one of these polls matched McCain up against John Edwards—a white southern man—in that hypothetical race the eventual Republican nominee easily beat the Democrat by eight points. The same poll showed McCain defeating Clinton by four points and losing to Obama by two points.[18]

In his analysis of some of these same polls—specifically those which Survey USA conducted from February 26–28, 2008—political scientist Todd Donovan explains that "the range of differences across states in the relative appeal of Clinton versus Obama is substantial." Moreover, with regard to race, he concludes that there is "some support for Senator Clinton's claim that she may have had stronger general election support among whites." While this increased support would have been "mainly in southern and border states," an analysis of the same polls for the northeast (Table 4.1) also shows Clinton with greater support among whites in 6 of the region's 12 states (with one tie), including the most populated states of New York, Pennsylvania, New Jersey, Massachusetts, and Maryland.[19] However, in all but two of these states—Vermont and West Virginia—the difference is within the margin of error. It is also important to remember that these polls are mere snapshots of the contests in these states. Indeed, both earlier and later polls in some of these states show different levels of white support for Barack Obama.

In the general election results in the northeast, the evidence appears to be mixed with regard to the question of whether white support for Obama was diminished compared to his most immediate Democratic predecessors. To be sure, the results do not show that white voters abandoned Obama in the dramatic numbers that Kinder and Dale-Riddle suggest for the national result. As Table 4.2 shows, white support in the region was consistent with the figures from 2004. So, for example, in Pennsylvania Obama garnered 4 more percentage points than John Kerry (55 to 51 percent) and he won the white vote by 3 percentage points more than Kerry (48 to 45 percent).[20] As Table 4.2 also shows, the regional average for white Democrats supporting Obama was 87 percent (two points above the national average).[21]

Table 4.1 White support for Clinton and Obama v. McCain in the northeast, February 2008

State	Clinton	Obama
Connecticut	47	51
Delaware	42	42
Maine	48	53
Maryland	45	41
Massachusetts	54	47
New Hampshire	41	46
New Jersey	43	37
New York	50	46
Pennsylvania	46	40
Rhode Island	54	51
Vermont	50	63
West Virginia	47	34

Source: Survey USA state polls

Table 4.2 White support for Obama in the northeast

State	% white Obama voters	Change from 2004	% white dems for Obama	Overall change from 2004
Connecticut	51	0	86	+7
Delaware	53	+8	86	+9
Maine	58	+5	89	+4
Maryland	47	+3	83	+6
Massachusetts	59	0	86	0
New Hampshire	54	+4	92	+4
New Jersey	49	+3	85	+4
New York	52	+3	85	+5
Pennsylvania	48	+3	85	+4
Rhode Island	58	+1	89	+4
Vermont	68	+10	96	+9
Washington, DC	86	+6	97	+4
West Virginia	41	−1	69	0
National	43	+2	85	+5

Source: Exit polls from 2004 and 2008

In comparison with the Democratic senate candidates in the northeastern states, all of whom were white, Obama did underperform against all but one incumbent among white voters in those particular states. However, he outperformed the two non-incumbents—one of whom won—among white voters and equaled the percentage total of one incumbent. By the same token, white support in the northeast was fairly flat for Obama when compared to his three most recent Democratic predecessors. According to exit polls, Obama captured 59 percent of the vote in the northeast. (His national percentage total was 52.9.) Comparatively, northeast support for his three

Democratic predecessors, all of whom reached national percentages in the high forties, was in the mid-fifties: Clinton's 55 percent in 1996, Gore's 56 percent in 2000, and Kerry's 55 percent in 2004.[22] But white support in the northeast for Obama was nearly identical to these three predecessors— 1996, 51 percent, 2000, 52 percent, 2004, 50 percent, and 2008, 52 percent— suggesting at least some white resistance to his candidacy.

So what does this all mean? It does seem to suggest that race did matter in the 2008 presidential election to some extent. Indeed, in some areas of the nation, the evidence suggests that Obama's race had a noticeable effect on his percentage totals. For example, Donovan's analysis "suggests that larger African American populations correlate with whites evaluating candidates in a manner that depressed white support for an African American candidate, particularly in areas where the Voting Rights Act has justified the use of majority-minority districts."[23] But even with this support for a "race effect," it is difficult to see how Obama could have captured 60 percent of the popular vote without the benefit of a much larger mobilization of voters than actually occurred.[24]

Understanding the Republican Resurgence

In the second part of the chapter, I consider President Obama's standing in the northeast following the Democratic Party's significant losses at the congressional level—particularly in the House of Representatives—in the 2010 midterm elections. As noted already, in these elections, the Democratic Party suffered some major setbacks in the region, losing a total of 15 House seats (16 losses and one pickup) and one Senate seat. Moreover, in early 2010, Republican Scott Brown captured a Senate seat in Massachusetts in a special election to replace the longtime liberal lion of the Senate, Ted Kennedy. In doing so, he ended the Democrats' filibuster-proof 60-seat majority in that body. By examining the results and exit polls for the 2010 election, I consider the causes of the Democrats' disappointing results in the region and the possibility the white voters may have been turned off by a party led by anAfrican American president.

In writing about the overall results of the 2010 midterm elections—in which the Democrats lost 63 House seats and 6 Senate seats—Kinder and Dale-Riddle once again emphasize the importance of Barack Obama's race in assessing the Democratic Party's poor showing. As they write:

> We found seven reputable forecasts of the 2010 House midterm elections that posted a prediction in advance of the voting. All the models predicted that the Democrats would lose seats in the House ... rang[ing] from twenty-two to fifty-two seats. That is, no model predicted as severe a loss as actually transpired. The models used to forecast the 2010 elections share three things in common. All presume that the fate of the president's party at the midterm depends upon economic performance. All ignore the fact that the president in 2010 is of African

descent. And all seriously underestimate the magnitude of the Democratic midterm disaster. Sounds familiar, does it not?[25]

To be sure, Kinder and Dale-Riddle are writing about the national results for the House, not specifically those in the northeast. Nevertheless, they raise an important point and provoke questions about the role of race in helping to explain the Democratic losses in this ideological liberal and politically Democratic region of the nation. After all, in the 2010 midterm elections, Republicans increased their representation in the northeast by 88 percent, more than in any other region of the country. What explains, to borrow the president's term, such a "shellacking" in the nation's bluest region?

One of the more striking aspects of the Democratic Party's 2010 losses in the House concerns the nature of the seats it lost. As Table 4.3 shows, Republicans had recently held 14 of the 16 congressional districts where Democratic candidates lost in the 2010 midterm elections. Recall, both 2006 and 2008 were considered "wave elections" for the Congress. In the course of those two years, Democrats picked up 18 House seats and three Senate seats in the northeast. Indeed, following the 2006 midterm elections, journalist Pam Belluck wrote of a political species that was on the verge of extinction in Washington.

> It was a species as endemic to New England as craggy seascapes and creamy clam chowder: the moderate Yankee Republican. Dignified in demeanor, independent in ideology and frequently blue in blood, they were politicians in the mold of Roosevelt and Rockefeller: socially tolerant, environmentally enthusiastic, people who liked government to keep its wallet close to its vest and its hands out of social issues like abortion and, in recent years, same-sex marriage.[26]

And two years later, after the Republican losses in the 2008 election, Yankee Republicans were gone from the House of Representatives for the first time since candidates started running under the party label. In neighboring New York, with just three of its 29 members, Republican representation in the House also neared extinction.

In 2010, things turned around a bit for the Republican Party in the northeast. But this should not be too surprising. As Table 4.3 shows, in many of the districts the GOP won in 2010, its candidates were quite competitive in 2008. Indeed, even in some districts where Barack Obama performed quite well, the Republican candidate barely lost. Given the closeness of these races and the Republican tradition in these districts, the GOP should have expected to take back at least some of these seats in the Democrats' difficult year of 2010. And in fact, even with these losses, the Democrats still held four more House seats and two more Senate seats in the northeast than they did before the 2006 midterm elections.

Unfortunately, there were no exit polls taken for these individual House races. However, those taken for the Senate races in the northeast are worthy

Table 4.3 GOP house pickups in the northeast, 2010

House district	Year previously held by GOP	2008 Obama percentage	2008 GOP percentage	2010 GOP percentage
MD-1	2009	40	48	54
NH-1	2007	53	46	54
NH-2	2007	56	42	48
NJ-3	2009	52	48	50
NY-13	2009	49	33	51
NY-19	2007	51	42	53
NY-20	2007	51	38	55
NY-24	2007	50	49	53
NY-25	2009	56	42	50
NY-29	2009	48	49	57
PA-3	2009	49	48	56
PA-7	2007	56	40	55
PA-8	2007	54	42	54
PA-10	2007	45	44	55
PA-11	1983	57	48	55
WV-1	1969	42	No candidate	50

Table 4.4 Partisan breakdown of House and Senate representation in the northeast

State	2005 Senate	2009 Senate	2011 Senate	2005 House		2009 House		2011 House	
				D	R	D	R	D	R
Connecticut	2 D	2 D	2 D	2	3	5		5	
Delaware	2 D	2 D	2 D		1		1	1	
Maine	2 R	2 R	2 R	2		2		2	
Maryland	2 D	2 D	2 D	6	2	7	1	6	2
Massachusetts	2 D	2 D	1 D 1 R	10		10		10	
New Hampshire	2 R	1 D 1R	1 D 1 R		2	2			2
New Jersey	2 D	2 D	2 D	7	6	8	5	7	6
New York	2 D	2 D	2 D	20	9	26	3	21	8
Pennsylvania	2 R	1 D 1 R	1 D 1 R	7	12	12	7	7	12
Rhode Island	1 D 1 R	2 D	2 D	2		2		2	
Vermont	2 D	2 D	2 D	1		1		1	
West Virginia	2 D	2 D	2 D	2	1	2	1	1	2
Totals	17 D 7 R	20 D 4 R	19 D 5 R	59	36	77	18	63	32

of consideration. Consider, for example, the state of the New York, the site of six of the Democrats' 16 losses in the 2010 midterm elections. Due to Hillary Clinton's move from the Senate to the State Department, there were two Senate races in the Empire State. Incumbents Chuck Schumer and newly appointed Kirsten Gillibrand, both of whom are white, faced fairly weak Republican opponents. And both won easily, with 66.3 and 62.9 percent of the vote, respectively. These figures are not out of the ordinary for Democratic senators in New York, at least with regard to recent elections. For example, in 2004 Schumer won 71.1 percent of the vote, the largest percentage for a candidate running statewide in history. And in 2006 Hillary Clinton captured 67 percent of the vote in her successful reelection bid. For his part, in 2008, Barack Obama's New York total matched Gillibrand's 2010 figure at 62.9 percent. With this in mind, it is useful to examine the exit polls from the two races with regard to the white vote. In 2008, white voters—making up 71 percent of the voting public—gave 52 percent of their support to Obama and 46 percent to McCain. In 2010 the percentages in the Gillibrand race were exactly the same. In the other senate race, Schumer performed slightly better with white voters with 55 percent, which does much to explain his higher overall figure.[27] Moreover, according to exit polls, New York voters of all races did not show any signs of abandoning the president or the Democratic Party. Of the 57 percent who said they voted Obama in 2008, 93 percent supported Schumer and 90 percent supported Gillibrand. Both candidates even performed fairly well among those who disapproved of the president's handling of the job, receiving 33 and 27 percent respectively of the 43 percent who voiced disapproval of Obama.

The senate race in the state of Pennsylvania—the site of five Democratic House losses—tells a slightly different story. In 2008 Obama won the state with 54.5 percent of the vote. Two years later, Democratic senatorial nominee Joe Sestak—a white congressman who defeated incumbent Arlen Specter in the primary—received 49 percent, losing to conservative Republican Pat Toomey by a slim 2 percent margin. Significantly, white voters made up a larger portion of the 2010 electorate (86 percent) than they had in 2008 (81 percent). Moreover, white support for Sestak was 5 percentage points less than Obama's four years earlier (43 to 48 percent). African American support was quite similar (93 percent for Sestak and 95 percent for Obama). However, the percentage of African American voters was down from two years earlier (9 percent in 2010 and 13 percent in 2008). This is quite significant. All else being equal, Sestak would have won the contest if the percentage of the white and African Americans voters had remained the same. But he was not able to overcome Toomey's support among whites given that white voters made up a noticeably larger percentage of all voters in 2010.

With the 11 Democratic House losses in New York and Pennsylvania making up the lion's share of the party's 16 losses in the northeast—and without exit polls in the House contests—these senate races shed the most light on the thinking of the voters in the 2010 midterm elections. And put simply, they hardly suggest the voters of these two states abandoned the president and his party because of his race. Historically, the midterm elections of a president's first term have been difficult for the incumbent's party. And the elections of 2010 were an obvious example of that pattern. To be sure, Obama's Democratic Party may have performed more poorly because of "racial resentment" as Kinder and Dale-Riddle suggest, but it seems more likely that the

Democratic losses stem from the nature of the turnout, the fact that Republicans won seats in swing districts that they had only recently lost, and the state of the economy, which was by far the most important issue to voters.

Conclusion: The New Normal?

In the six elections between 1964 and 1984, three and possible four qualify as landslides: 1964, 1972, and 1984, and arguably, 1980. In the six elections since 1984, none easily fits that description. The largest percentage victory came in 1996 when incumbent Bill Clinton beat Kansas Senator Bob Dole by 8.5 percentage points. But Dole still won 19 states, some by substantial margins. In the last landslide election, Ronald Reagan captured 49 of the 50 states, including all 12 in the northeast. He won Connecticut, Maine, and New Jersey—which today are solidly blue—by more than 20 percentage points. He won New York by almost 10 percentage points. In 2008 such a showing by Republican John McCain would have been virtually unimaginable. Whatever the causes, and there are many thoughts on the matter, America has become a much more divided nation on election day than in the days of landslide elections. And it is a closely divided nation as well. Indeed, for much of the time since the 1994 Republican takeover of Congress, both the House and the Senate have been fairly evenly divided, with one party controlling with uncertain majorities. What does this mean in terms of evaluating Barack Obama's victory in 2008 and the Democratic Party's failures of 2010? The relative closeness of Obama's victory—at least according to some—and the Democrats' loss of the House in 2010 may be more about the nation's red/blue political and ideological divisions than the racial divisions that still exist throughout the land. Put simply, it appears that far fewer voters are willing to consider support for the alternative party no matter how great the failures of the one they have supported previously.

Notes

1 Fearing a primary challenge from the right, another northeast Republican senator, Arlen Spector of Pennsylvania, switched parties in 2009.
2 Clinton noted: "I have a much broader base to build a winning coalition on." To support the claim, she cited an Associated Press article "that found how Senator Obama's support among working, hard-working Americans, white Americans, is weakening again, and how whites in [Indiana and North Carolina] who had not completed college were supporting me." Kiely, Kathy and Lawrence, Jill. "Clinton makes case for wide appeal," *USA Today*, May 8, 2008; Phillips, Kate. "Clinton touts white support," *New York Times* website, May 8, 2008.
3 Blazina, Ed. "Murtha says Obama will win Pennsylvania despite Racism," *Pittsburgh Post-Gazette*, October 16, 2008; additional 'redneck' comments available on video at www.youtube.com/watch?v=DoPabBvVRpg

4   Kinder, Donald R. and Dale-Riddle, Allison. *The End of Race? Obama, 2008, and racial politics in America* (New Haven, NJ: Yale University Press, 2012), pp. 98–9.
5   Ibid., pp. 99, 108, 115–16.
6   Nie, Norman H., Verba, Sidney, and Petrocik, John R. *The Changing American Voter*, enlarged edn (Cambridge, MA: Harvard University Press, 1979), pp. 360–61.
7   See also Leuchtenburg, William E. "When the people spoke, what did they say? The election of 1936 and the Ackerman thesis," *Yale Law Journal* (1999): 108, 2077–114.
8   1916 total vote: 18,535,022; 1920 total vote: 26,768,613; percentage increase 44.4 points.
9   See, for example, Anderson, Kristi. *The Creation of a Democratic Majority, 1928–1936* (Chicago: University of Chicago Press, 1979); Sundquist, James. *Dynamics of the Party System: alignment and realignment of political parties in the United States* (Washington, DC: Brookings Institution Press, 1983).
10 2004 total vote: 122,293,548; 2008 total vote: 131,463,122; percentage increase 7.5 points. 1996 total vote: 96,275,401; 2000 total vote: 105,417,475: percentage increase 9.5 points.
11 Kinder and Dale-Riddle. *The End of Race?* pp. 116–17.
12 Leuchtenburg, William E. *Franklin D. Roosevelt and the New Deal, 1932–1940* (New York: Harper & Row, 1963), pp. 1–2.
13 To be sure, the unpopularity of war in a foreign land was not a concern in 1932. But, despite Americans' dissatisfaction with the war in Iraq, the issue was not a major a concern to voters in 2008 as many expected it would be in the buildup to the general election. Specifically, according to exit polls, only 10 percent of voters considered the war in Iraq the most important issue; 63 percent considered the economy the most important issue. For the other choices, the percentages were as follows: health care, 9 percent; terrorism, 9 percent; energy policy, 7 percent.
14 After the 1912 elections, GOP representation in the House and Senate was 134 and 44, respectively. After the 1920 elections, it had increased to 302 (↑125%) and 59 (↑34%), respectively. After the 1920 elections, Democratic representation in the House and Senate was 131 and 37, respectively. After the 1932 elections, it had increased to 313 (↑139%) and 59 (↑60%), respectively. After the 2000 elections, Democratic representation in the House and Senate was 212 and 46, respectively. After the 2008 elections, it had increased to 257 (↑21%) and 60 (↑30%), respectively.
15 1924 total vote: 29,095,023; 1928 total vote: 36,805,951; percent increase 26.5 percent.
16 Kinder and Dale-Riddle. *The End of Race?* pp. 155, 160.
17 All polls available at realclearpolitics.com as of March 1, 2012.
18 Hotline/FD, 1/10-1/12/2008.
19 Donovan, Todd. "Obama and the white vote," in Mazama, Ama and Asante, Molefi Kete, eds. *Obama: political frontiers and racial agenda* (Washington, DC: CQ Press, 2012), pp. 193–212, 198–9.
20 Connecticut is a clear exception since Obama won the state by 7 percentage points more than Kerry, but did not improve among white voters.
21 Material in this paragraph is drawn from my chapter "The northeast: blue, deep blue," in *Winning the White House 2008*, McMahon, Kevin J., Rankin, David M., Beachler, Donald W., and White, John Kenneth (New York: Palgrave Macmillan, 2009), pp. 81–102.
22 Bill Clinton at 49.2 percent in 1996, Al Gore at 48.4 percent in 2000, and John Kerry at 48.3 percent in 2004. Clinton's 1992 national percentage total was 43.0 percent.
23 Donovan, pp. 2012, 208.

24 Kinder and Dale-Riddle do suggest that white turnout was less in 2008 because of Obama's race. While their model suggests that whites should "have made up 77.9 percent of the 2008 electorate," they in fact made up slightly less, 76.3 percent. More important for Kinder and Dale-Riddle's conclusion is white support for Obama. It was 43.3 percent, but they suggest that, without the "race penalty," it would have been 55.5 percent, a figure not seen for a Democratic presidential candidate since 1964. Kinder and Dale-Riddle. *The End of Race?* pp. 104–105.

25 Kinder and Dale-Riddle. *The End of Race?*, p. 155.

26 Belluck, Pam. "A Republican breed loses its place in New England as voters seek change," *New York Times*, November 26, 2006.

27 In the Schumer exit poll, white voters made up slightly less—70 percent—of the overall total.

5 Backlash

Racism and the Presidency of Barack Obama

Heidi Beirich and Evelyn Schlatter

The nomination and election of Barack Obama to the presidency was a major breakthrough in race relations for the United States. Only some 40 years after segregation and Jim Crow were abolished by the 1964 Civil Rights Act, a black man would serve in America's White House. As inspiring as the election was—especially since more than 40 million white Americans voted for Obama—the months leading up to the inauguration also revealed a true ugliness in American society.

The election unleashed a wave of Obama-related hate crimes and domestic terrorist incidents and spurred the growth of radical right movements that were at least partly driven by racial resentment. Interest in joining hate and antigovernment groups soared, beginning in 2008. At least two serious attempts on Obama's life by individuals motivated by white supremacist beliefs took place during the campaign and the day after Obama's inauguration, a man with neo-Nazi leanings went on a killing spree in Massachusetts in which he targeted African immigrants and Jews.[1]

Scores of racially charged incidents—beatings, effigy burnings, racist graffiti, threats, and intimidation—were reported across the country after the election. Extremists also exploited the economic crisis, spreading propaganda blaming minorities and immigrants, and their supposed handmaiden Obama, for the subprime mortgage meltdown.[2]

Infuriated by the election's outcome, hate groups of various stripes saw increasing interest in their issues and an uptick in recruitment. On the night of the election, servers crashed due to heavy web traffic on several hate sites. Overall, the election injected a particular urgency into the white supremacist movement, and served as a stark reminder to those in it that demographic change, as symbolized by Obama's rise, will eventually signal the death knell of the hate movement, given that sometime after 2040 the U.S. Census Bureau predicts whites will become a minority population.

This forecasted demographic shift has also helped hate group growth to some extent, at least in the short term. Since 2008 the number of hate groups has continued to rise, reaching 1,018 in 2011 (the rise, largely prompted by changing demographics due to non-white immigration, began in 2000, when the Southern Poverty Law Center counted 602 hate groups).[3] Committed racists are not quietly accepting their fate. The result has been a dangerous new trend: Obama-inspired hate crimes and domestic terrorism that will likely last far beyond the Obama presidency as America's demographics become more diverse.[4]

Obama's election has also been a boon to antigovernment activists, particularly those active in militias and paramilitary groups. His election seemed to bring back to life a movement that had been moribund during the George W. Bush presidency. The era of the Bill Clinton presidency, which saw a "liberal" president disliked by the far right enact such things as gun control, was also a hotbed of antigovernment activity, but the rise in antigovernment groups since Obama took office is unprecedented.

According to the Southern Poverty Law Center's (SPLC) count, antigovernment groups reached a high of 858 in 1996. That white-hot enmity at the federal government contributed to the Oklahoma City bombing in 1995, whose perpetrator Timothy McVeigh was inspired by both racist and antigovernment ideologies.

Under Obama, America is seeing a repeat of that era, but on steroids. The number of antigovernment groups hit an all-time high in 2011 of 1,274 according to the SPLC.[5] As in the Clinton era, a president perceived as liberal and, in some cases, as "foreign," is fueling both antigovernment activism and resurgent domestic terrorism. The antigovernment movement this time has expressed itself in additional ways, from Tea Party activists to "birthers." In essence, Obama's election has engendered a massive expansion in America's far right.

The ferment has not escaped those who study the radical right. "I think that Barack Obama—as the first black president, with an unusual life story and heritage and, of course, that infamous middle name—is a symbol for broader anxiety about major cultural change in America," political journalist Will Bunch noted in August 2010:

> This summer we've seen a powerful conflating of xenophobia about Mexican immigrants and Muslims and these notions that Obama is a Muslim or a Kenyan. That has helped to weaken the Obama presidency, and I don't think it would have played out the same way with a white president.[6]

Evidence seems to suggest he is correct.

The Far Right's Reaction to Obama's Election

While many in America were celebrating the election of the first African American to the presidency, the far right was apoplectic, particularly in the weeks after the election and up to Obama's inauguration, when threats against the first black man to be elected U.S. president grew more heated. New Jersey-based neo-Nazi Hal Turner provides an example of this. On his blog, Turner suggested that it would be a good thing to use an unmanned drone carrying explosives to attack inaugural crowds. He wrote that a mass murder of those attending the festivities "would be a public service." "I won't say what may happen Tuesday [the date of Obama's inauguration] but I will say this," Turner continued on his blog, "After Tuesday, the name Hal Turner may live in infamy. Let it be known that I saw what was necessary and decided to do what had to be done. I make no apology to those affected or their families."[7]

Turner was just one of many extremists to post such threats. The comments entered into Turner's site by his fellow extremists were similarly vicious, much like those that popped up throughout the racist internet underworld. "Why talk about it?" asked "Reck Less Abandon" in a comment after Turner's post suggesting ways of attacking the inaugural ceremonies. "JUST FUCKING DO IT." Another poster, "PragmaticSaxon," proposed adding an explosive gas to "bubonic plague or anthrax" in the balloons: "The exploding balloons will spread the pathogens and have massive effect on the masses of useless feeders that put that fucking nigger in office," he wrote.

And it wasn't just bona fide extremists who were raging about Obama. During later stages of the campaign, angry supporters of John McCain and Sarah Palin had reportedly shouted "terrorism," "treason," and perhaps "Kill him!" at an Obama campaign rally.[8] Another even screamed "nigger" at a black cameraman, telling him, "Sit down, boy!" The head of the Hillsborough County, Florida, Republican Party sent an email warning members of "the threat" of "carloads of black Obama supporters coming from the inner city to cast their votes."[9] A reporter who had covered every presidential election since 1980 was on record saying that he had never seen such fury on the campaign trail.[10] Similar scenes were reported nationwide.[11]

And there was evidence of increasing interest in hate groups in the months after the election, a trend clearly fueled by the general rage Obama's nomination and election caused. "The League of the South is reporting a surge in new members within hours of the results from yesterday's elections," proclaimed an email that the neo-Confederate hate group sent to supporters the day after the election. "League president, Dr. Michael Hill, stated that it is from an awakening of many Southerners that the constitutional Republic is now dead and has been replaced with a national socialist empire."[12]

Don Black, a former Klansman who runs the oldest and largest white supremacist hate site Stormfront, boasted in an online post just after the election that his website was seeing six times its usual traffic. "There are a lot of angry White people out there looking for answers," he wrote. "Let's show them. We will not be defeated." Billy Roper, then-chairman of the neo-Nazi group White Revolution, predicted just after the election that "more and more white Americans [would be] waking up" and instructed followers to be prepared. "[W]e are on the crest of [the storm's] wave. People will be coming forward, shaking the cobwebs from their numbed minds, and they will need us to lead them."[13]

Klansman Thomas Robb, leader of an Arkansas-based Ku Klux Klan group, announced just after the election on his blog that Obama had become America's first "mulatto" president. He then invited readers to click on a link for an application to join his Knights Party. "If you want to do something to help provide a future for you [sic] children then you need to become part of a movement working for our people. We are not asking you to hate anyone! We are not asking us to commit an illegal act. We are not asking you to hurt anyone. We just want you to love your people and do that which your grandfathers did—give your children a bright future."[14]

But it wasn't all doom and gloom in hate circles in the wake of the election. Some sections of the white supremacist movement adopted a surprising attitude: electing America's first black president may well be a very good thing. A growing number of white supremacists came to see that a black man in the Oval Office would shock white America, hopefully drive millions to their cause, and perhaps even set off a race war that, they hoped, would ultimately end in Aryan victory.

"Thomas Dixon Jr.," a Stormfront poster using the name of the racist author who wrote the classic novel *The Clansman* (1905), put it like this: "As WLP [William Luther Pierce, the late leader of the neo-Nazi National Alliance] would say ... 'What is bad for the system is good for us'." "Obama," added "The Patriot" in the same thread, "would be better for our cause in the long run, no doubt about it."

User "Darthvader" wrote on the neo-Nazi Vanguard News Network web forum that "He will make things so bad for white people that hopefully they will finally realize how stupid they were for admiring these jigaboos all these years." He continued: "I believe in the motto 'Worse is Better' and Obama certainly fits that description." Another poster on the same thread chimed in with this: "I hope Obama wins because in four years, white people just might be pissed off enough to actually do something. ... White people aren't going to do a thing until their toys are taken away from them. So things have to be worse for things to be better."[15]

David Duke, the neo-Nazi and former Klan boss who once served in the Louisiana House of Representatives, saw clear advantages to an Obama victory. "Obama will be a signal, a clear signal for millions of our people," Duke wrote in an essay entitled "A Black Flag for White America."[16] He continued in that vein throughout the essay:

> Obama is like that new big dark spot on your arm that finally sends you to the doctor for some real medicine. ... Obama is the pain that let's [sic] your body know that something is dreadfully wrong. ... My bet is that whether Obama wins or loses in November, millions of European Americans will inevitably react with new awareness of their heritage and the need for them to defend and advance it.[17]

This is not an idle belief on the part of these extremists. The Department of Homeland Security warned about the dangers of increasing right-wing extremism in terms of terrorism and hate violence in a 2009 report. The report said that these extremists were "harnessing this historical election as a recruitment tool."[18]

Violence and Threats

Federal authorities viewed the threats to Obama as legitimate, and he was given Secret Service protection earlier than any presidential candidate.[19] Following the election, he received more threats than any previous president-elect.[20] Direct threats and assassination plots made the Secret Service's efforts the only sensible route to take.[21] A 2009 Department of Homeland Security report backed up that position. The report, which argued that right-wing extremists were finding current conditions fertile ground for their activities, specifically cited "the election of the first African American president" and the "economic downturn" as "unique drivers for rightwing radicalization and recruitment."[22]

The list of threats was extensive. Just days before the inauguration, federal authorities arrested a Wisconsin man for threatening to assassinate Obama in a posting to a website.[23] A more serious problem arose in the form of organized assassination plots against Obama by racists and members of racist groups. The first such plot broken up by authorities was to take place during the Democratic Party's National Convention held in Denver, Colorado, in August 2008. The plot was allegedly perpetrated by three men, who were later found to have been drug addicts, who planned to shoot Obama with a high-powered rifle during his appearance at the convention.[24] The alleged motive for the attempted assassination was a white supremacist belief that an African American should not be elected president. One of the perpetrators allegedly said: "No nigger should ever live in the White House."[25]

In October 2008 the ATF foiled another alleged plot to assassinate Obama that involved a planned multi-state "killing spree." Agents arrested two men, Daniel Cowart of Bells, Tennessee, and Paul Schlesselman of West Helena, Arkansas, and charged them with possession of an unregistered firearm, conspiracy to steal firearms, and threatening a candidate for president. According to an affidavit filed by an ATF special agent, the men met through the internet and planned to shoot 88 African Americans and behead another 14 ("88," an important number in skinhead numerology, means "Heil Hitler," as "H" is the eighth letter of the alphabet; "14" refers to the "14 Words," a racist slogan that originated with the late white supremacist terrorist David Lane). Targets included a predominantly African American high school. At the end of the alleged spree, the men intended to try to kill Obama. One of the suspects, Cowart, was a known member of the racist skinhead group, Supreme White Alliance, formed at the beginning of 2008.[26]

The election also led to an increase in hate violence directed at African Americans and those perceived to be Obama supporters. The FBI's 2008 *Hate Crime Statistics* report reflected the turmoil that took place at the time of the election.[27] Overall, the number of hate crimes was up slightly from

2007, by 2 percent. But one of the biggest jumps was in the number of anti-black hate crimes, which went up from 2,658 in 2007 to 2,876 in 2008, a rise of nearly 8 percent.

In the weeks before and after the election, dozens of hate crimes occurred across the country, most representing a racist backlash to the election of America's first African American president. Hate incidents related to the election occurred in all parts of the country. An interracial couple in Apolacan Township, Pennsylvania, who supported Obama, found the remains of a burnt cross in their garden. In Madison County, Idaho, elementary school children allegedly chanted "assassinate Obama" on a school bus. In Mount Desert Island, Maine, black effigies were reportedly hanged with nooses.[28]

Some of the election-related hate crimes were violent. Five reported attacks by white supremacists on blacks and Latinos in California's San Jacinto Valley were what police described as a reaction to the election. And on Staten Island, two 18-year-olds were among a group of men who yelled "Obama" as they assaulted a black teenager with a baseball bat just hours after Obama clinched the presidency.[29]

One of the most widely publicized incidents involved the burning of a black church, the Macedonia Church of God in Christ, in Springfield, Massachusetts, just a few hours after Obama's win was confirmed. At the time of the burning, federal investigators called the act a probable hate crime.[30] The Department of Justice eventually released a statement about arrests in the Springfield case and condemned the acts as motivated by "racism," even though the city of Springfield reported no hate crimes in the fourth quarter of 2008.

Following the election, there was also an outbreak of more systematic violence—domestic terrorist acts perpetrated by members of, or those connected to, extremist groups or ideologies. Some of the attempted terrorist plots involved assassination attempts against Obama, but others were simply spurred by general rage at the outcome of the elections.

James G. Cummings, a neo-Nazi who was amassing a cache of radioactive materials suitable for building a "dirty bomb" ended up being shot to death by his wife, Amber, in December 2009. The "dirty bomb" reference was in a leaked FBI intelligence report.[31] During a search of the Belfast, Maine, house where Cummings lived with his wife, investigators reportedly discovered instructions for making a dirty bomb, along with four one-gallon containers filled with a mix of uranium and thorium, both of which are radioactive, along with highly toxic beryllium powder. The containers also held a hydrogen peroxide-based solution for making peroxide-based explosives, along with lithium metal, thermite, magnesium ribbon, black iron oxide, and other substances that are used to amplify the effects of homemade explosives. Amber Cummings reportedly told police that her husband was "very upset" about Obama's election.

Unfortunately, during the last four years, the outbreak of domestic terrorism has not abated. The SPLC has documented 36 separate domestic terrorist plots since 2008. Many of them occurred just after the election, including the April 2009 shooting of law enforcement officers by a racist in Pittsburgh, Pennsylvania; a May 2009 shooting of an abortion doctor in Wichita, Kansas; and a June 2009 shooting at the Holocaust Memorial Museum in Washington, DC, by a neo-Nazi. Directly tied to the election was a murder and rape spree targeting African immigrants and Jews by Keith Luke, a neo-Nazi, in Brockton, Massachusetts, that took place the day after the inauguration.[32]

Antigovernment "Patriot" Groups

Another aspect of the election's fallout has been the stunning growth that has occurred in the antigovernment "Patriot" movement—conspiracy-minded groups that see the federal government as their primary enemy—over the last three years. Such organizations are not necessarily racist, although anti-Obama sentiment among them is common. They are typified by extreme conspiracy mongering about things like secret government concentration camps (to imprison American citizens), an impending New World Order (that will take away individual freedoms), and violent government gun confiscations.

The antigovernment Patriot movement first emerged in 1994, as a response to what was seen as violent government repression of dissident groups at Ruby Ridge, Idaho, in 1992 and near Waco, Texas, in 1993, combined with general anger about gun control and the Democratic Clinton administration. It peaked in 1996, a year after the Oklahoma City bombing, with 858 groups, then began to fade. By the turn of the millennium, the Patriot movement was reduced to fewer than 150 relatively inactive groups.[33]

The movement came roaring back to life beginning in late 2008, just as the American economy entered official recession. Barack Obama's appearance on the political scene as the Democratic nominee and, ultimately, the president-elect helped fuel a right-wing resurgence.[34] Many Americans, infused with populist fury about the government providing bank and auto industry bailouts as well as a feeling that somehow, the country was "being lost," joined antigovernment groups.

Consequently, the swelling of the Patriot movement has been astounding. From 149 groups in 2008, the number of patriot organizations skyrocketed to 512 in 2009, shot up again in 2010 to 824, and then, in 2011, jumped to 1,274. That works out to a staggering 755 percent growth rate in three years. The 2011 total was more than 400 groups higher than the prior all-time high, in 1996.[35]

Violence has also followed the movement's ascendancy. Many of the domestic terrorism plots that have occurred since the election were perpetrated by organizations that make up this movement. In March 2011, Alaska Peacemakers Militia leader Francis "Schaeffer" Cox and four followers were arrested on weapons and conspiracy charges related to an alleged plan to kill Alaska state troopers and a judge. A state court later ruled that hundreds of hours of secret recordings made by informants would not be admissible, leading to the freeing of one of Cox's followers. Cox, however, was convicted on nine counts in 2012 that included conspiring to kill a judge.[36]

Other antigovernment plots included one in Georgia. In November 2011 the FBI arrested four members of a Georgia militia group who were accused of a wide-ranging plot to attack cities with the deadly toxin ricin and kill federal law enforcement officials and IRS agents. As one of the plotters said: "The first ones that need to die are the ones in the federal buildings." The men were in their late sixties and seventies, but their concrete actions included an attempt to purchase a briefcase-sized bomb, casing two buildings as potential bombing targets, and trying to manufacture ricin.[37]

A bizarre subset of the antigovernment movement has also been on the rise, inspired by the downturn in the economy as well as a president who seems "other." "Sovereign citizens," whose ideology first developed in white supremacist groups, generally do not believe that they are subject to federal or even local laws. They do not feel they have to pay taxes or comply with requirements for documents like drivers' licenses and vehicle registrations. They also typically believe that filing certain documents with courts will relieve them of debt or bankruptcy proceedings, or even bring them millions of dollars from secret government accounts. As a result, thousands of pages of garbled and nonsensical legalistic paperwork are clogging up American court systems. The sovereigns' claims are bogus, of course, but they have attracted thousands into the movement with promises of easy money and bilking the government during a time of real financial hardship for many Americans.

Sovereign citizen beliefs have brought them into regular conflict with law enforcement officials, seen most dramatically on May 20, 2010, when a father–son team of sovereigns murdered two West Memphis, Arkansas, officers during a traffic stop.[38] And officials have had other encounters. In September 2012 the FBI issued a bulletin to law enforcement officials entitled "Sovereign citizens: a growing domestic threat to law enforcement," which describes the movement as "domestic terrorist."[39] The bulletin notes that sovereigns have killed six law enforcement officers since 2000 and that Terry Nichols, convicted in the Oklahoma City bombing, was a sovereign. The largest group of organized sovereigns, the Alabama-based Republic for the united [sic] States of America (RuSA), took a new step in 2011 toward organizing a kind of government-in-waiting by adding a "Congress" with voting representatives in 49 states. The group says it is in the process of "reinhabiting" the government.[40]

These extreme sentiments against the federal government have leaked into the mainstream, so now some mainstream politicians are spouting the same antigovernment rhetoric as those in the Patriot movement. A Rasmussen Reports poll in spring 2010 showed that 75 percent of likely American voters were "angry" or "very angry" at the policies of the federal government, up from 66 percent in September.[41] The poll was taken not long after former Republican vice presidential candidate Sarah Palin told the first

National Tea Party Convention in Nashville in February 2010 that: "America is ready for another revolution."[42]

The Rasmussen poll also found that 88 percent of "mainstream voters" were angry, but 84 percent of the "political class" was not—another indication of how leaders are widely seen as completely out of touch. The numbers are harrowing, and hearken back to the period around the 1995 bombing of the Oklahoma City federal building, when the antigovernment movement was seething. A few days after that attack left 168 men, women, and children dead, a *USA Today* poll found that fully 39 percent of Americans agreed with the proposition that the federal government was "so large and powerful that it poses an immediate threat to the rights and freedoms of ordinary citizens."[43]

In March 2010 a CNN Opinion Research Corporation poll asked precisely the same question and found that 56 percent of Americans now agree with that statement—a simply astonishing measure of how angry and suspicious Americans have become, even when compared to the period of the mass murder in Oklahoma. The Oklahoma attack was the culmination of political anger against the government that had been building for years over issues such as gun control, environmental regulation, the outsourcing of jobs, and the purported crushing of dissent. Today, the fury is building again, this time over bailouts of banks and the auto industry, health insurance, the economy, government spending, and the country's changing demographics, particularly as represented in the person of Barack Obama.[44]

The "Birthers"

Arguably one of the most powerful conspiracy theories that erupted right after the Obama election was what has come to be called "birtherism," or the belief that Obama is not a legitimate American. To those who believe this conspiracy (the so-called "birthers"), the president's birth certificate from Hawaii is somehow forged, and he is a "foreign" influence that has infiltrated the American political system. The theory is patently racist and xenophobic, playing off Obama's foreign-sounding name and his skin color to paint him as a foreign organism in the American body politic. "Birthers" thus view the president as a "Manchurian candidate" of sorts, some kind of sleeper agent placed here years ago by foreign, often "Islamic," interests that now have finally managed to seize control of the nation's highest office.

The "birther" claims were first introduced during the 2008 campaign. Right-wing polemicist Jerome Corsi—best known for his "Swift Boat" distortion of the Vietnam war record of then-presidential candidate John Kerry—has written two books questioning Obama's origins.[45] These claims quickly spread from the conspiracy-laden dens of the radical right into the talking points of conservative media pundits and politicians, many of whom gave the idea credence, including millionaire Donald Trump, who for a brief time in 2011 was running for president.[46] Former vice presidential candidate Sarah Palin said questions about Obama's citizenship were "fair game."[47] U.S.

Republican Michele Bachmann (R-Minnesota), who ran for president in the Republican primaries, questioned the president's nationality, too, although she later seemed to soften her stance.[48]

Others tried to pass legislation that would require presidential candidates appearing on state ballots to produce a birth certificate. Arizona state senator Carl Seel introduced such a bill. It was initially vetoed by Arizona Governor Jan Brewer, but eventually passed the state legislature.[49] Congress, too, has played a role in spreading the conspiracy. In March 2009 Representative Bill Posey, a newly elected Republican from Florida's 15th congressional district, introduced a bill, H.R. 1503, in the U.S. House of Representatives. Had this bill been enacted into law, it would have amended the Federal Election Campaign Act of 1971 to require candidates for the presidency "to include with the [campaign] committee's statement of organization a copy of the candidate's birth certificate" plus supporting documentation.[50] Ultimately, 12 Republican congressmen became co-sponsors of the bill.

"Birtherism" has had some success at undermining President Obama. Polls have shown large numbers of Americans believe in various aspects of the conspiracy. In March 2011 a Harris poll found that 25 percent of respondents believed Obama was not born in the U.S.[51] In July 2010 a CNN poll found that 27 percent doubted Obama was born in the U.S. or were certain that he was not.[52] All polls have shown that these beliefs are far higher among Republicans than Democrats.

In 2011 in what the *New York Times* called "a profoundly low and debasing moment in American political life," Obama released the missing piece of the "birther" conspiracy puzzle—his "long-form" birth certificate[53] which confirmed the president's birthplace (Hawaii) and the identities of his parents. But the clamor surrounding Obama's citizenship only intensified, with calls to "prove" that this birth certificate was "real."

WorldNetDaily.com (WND), the right-wing conspiracy and antigovernment website that has been at the forefront of the "birther" conspiracy (Corsi is a staff reporter at WND), reported that the nation's first law enforcement investigation into the president's birth certificate was under way by Arizona's Maricopa County Sheriff Joe Arpaio, who bills himself as "America's toughest sheriff" and who is currently embroiled in a U.S. Department of Justice lawsuit accused of discrimination against Latinos and racial profiling.[54]

WND's founder Joseph Farah—who has sponsored billboards with the text "Where's the birth certificate?"—called for a "skeptical public" to continue to press Obama on his parentage and on why he "continues to cultivate a culture of secrecy around his life." Farah continued: "It would be a big mistake for everyone to jump to a conclusion now based on the release of this document, which raises as many questions as it answers."[55]

Orly Taitz, a California lawyer and dentist, has also been a driving force behind the "birther" movement. Often described as the "Queen of the Birthers," she ended up in a surreal shouting match on the network news channel MSNBC in April 2011. She demanded that the camera zoom in on a copy of Obama's draft records, because these offered new proof, she claimed, of a fraudulent presidency. The interview quickly devolved from there, and the channel cut her feed. "I invited a crazy person on the show to see if a crazy person faced with the thing that the crazy person was trying to get for two and a half years could say something responsive, something human," host Lawrence O'Donnell said. In the end, she couldn't.[56]

Another aspect of the "birther" conspiracy is that Obama is actually Muslim (which, to "birthers," is a bad thing), supposedly because of his Kenyan father or because of his year of elementary school in Indonesia, where his mother was pursuing graduate research on poverty. This claim further "otherizes" the president, and fuels "Manchurian candidate" arguments. It also helped feed a wave of anti-Muslim sentiment that surfaced in the United States after the 10th anniversary of the 9/11 attacks.

In the wake of this hysteria, anti-Muslim hate crimes were reported across the country. At the same time, protests were launched against mosques, and lawmakers in more than a dozen states introduced legislation to ban the use of Islamic religious law, called sharia, in the U.S. legal system— a completely unfounded fear. Nevertheless, extremists have tried to paint Obama as Muslim, which, in their circles, carries the idea that Muslims, too, are foreigners on American soil.[57]

The Rise of the Tea Parties

The Obama presidency was accompanied by a major backlash in terms of right-wing populism, in addition to the reaction it engendered on the radical right. Primary to this phenomenon was the rise of the so-called "Tea Parties," a diffuse movement made up of several groups that address a variety of issues, from battling tax hikes (some in the movement claim the "tea" is an acronym for "taxed enough already") to what they view as overreaching by the federal government. Although not an official political party (people with its support generally run for office as Republicans), the movement has served as an umbrella for a variety of right-wing populist and antigovernment ideas, and even as a recruiting ground for white nationalists.

Various accounts exist as to what and/or who started the Tea Parties and whether or not the movement has been bankrolled by the billionaire conservative brothers, David and Charles Koch. According to *New York Times* reporter Kate Zernike, the tea party movement erupted early in the Obama presidency, after an announcement was made in February 2009 by the new administration to help bail out homeowners who had defaulted on their mortgages. In her 2010 book *Boiling Mad*, Kate Zernike claims that the original seed of the Tea Party movement was a woman named Keli Carender, who was frustrated with the government stimulus package, bank bailouts, and the economic collapse. So she organized a protest in Seattle, Washington, by calling up a conservative radio host and emailing conservative pundit Michelle Malkin. Both gave her a plug for her protest, which drew 200 people. About a week after that, Zernike says, the incident that further sparked the movement occurred.[58]

This was network television CNBC reporter Rick Santelli's "rant" (it is referred to in Tea Party lore as "the rant") that occurred in February 2009 on the floor of the Chicago Board of Trade. Santelli was angry about Obama's proposal to help homeowners who could no longer afford their mortgages, and he proposed the idea of having a Tea Party in Chicago on the shores of Lake Michigan along the lines of the historic Boston Tea Party, in which American colonists dressed as Indians threw boxes of British tea into Boston harbor to protest what they felt were unfair taxes and unfair government practices. Santelli felt that people who could not pay their mortgages deserved no such help, and the rest of America should not have to pay for them, either.[59]

Right-wing populists took up his call, and quickly began to organize protests against the Obama administration's policies. The first protests were planned for April 15, 2009, the day when Americans have to file tax returns. The April 15 protests included many aspects that were racialized and ugly. There were signs held up that depicted Obama as Hitler. Speakers complained that Obama was destroying the country and taking away civil liberties. Racist images of the president and warlike rhetoric were common at the events.[60]

The Tea Parties hit a boiling point in the summer of 2009 after the president announced his intention to pass a massive health care overhaul whose provisions included extending health insurance coverage to all Americans. Sentiment among the Tea Parties became particularly angry as proponents of Tea Party ideas claimed the government was trying to "ration" healthcare and judge who would be "eligible" for it, relegating some to so-called "death panels" while other, more fortunate people, would get healthcare.[61]

Activists stressed the idea that Obama was creating a Nazi or socialist state, and that he was trying to destroy the country.[62] Town hall meetings held by Obama and other politicians to describe the new health care plan drew gun-toting activists, racist signs, and screaming matches. Many of the meetings ended in chaos, others with threats of violence. At an event in Hagerstown, Maryland, held by Senator Ben Cardin, a man held up a sign that read "Death to Obama" and "Death to Michelle and her two stupid kids."[63]

Although Tea Party movement members often deny it, racism has been a continuing theme at Tea Party events and an underlying current within the movement. For example, Tea Party-affiliated politicians and activists have pushed more challenges to the Voting Rights Act of 1965 since 2010 than in the past 40 years.[64] Other incidents demonstrated racially charged speech. In Ohio, scheduled speakers at a Tea Party rally organized by leader Brian "Sonny" Thomas fled after he suggested in a tweet that he wanted to shoot Latino immigrants—or, as he wrote, "spicks" [sic].[65] Thomas' Tea Party site also linked to White-pride.org, and CNN found a photo of him wearing a "White Pride" T-shirt. The Anti-Defamation League (ADL) documented widespread evidence of racism in Tea Party events in a November 2009 report.

In addition to signs questioning Obama's birth certificate and comparisons of President Obama to Hitler, there were also racist signs and even some signs that promoted implicit or explicit violence against the government. One sign called the President 'parasite in chief,' suggesting that he was feeding off the country for his own benefit. Many attendees [at September 12, 2009 rallies] shouted 'liar, liar, liar,' echoing Representative Joe Wilson's outburst [at Obama] during the joint session of Congress, the ADL reported.[66]

The radicalism expressed by the tea parties in general, and especially over the summer of 2009 in reaction to what came to be known by right-wing activists pejoratively as "Obamacare," quickly infiltrated the American mainstream. Polled by CBS and the *New York Times* in the spring of 2010, some 18 percent of Americans described themselves as supporters of the tea parties.[67] Sounding in many ways like furious, government-hating patriot activists, they described their top issues as opposition to the health care reform bill (viewed as a "socialist" overreaching of the government), a belief that the government does not represent real Americans, high levels of government spending and the economy. Like the patriots, they were far more likely than most to call themselves "angry."

Evidence surfaced that race was playing a part in the tea party movement, even as it began to build real political power in the grassroots of the Republican party. Just 1 percent of Tea Party supporters are black, the 2010 polls found, compared to more than 12 percent of the general population. Nine out of 10 disapproved of President Obama's job performance. Asked why they did not like the president, 19 percent said they just did not like him, 11 percent suggested he was moving the country toward "socialism," and 9 percent said he was dishonest. Fifty-two percent thought too much had been made of black people's problems, about twice the proportion of all Americans.[68]

Another poll by the University of Washington Institute for the Study of Ethnicity, Race & Sexuality found that white supporters of the Tea Parties were 25 percent more "racially resentful" than those who were not supporters.[69] White backers of the Tea Parties were less likely to believe that African Americans are intelligent, hardworking, or trustworthy, and their perceptions of Latinos were similar. As journalist and political commenter E.J. Dionne of the *Washington Post* rightly pointed out in an op-ed about the Tea Party poll, "Part of the anger at President Obama does appear to be driven by racial concerns." He noted that the poll's findings suggest that the Tea Party is essentially the reappearance of "an old anti-government far right" and that, according to the *New York Times*, supporters tend to be Republican married white men older than 45 who are better educated and more affluent than Americans as a whole.[70]

In October 2010 the first major report on racism in the tea parties was published by the Institute for Research and Education on Human Rights, *Tea Party Nationalism: a critical examination of the Tea Party movement and the size, scope, and focus of its national factions.*[71] Written and researched by longtime scholars of the far right Devin Burghart and Leonard Zeskind, the report examines the six major Tea Party groupings, and it found associations between Tea Party organizations and extremists from anti-immigration activists to militia leaders to white nationalists. Groups with known anti-Semitic agendas come up often and prominently in the report, which also catalogs numerous vitriolic attacks by Tea Party members using anti-Muslim and Islamophobic rhetoric.

The report names several figures who have played prominent roles in the Tea Party movement and who have histories of hate speech or associations with hate organizations. It also gives several examples of extremism in the Tea Party leadership. For example, former Tea Party Express Chairman Mark Williams resigned from the organization in June 2010 after a series of racially volatile comments, including calling slavery "a great gig" in a satirical piece he authored. He referred to President Obama as "a Nazi, a half-white racist, a half-black racist and an Indonesian Muslim turned welfare fraud."[72]

Other individuals with links to the white supremacist Council of Conservative Citizens are involved in the Tea Party, as are members of American Third Position (A3P; now American Freedom Party), a white nationalist political party founded by racist skinheads in California. According to Media Matters, A3P members organized, co-sponsored, or freely distributed literature at "no fewer than 10 Tea Party rallies in 6 states from 2010 to 2011."[73]

Burghart and Zeskind further argue that the movement as a whole is based on "a form of American nationalism [that] does not include all Americans, and separates itself from those it regards as insufficiently real Americans'." In addition, "a bright white line of racism threads through this nationalism [in which] race and religion are powerful determinants of national identity [and] mark the border between 'self' and 'other'."[74]

In about a year, Tea Party activists created a groundswell of right-wing rage that had a huge impact in the 2010 elections, which resulted in the Republican Party gaining a majority in the House of Representatives. Some of the new members of the House were themselves Tea Party members or sympathizers who created a "Tea Party Caucus" in Congress. However, public opinion quickly soured on both the Tea Party and Congress—most notably during the debt ceiling crisis in the summer of 2011, when the more conservative members of the GOP (including the strident tea partiers) refused to vote to raise the debt ceiling, which placed the U.S. in danger of losing its credit rating. The debt ceiling is a routine legislative process, done 18 times during the Reagan administration, nine under the first President Bush, six under Clinton, and seven during the second Bush administration. But under Obama, and with the new tea party factions in Congress, it became a heated battle.[75]

That may have helped stall the Tea Party, which was criticized for its obstructionism with regard to the debt ceiling. In August 2011 a *New York Times*/CBS poll found that an unfavorable view of the Tea Party was higher than when the question was first asked in 2010. Forty percent of people polled in August 2011 had an unfavorable view of the Tea Party.[76] By spring 2012 support for the Tea Party had stalled. An ABC poll by Langer Research found that six in 10 Americans are not interested in additional information about the Tea Party. Forty-one percent are not interested at all, while only 9 percent are "very" interested. Strong opponents outnumber strong supporters by two to one, and the majority of its support still comes from Republicans, especially conservative Republicans (81 percent in that category are supportive of the Tea Party).[77]

Regardless, Tea Partiers are still seething with anger at the American government. Their sentiments are similar to the general antigovernment movement, particularly apparent after the Supreme Court ruled in June 2012 that the health care mandate included in Obama's plan was constitutional. Many on the right were aghast, and claimed that a mandate took away personal freedoms and liberties, and was a step to a dictatorship. Some of the rhetoric carried fears and warnings about impending violence.

Mike Vanderboegh, an antigovernment activist and militia leader who in 2010 reacted to the imminent passage of the health care law by calling on Americans to break the windows of local Democratic Party offices around the country, predicted on his blog that the court's ruling would result in violence. "The health care law carries ... the hard steel fist of government violence at the center," Vanderboegh wrote. "If we refuse to obey, we will be fined. If we refuse to pay the fine, we will in time be jailed. If we refuse to report meekly to jail, we will be sent for by armed men. And if we refuse their violent invitation at the doorsteps of our own homes we will be killed—unless we kill them first."[78]

Also invoking the specter of violence was a more mainstream Republican, former Michigan GOP spokesman Matt Davis, who wondered in an email to fellow conservatives first reported by *Michigan Capitol Confidential*, "If the Supreme Court's decision Thursday paves the way for unprecedented intrusion into personal decisions, than [sic] has the Republic all but ceased to exist? If so, then is armed rebellion today justified? God willing, this oppression will be lifted and America free again before the first shot is fired."[79]

Conclusion

Several factors in American politics, economics, and society are currently driving the expansion of the country's radical right. At the most macro level, the growth of right-wing radicalization—a phenomenon that is plainly evident in Europe as well as the United States—is related directly to political and, especially, economic globalization. As the nation-state has diminished in importance since the end of the Cold War, Western economies have opened up, not only to capital from abroad but also to labor. In concrete terms that has meant major immigration flows, many of which have drastically altered the demographics of formerly homogenous populations. In Europe and the U.S., historically white-dominated countries, demographic shifts have altered that.

At the same time, globalization has caused major economic dislocations in the West as certain industries and production move to less developed countries.

In 2011 and 2012, as the American election season heated up, many politicians and other public figures on the political right attacked Muslims and perennial right-wing targets, including lesbian, gay, bisexual, transgender and queer (LGBTQ) people and other minorities. How this plays out is difficult to predict, given the unsettled nature of the presidential campaign and the animus toward President Obama and the government that is rooted in both economic and racial anger. But what may end up affecting the American radical right more than any other single factor in coming years is another term for Obama. The primaries and campaign did not slow down the attacks on the nation's first black president based on complete falsehoods—that he is a secret Muslim, a Kenyan, a radical leftist bent on destroying America—and it is likely that the radical right will further spread this poisonous rhetoric. Following Obama's reelection, the reaction of the extreme right, already angry and perceiving itself on the defensive, could result in even more tumultuous and troubling reactions.

Notes

1 Holthouse, David. "Was alleged Massachusetts spree killer a neo-Nazi? Keith Luke makes it official," *Hatewatch* blog, May 11, 2009, www.splcenter.org/blog /2009/05/11/was-alleged-massachusetts-spree-killer-a-neo-nazi-keith-luke-makes -it-official/. *Hatewatch* is the blog of the Southern Poverty Law Center's Intelligence Project.

2 Keller, Larry. "HUD debunks false statistic about how many bad mortgages illegal immigrants hold," *Intelligence Report* 133, Spring 2009, www.splcenter.org/ get-informed/intelligence-report/browse-all-issues/2009/spring/minority-meltdown.

3 2011 SPLC annual hate count. Numbers available also in Potok, Mark. "The 'patriot' movement explodes," *Intelligence Report* 145, Spring 2012, www.splcen-ter.org/get-informed/intelligence-report/browse-all-issues/2012/spring/the-year-in-hate-and-extremism. Potok is a former director of the Intelligence Project at SPLC. He is currently a senior fellow there.

4 Harvard sociologist Robert Putnam has written extensively about how demographic diversity leads to a loss of trust in communities. Putnam, Robert. *Bowling Alone: the collapse and revival of American community* (New York: Simon & Schuster, 2000). Putnam, Robert. "*E pluribus unum*: diversity and community in the twenty-first century," the 2006 Johan Skytte Prize Lecture, *Scandinavian Political Studies* (2007). 30, 2, 137–74.

5 2011 SPLC hate count. Each year, the SPLC tallies groups in different categories and publishes this report with the spring issue of the *Intelligence Report*. Categories include groups that are designated as "hate groups," including the categories white supremacist, anti-immigrant, and anti-gay. Other group categories include antigovernment, within which are various subcategories. Antigovernment groups are not necessarily listed as hate groups. For the most recent group tally, see www.splcenter.org/get-informed/intelligence-report/browse-all-issues/ 2012/spring.

6 What Will Bunch learned is the subject of his third book, *The Backlash: right-wing radicals, high-def hucksters, and paranoid politics in the age of Obama*

(New York: Harper, 2010). See also SPLC interview with Bunch at *Hatewatch*, www.splcenter.org/blog/2010/08/30/author-interview-journalist-probes-back-lash-under-obama/

7   Potok, Mark. "Threats against Obama growing as inauguration nears," *Hatewatch* blog, January 18, 2009, www.splcenter.org/blog/2010/08/30/author-inter-view-journalist-probes-backlash-under-obama/

8   Weiner, Rachel. "Obama hatred at McCain-Palin pallies: 'terrorist,' 'kill him!'," www.huffingtonpost.com/2008/10/06/mccain-does-nothing-as-cr_n_132366.html

9   *The Buzz* in the *Tampa Bay Times*, "GOP e-mail raises charges of racism," October 30, 2008.

10 Potok, Mark. "The radical right's reaction to the election of Barack Obama," /intelligence-report/browse-all-issues/2008/winter/after-the-election

11 Ibid.

12 Scherr, Sonia. "Hate groups claim Obama win is sparking recruitment surge," *Hatewatch* blog, (November 6, 2008, www.splcenter.org/blog/2008/11/06/hate-groups-claim-obama-win-is-sparking-recruitment-surge/. See also SPLC, "In their words: hating Barack Obama," *Intelligence Report* 133, Spring 2009, www.splcenter.org/get-informed/intelligence-report/browse-all-issues/2009/spring/white-heat/in-their-words-hating-bara

13 Ibid. Billy Roper shut down his group, White Revolution, in 2011. He then joined the Knights Party (a Klan group in Arkansas) under the direction of Thom Robb. Text of his essay, "White America, this IS your WAKE UP CALL" is on file at SPLC. It was also posted by a guest user at a health forum, of all places, www.health-forums.com/misc-fitness-weights/re-white-america-your-wake-up-call-billy-roper-66966.html

14 Ibid. Original can be found at www.kkk.bz/Obamalert.htm

15 Beirich, Heidi and Potok, Mark, "Not all white supremacists oppose black president," http://www.splcenter.org/get-informed/intelligence-report/browse-all-issues/2008/fall/silver-lining

16 Duke, David. "A black flag for white America," *Incogman* blog, June 6, 2008, http://incogman.net/06/2008/david-duke-a-black-flag-for-white-america/

17 Ibid.

18 U.S. Department of Homeland Security (hereafter DHS), "Rightwing extremism: current economic and political climate fueling resurgence in radicalization and recruitment," April 7, 2009, 3, www.fas.org/irp/eprint/rightwing.pdf

19 Bender, Bryan. "Secret Service strained as leaders face more threats," *Boston Globe*, October 18, 2009, www.boston.com/news/nation/washington/ articles/2009/10/18/secret_service_under_strain_as_leaders_face_more_threats/

20 Keller, Larry. "Racist backlash greets President Barack Obama," *Intelligence Report* 133, Spring 2009, www.splcenter.org/get-informed/intelligence-report/browse-all-issues/2009/spring/white-heat

21 *Wikipedia* devotes several pages to detailing assassination threats against President Obama. For more, readen. wikipedia.org/wiki/Barack_Obama_assassination_threats

22 DHS, "Rightwing extremism," 2.

23 Talbott, Chris. "Steven Joseph Christopher charged with threatening Obama on the internet," *Huffington Post*, January 16, 2009, www.huffingtonpost.com/2009/01/16/ steven-joseph-christopher_n_158703.html

24 Burnett, Sara. "Probe into purported Obama plot reveals details," *Rocky Mountain News*, September 3, 2008, www.rockymountainnews.com/news/2008/sep/03/drug-suspect-wanted-shoot-obama-invesco/#

25 Friedman, Dan and Maggs, John. "Authorities play down plot against Obama," *Government Executive*, August 27, 2008. U.S. attorney Troy Eid dismissed reports of a plot to kill the president, calling threats made by two men "racist

rantings" by two men "high on meth" and "not a credible threat," www
.govexec.com/defense/2008/08/authorities-play-down-plot-against-obama/27545/

26 NBC.com (formerly MSNBC.com), "Obama plot arrests shocks suspects'
neighbors," October 28, 2008, www.msnbc.msn.com/id/27416974/t/obama-plot-
arrests-shock-suspects-neighbors/#.UA8RdGhgNHg; Potok, Mark. "Alleged
plotter against Obama was member of Supreme White Alliance," *Hatewatch* blog,
October 28, 2008, www.splcenter.org/blog/2008/10/28/alleged-plotter-against-
obama-was-member-of-supreme-white-alliance

27 U.S. Federal Bureau of Investigation (hereafter FBI), "2008 hate crimes statistics,"
www.fbi.gov/about-us/cjis/ucr/hate-crime/2008/

28 Beirich, Heidi. "Anti-black hate crimes rise, data remains flawed," *Hatewatch*,
November 24, 2009, www.splcenter.org/blog/2009/11/24/anti-black-hate-crimes-
rise-data-remains-flawed/

29 Rosen, Daniel Edward. "Staten Island teens arrested in anti-Obama attack,"
Newsday, Long Island edition, November 15, 2008, www.newsday.com/news
/nation/staten-island-teens-arrested-in-anti-obama-attack-1.883726

30 Graham, George. "Post-election church arson at predominantly black parish probed
as possible hate crime," *The Republican*, (November 5, 2008, www .masslive.
com/news/index.ssf/2008/11/suspicious_blaze_destroys_tink.html. Three white
men were arrested and later convicted for the crime. Two pleaded guilty and one
was found guilty in a jury trial. Testimony at the trial indicated the men had used
racial slurs in the past, and were alarmed about a black man becoming president.
See Tuthill, Paul. "Three now convicted in church burning," WAMC Northeast
Public Radio, April 15, 2011, wamc.org/post/three-now-convicted-church-burning

31 Holthouse, David. "Slain neo-Nazi, angry over Obama victory, reportedly
prepared 'dirty bomb' components," *Hatewatch* blog, February 11, 2009, www
.splcenter.org/blog/2009/02/11/slain-neo-nazi-angry-over-obama-victory-repor
tedly-prepared-dirty-bomb-components/

32 For a list of all domestic terrorist plots since 1995, see SPLC, "Terror from
the right," www.splcenter.org/get-informed/publications/terror-from-the-right

33 SPLC group counts, on file at SPLC.

34 SPLC, "The second wave: return of the militias," August 2009, www.splcenter
.org/get-informed/publications/splc-report-return-of-the-militias

35 Potok, Mark. "The 'patriot' movement explodes."

36 Morlin, Bill. "Alaska militiamen convicted in antigovernment conspiracy,"
Hatewatch blog, June 19, 2012, www.splcenter.org/blog/2012/06/19/alaska
-militiamen-convicted-in-antigovernment-murder-conspiracy/

37 Potok, Mark. "Georgia militiamen arrested in major domestic terror plot,"
Hatewatch blog, November 2, 2011, www.splcenter.org/blog/2011/11/02/georgia
-militiamen-arrested-in-major-domestic-terror-plot/. Two members later pleaded
guilty to conspiracy charges. See Morlin, Bill. "Key members of Georgia militia
plead guilty in terror plot," *Hatewatch* blog, April 10, 2012, www.splcenter.org/
blog/2012/04/10/leader-of-georgia-militia-accomplice-plead-in-terror-plot/

38 MacNab, J.J. "'Sovereign' Citizen Kane," *Intelligence Report* 139, Fall 2010,
www.splcenter.org/get-informed/intelligence-report/browse-all-issues/2010/fall
/sovereign-citizen-kane. MacNab also details the bizarre and murky beliefs of
the sovereign movement.

39 FBI Counterterrorism Analysis Section, "Sovereign citizens: a growing domestic
threat to law enforcement," *Law Enforcement Bulletin*, September 2011, www.
fbi.gov/stats-services/publications/law-enforcement-bulletin/september-2011/
sovereign-citizens

40 SPLC has covered RuSA extensively. See, for example, Lenz, Ryan. "'Sovereign'
president," *Intelligence Report* 143, Fall 2011, www.splcenter.org/get-informed/
intelligence-Report/browse-all-issues/2011/fall/-sovereign-president;Lenz.

"Republic for the united [sic] States of America plagued by criminality," *Intelligence Report* 146, Summer 2012, www.splcenter.org/get-informed/intelligence-report/browse-all-issues/2012/summer/sins-of-the-sovereigns. One Republican in Iowa dropped out of an election campaign in order to become a "senator" in the RuSA government. Lenz. "Iowa senate candidate drops out, becomes 'senator' in Sovereign Group," *Hatewatch* blog, July 17, 2012, www.splcenter.org/blog/2012/07/17/iowa-senate-candidate-drops-out-becomes-senator-in-sovereign-group/

41   Rasmussen Reports, "75% are angry at government's current policies," February 8, 2010, www.rasmussenreports.com/public_content/politics/general_politics/february_2010/75_are_angry_at_government_s_current_policies. See also "Poll: 75% 'angry' at government," *Politico*, February 8, 2010, www.politico.com/news/stories/0210/32680.html

42   "Palin to Tea Party: America ready for another revolution," *CNN.com*, February 6, 2010, http://articles.cnn.com/2010-02-06/politics/palin.tea.party _1_tea-party-convention-sarah-palin-republican-vice-presidential-nominee?_s=PM:POLITICS

43   Potok, Mark. "They say they want a revolution," *Intelligence Report* 137, Spring 2010, www.splcenter.org/get-informed/intelligence-report/browse-all-issues/2010/spring/ they-say-they-want-a-revolution

44   Steinhauser, Paul. "CNN poll: majority think government poses threat to citizens' rights," *CNN Politics*, February 26, 2010, http://articles.cnn.com/2010-02-26/politics/citizens.rights.poll_1_national-poll-cnn-poll-survey?_s = PM:POLITICS

45   Corsi, Jerome. *The Obama Nation* (New York: Pocket Star Books, 2010); Corsi. *Where's the Birth Certificate? The case that Barack Obama is not eligible to be president* (World Net Daily Books, 2011). For information about the "swift boat" attacks on John Kerry, see Black, Duncan. "MMFA investigates: who is Jerome Corsi, co-author of swift boat vets attack book?," *Media Matters for America* site, August 6, 2004, http://mediamatters.org/research/2004/08/06/mmfa-investigates-who-is-jerome-corsi-co-author/131607.Corsi's co-written book (with John O'Neill) that attacked John Kerry is *Unfit for Command: swift boat veterans speak out against John Kerry* (Washington, DC: Regnery Publishing, 2004).

46   Trump appeared several times on network stations for interviews in which he voiced his "concerns" about the president's birth certificate, and even started attracting criticism from fellow Republicans. Puzzanghera, Jim. "Republicans criticize Donald Trump on 'birther' issue," *Los Angeles Times*, May 2, 2011, http://articles.latimes.com/2011/may/02/nation/la-na-gop-birthers-trump -20110502. Trump also took credit for getting the president to release his long-form birth certificate, although he hinted that it might be a fake. Madison, Lucy. "Trump takes credit for Obama birth certificate release, but wonders 'is it real?'," *Political Hotsheet*, CBS News, April 27, 2011, www.cbsnews.com/8301-503544_162-20057854-503544.html

47   Smith, Ben. "Palin: Obama birth certificate a 'fair question'," *Politico*, December 3, 2009), www.politico.com/blogs/bensmith/1209/Palin_Obama_birth_ certificate_a_fair_question.html

48   Marr, Kendra. "Michele Bachmann: 'no birth flap for me'," *Politico*, March 15, 2011. Bachmann, who generally sidestepped questions regarding the president's citizenship, was interviewed by conservative radio host Jeff Katz. She told him that the first thing she would do in an initial presidential debate if she were running for office would be to offer her birth certificate, see www.politico.com/news/stories/0311/51245.html#ixzz1Ghinodu3

49   Condon, Stephanie. "'Birther' bill passes in Arizona legislature," *Political Hotsheet*, CBS News, April 15, 2011, www.cbsnews.com/8301-503544_162-20054236-503544.html

50   Smith, Ben. "'Birther' bill hits Congress," *Politico*, March 13, 2009, www.politico.com/blogs/bensmith/0309/Birther_bill_hits_Congress.html

51   Harris Polls, "'Wing nuts' and President Obama," www.harrisinteractive.com/
     NewsRoom/HarrisPolls/tabid/447/ctl/ReadCustom%20Default/mid/1508/Arti-
     cleId/223/Default.aspx
52   "CNN poll: quarter doubt Obama was born in the U.S.," *Political Ticker*, CNN
     Politics, August 4, 2010, http://politicalticker.blogs.cnn.com/2010/08/04/cnn
     -poll-quarter-doubt-president-was-born-in-u-s/?fbid=2s_9mn_pZ17; the poll is
     available at http://i2.cdn.turner.com/cnn/2010/images/08/04/rel10k1a.pdf
53   Editorial, "A certificate of embarrassment," *New York Times*, April 27, 2011,
     www.nytimes.com/2011/04/28/opinion/28thu1.html
54   Tashman, Brian. "WorldNetDaily and Sheriff Joe's very profitable 'birther' investi-
     gation," *Right Wing Watch* blog, January 6, 2012, www.rightwingwatch.org/
     content/worldnetdaily-and-sheriff-joes-very-profitable-birther-investigation;
     Santos, Fernanda and Savage, Charlie. "Lawsuit says sheriff discriminated
     against Latinos," *New York Times*, May 10, 2012, www.nytimes.com/2012/05/
     11/us/justice-department-sues-arizona-sheriff-joe-arpaio.html. The lawsuit alle-
     ges a "pattern of unlawful discrimination" by law enforcement. Arpaio is
     accused of running an agency in which suspicion and grounds for arrest were
     influenced by ethnicity and/or poor English skills. The U.S. Department of Justice
     alleges that Arpaio waged a campaign against illegal immigration aimed speci-
     fically at Latinos, regardless of their status or citizenship and that he sought to
     silence his opponents through retaliation that included filing baseless lawsuits.
55   Unruh, Bob. "White House releases Obama 'birth certificate'," *World Net
     Daily*, April 27, 2011, www.wnd.com/2011/04/292165/
56   "Lawrence O'Donnell and birther Orly Taitz have wild shoutfest about
     Obama," *Huffington Post*, April 28, 2011, www.huffingtonpost.com/2011/04/28/
     lawrence-odonnell-orly-taitz-birther_n_854769.html
57   SPLC has documented growing anti-Muslim/anti-Islam sentiment on its *Hate-
     watch* blog and its *Intelligence Report*. See, for example, Steinback, Robert.
     "Jihad against Islam," *Intelligence Report* 142, Summer 2011; and Steinback,
     "The anti-Muslim inner circle," in *Intelligence Report* 142. A poll released in
     July 2012 found that 17 percent of registered American voters believe President
     Obama is a Muslim, a steady figure since 2008. But the belief had doubled among
     Republicans. In 2008 16 percent of Republicans believed he was a Muslim. In
     the latest poll, 30 percent do. The poll was conducted by the Pew Forum on
     Religion and Public Life, from June 28–July 9, 2012, www.pewforum.org/Politics-
     and-Elections/Little-Voter-Discomfort-with-Romney's-Mormon-Religion.aspx
58   *All Things Considered* radio show, "'Boiling mad': a tea party origin story,"
     National Public Radio, September 15, 2010, www.npr.org/templates/story/story.
     php?storyId=129865403. See also Zernike, Kate. *Boiling Mad: inside Tea Party
     America* (New York: Times Books, 2010); Skopcol, Theda and Williamson, Vanessa.
     The Tea Party and the Remaking of Republican Conservatism (Cambridge, MA:
     Harvard University Press, 2012). Others suggest that the billionaire Koch brothers
     (Charles and David) have worked closely with the Tea Party movement from its
     inception, and bankrolled it. See Mayer, Jane. "Covert operations: the billionaire
     brothers who are waging a war against Obama," *New Yorker*, August 30,
     2010, www.newyorker.com/reporting/2010/08/30/100830fa_fact_mayer
59   "The rant," www.youtube.com/watch?v=APAD7537RN0. The so-called
     Boston Tea Party event occurred December 16, 1773 when a group of disguised
     Bostonians snuck aboard British ships in Boston harbor and dumped 46 tons of
     tea into the water. The incident set the stage for looming war between the
     American colonists and England. See Carp, Benjamin L. *Defiance of the Patriots: the
     Boston Tea Party and the making of America* (New Haven, NJ: Yale University
     Press, 2011). The modern incarnation of the Tea Party draws heavily on
     America's colonial symbols.

60 Anti-Defamation League (hereafter ADL), "Rage grows in America: anti-government conspiracies," November 2009, 4–5, www.adl.org/special_reports/rage-grows-in-America/

61 The so-called "death panel" meme appears to have its origins with the religious right-wing legal organization, Liberty Counsel. Vice presidential candidate Sarah Palin, however, popularized it with an infamous post on Facebook in which she claimed that the Obama health care plan would implement death panels that would decide who was a "productive member of society" and thus who was "worthy of healthcare." See the post at the NPR *Science Desk* blog, "'Death panels' debunked: Sen. Johnny Isakson," August 11, 2009, www.npr.org/blogs/health/2009/08/death_panels_debunked_sen_john.html. According to a blog by Sue Sturgis at the Institute for Southern Studies, Palin appears to have gotten the "death panel" idea from a set of talking points put out by the Liberty Counsel, which claimed that part of the Obama health care act was going to ration health care for the elderly (thus determine "who lives and who dies") and that the government will mandate "how your life ends," www.lc.org/index.cfm?PID=19319. Sturgis, Sue. "Far-right religious group behind 'death panels' myth linked to other health reform distortions," Institute for Southern Studies, August 11, 2009, www.southernstudies.org/2009/08/far-right-religious-group-behind-death-panels-myth-linked-to-other-health-reform-distortions. The Liberty Counsel is associated with Jerry Falwell's Liberty University and has offered legal counsel to various individuals and organizations who feel their "religious liberties" are being diminished or curtailed.

62 Comparisons of Obama to Hitler riddled Tea Party events and other right-wing quarters. See Lederman, Noah. "Playing the Nazi card: comparing Obama to Hitler becomes a standard right-wing trope," *Fairness and Accuracy in Reporting*, March 2010, www.fair.org/index.php?page=4022

63 ADL, "Rage grows in America," p. 7. Reports of these town hall meetings are too numerous to list. See the ADL report, but also see, for example, Krushaar, Josh and Lerer, Lisa. "Health care town hall anger rages on," *Politico*, August 12, 2009, www.politico.com/news/stories/0809/26049.html; Bigg, Matthew and Carey, Nick. "Protestors disrupt town-hall healthcare talks," *Reuters*, August 8, 2009, www.reuters.com/article/2009/08/08/us-usa-healthcare-townhalls-idUS-TRE5765QH20090808; Saul, Michael. "Rage boils over at town hall meetings over health care," *New York Daily News*, August 8, 2009, http://articles.nydailynews.com/2009-08-12/news/17934349_1_health-care-event-in-new-hampshire-president-obama

64 *Reuters*, "Voting rights act petitions reach Supreme Court," *Chicago Tribune*, July 20, 2012, www.chicagotribune.com/news/sns-rt-us-usa-voting-rights-challengebre86j16u-20120720,0,7296229.story

65 The term "spic" is a derogatory reference to Hispanics.

66 ADL report, p. 9.

67 Potok, Mark. "Unsweet tea: exploring the ideas of the antigovernment movement," editorial, *Intelligence Report* 138, Summer 2010, www.splcenter.org/get-informed/intelligence-report/browse-all-issues/2010/summer/unsweet-tea

68 Montopoli, Brian, "Tea Party supporters: who they are and what they believe," CBSNews.com, April 14, 2010.

69 The University of Washington Institute for the Study of Ethnicity, Race & Sexuality has conducted various surveys that deal with American attitudes toward race and politics. These include "Tea Party attitudes in Washington State," "Tea Party views on equality, liberty and Obama," and "Is America now a post-racial society?" http://depts.washington.edu/uwiser/racepolitics.html

70 Dionne, Jr., E.J. "The Tea Party: populism of the privileged," *Washington Post*, April 19, 2010, www.washingtonpost.com/wp-dyn/content/article/2010/04/18/AR201004 1802724.html

71 Burghart, Devin and Zeskin, Leonard. "Tea Party Nationalism," Institute for Research and Education on Human Rights (hereafter IREHR), October 2010, www.irehr.org/issue-areas/tea-party-nationalism

72 Burghart, Devin. "Tea Party express (again) gives platform to bigot," September 12, 2011, www.irehr.org/issue-areas/tea-party-nationalism/tea-party-news-and-analysis/item/366-tea-party-express-again-gives-platform-to-bigot

73 Holthouse, David. "'Fertile ground': white nationalists organize within Tea Party," *Media Matters* blog, August 3, 2011, mediamatters.org/blog/2011/08/03/fertile-ground-white-nationalists-organize-with/180982. For information on A3P, see the SPLC Intelligence Files entry, www.splcenter.org/get-informed/intelligence-files/groups/american-third-position. Another major tea party organization, Tea Party Nation (TPN), has its own problems with racism creeping into its rhetoric. In March 2011 TPN sent out an email to its members written by Islamophobe Rich Swier, in which he lamented the falling birthrate of "native-born" Americans compared to immigrants and that American culture was going to perish because the "White Anglo-Saxon Protestant (WASP) population is headed for extinction." Tashman, Brian. *Right Wing Watch* blog, March 29, 2011, www.rightwingwatch.org/content/tea-party-group-warns-white-extinction-america. More recently TPN president Judson Phillips posted a blog on the site claiming that Obama smoked crack and had sex with a man during his days in Chicago. TPN blog was posted at www.teapartynation.com/forum/topics/mr-obama-release-your-records

74 Burghart and Zeskin. "Tea Party nationalism."

75 Schlesinger, Robert. "Both sides aren't to blame for debt ceiling crisis," *U.S. News and World Report*, July 29, 2011, www.usnews.com/opinion/blogs/robert-schlesinger/2011/07/29/both-sides-arent-to-blame-for-debt-ceiling-crisis. Schlesinger places blame on the GOP, and notes the Tea Party role in it. See also Hornick, Ed. "The 'big headache': Boehner backed into corner by Tea Party, Obama," *CNN Politics*, July 26, 2011, http://articles.cnn.com/2011-07 -26/politics/tea.party.boehner_1_tea-party-debt-ceiling-debt-limit-vote?_s=PM:POLITICS

76 Zernike, Kate. "Poll shows negative view of the Tea Party on the rise," *New York Times*, August 5, 2011, www.nytimes.com/2011/08/05/us/politics/05tea-party.html

77 Langer, Gary. "Tea Party movement looks stalled; half like it less as they hear more," *ABC News*, April 15, 2012, http://abcnews.go.com/blogs/politics/2012/04/tea-party-movement-looks-stalled-half-like-it-less-as-they-hear-more/; see also Clement, Scott. "Tea Party support stable, but interest is waning," *Washington Post*, April 15, 2012, www.washingtonpost.com/blogs/behind-the-numbers/post/tea-party-support-stable-but-interest-is-waning/2012/04/14/gIQAPXyKHT blog.html

78 Vanderboegh, Mike. "Black Thursday," *Sipsey Street Irregulars* blog, June 28, 2012, http://sipseystreetirregulars.blogspot.com/2012/06/black-thursday.html. See also Nelson, Leah. "Dawn of 'red America': extremists react to SCOTUS ruling," *Hatewatch* blog, June 29, 2012, www.splcenter.org/blog/2012/06/29/dawn-of-red-america-extremists-react-to-scotus-ruling/

79 Ganter, Tom: "'Is armed rebellion now justified?' Lansing attorney does not like Supreme Court Obamacare ruling," *Michigan Capitol Confidential*, June 28, 2012, www.michigancapitolconfidential.com/17151. Ganter is a former GOP spokesman.

6 Barack Obama and the Future of American Racial Politics[1]

Rogers M. Smith and Desmond S. King[2]

Both within academia and in popular political discourse, the rise of Barack Obama to the presidency has been accompanied by much debate over whether his success represents a kind of "post-racial" politics and is the harbinger of a post-racial era in American politics (e.g. Connerly 2008; Bobo and Dawson 2008, p. 1; Sinclair-Chapman and Price 2008, p. 739; Street 2008). And though there is great skepticism, particularly in academia, about whether the United States is genuinely moving beyond a politics shaped by racial divisions, even skeptics do accept that Obama ran a post-racial or at least a "race-neutral" campaign (Baiocchi 2008; Sinclair-Chapman and Price 2008, p. 741). Here, we seek not to challenge but to give greater specificity to these contentions by analyzing the 2008 presidential campaign strategies and the prospects for race in the nation's future through the lens of what we have argued to be the basic structure of American racial politics: the continuing clashes between America's rival racial institutional orders (King and Smith 2005; King and Smith 2008).

Was it a Post-Racial Election?

In order to understand why it makes sense to analyze the present and future in these terms, we should first ask why we should not simply accept that America has already entered an era of post-racial politics. After all, a major party nominated and elected a presidential candidate commonly seen as black, and neither that candidate nor his opponent focused on race or racial issues as central to the campaign or the policy choices facing the country. Surely this silence about race and racial policies is a defining characteristic of a post-racial politics?

We agree that a post-racial politics would display such silence. But as the 19th-century gag rule showed, race may be excluded from discussion for different reasons; and we argue that modern alliances on racial issues, not the absence of racial concerns, moved discussions of race to the margins of both campaigns in 2008. In considering why we should reject the possibility that the election was genuinely post-racial, note that not only was Barack Obama the first non-white candidate ever to be nominated by a major party in the United States for either president or vice president, although all humanity probably originated in Africa, Obama was the first person of known, modern African descent to be nominated and elected in any country with a European-descended majority population anywhere in the world, including all of North America, South America, and Australasia, as well as Europe. Many of those nations have far from trivial percentages of African-descended members. It is simply inconceivable that such a broad pattern of political exclusion dating back for more than six centuries could be altered without consciousness of race playing a significant part.

It may be said, however, that although Americans grasped the momentous novelty of Obama's candidacy, racial equity in the United States has improved so greatly that it is understandable that neither candidate focused on race or race-related problems. That contention is, if anything, even more of a non-starter. The familiar, painful litany of America's continuing severe material racial gaps encompasses virtually every dimension of life, from economic well-being to health to housing to education to the criminal justice system. And though the U.S. has become a more multiracial nation and is becoming still more so, the sharpest divides remain between blacks and whites. We summarize those gaps only because they must remain a baseline for any credible analysis of American racial politics.

Economic Well-Being

In 2007, as the current deep recession was just beginning, the poverty rate among African Americans was already 24.5 percent, almost three times what it was for non-Hispanic whites (8.2 percent) (U.S. Census 2008); 11.2 percent of blacks were in deep poverty, with incomes less than 50 percent of the official poverty rate, compared with 3.4 percent for non-Hispanic whites. And significant inequalities persisted above the poverty line: African American median household income in 2007 was 62 percent of the median non-Hispanic white household income (Danzinger and Danzinger 2006, pp. 16, 27). African American family members also had to work for longer hours and more weeks a year to achieve their incomes: Thomas M. Shapiro estimates that in 2000, middle-income black families had to work the equivalent of 12 more weeks a year than white families to earn the same money (Shapiro 2004, p. 7). And as Shapiro and Melvin Oliver have long argued, when we move from income to wealth, the disparities become sharper still. By 2004, the "black–white median net worth ratio" was 0.10, meaning that blacks controlled 10 cents of net assets for every dollar of net worth possessed by whites (Oliver and Shapiro 2006, p. 204).

Health

Blacks today remain nearly twice as likely as whites to lack health insurance, 19.5 percent to 10.4 percent (U.S. Census 2008). The black infant mortality rate is more than twice that of whites—13.7 per 1,000 births, versus 5.7 and 5.6, respectively—and life expectancy for black men is six years fewer than for white men, while for black women it is five years fewer than for white women (U.S. Department of Health and Human Services 2007, pp. 50, 167). Stress-related chronic diseases are a prominent source of these lower life expectancies (Geronimus and Thomson 2004, p. 249). These worrying statistics arise in part from other inequalities, such as differing labor market opportunities and participation rates. In 2000 roughly 33 percent of male blacks over 18 were not participating in the labor force, compared with 15 percent of male whites—a ratio that held for men in their prime earning years, 31–50 (Katz, Stern, and Fader 2005, p. 82).

Housing

There is still a large gap between black household heads who own their own homes (48.4 percent in 2003) and whites who do so (75 percent), and the gap actually grew between 1990 and 2003, even though home ownership also rose in both groups (Center for Responsible Lending, 2004; Katz, Stern, and Fader 2005, p. 104). That disparate home ownership is not equally stable, either. The Center for Responsible Lending has reported that in 2002, blacks were "3.6 times as likely as whites to receive a home purchase loan from a subprime lender, and 4.1 times as likely as whites to receive a refinance loan from a subprime lender" (Center for Responsible Lending 2004). The higher rates of subprime lending persist even at higher income levels (Fernandez 2007). These circumstances have made it inevitable for blacks to be especially likely to lose their homes during the current foreclosure crisis.

Education

As the Supreme Court has become increasingly reluctant to view patterns of school segregation as constitutional violations, American schools have become still more segregated: "the percentage of black students attending majority nonwhite schools increased in all regions from 66 percent in 1991 to 73 percent in 2003–4" (Orfield and Lee 2006, p. 9). If all students were reaching the same levels of educational attainment, that trend might not cause such concern. But in 2000, just 12 percent of black men aged 24–30 had graduated from college compared to 30 percent of white men, while black women graduated at the rate of 15 percent, in comparison with a graduate rate of 33 percent for white women (Katz, Stern, and Fader 2005, pp. 93–4). Separate is still too strongly associated with unequal in American education as a whole.

Incarceration

Perhaps most notoriously, African Americans have been massively disproportionately affected by the American explosion in incarceration in the last three decades—the rise of what has become known as the "prison industrial complex" (Schlosser 1998). By 2005 black men were incarcerated at a rate of 4,682 per 100,000, compared to 709 per 100,000 for white men; and black women were incarcerated at a rate of 347 per 100,000, compared to 88 per 100,000 for white women (Katz, Stern, and Fader 2005, p. 128).

Cumulatively, these statistics make it impossible to conclude that there are no longer significant race-related policy issues in the modern United States. To understand why both major candidates largely shied away from discussions of race and the racial dimensions of policy issues, and what these circumstances portend for the future under President Obama, we must grasp the structure of racial politics in America today.

Racial Institutional Orders

We contend that this structure is comprised today as in the past by what we have termed rival "racial institutional orders." These orders are durable alliances of political actors, activist groups, and governing institutions united by agreement on the central racial issue of the eras in American politics that their conflicts help to define. They seek political power to resist or advance the measures to promote greater material racial equality that are politically pivotal in their eras (King and Smith 2005). There have so far been three eras of rival racial orders, interspersed with periods of transition. In each of these eras, one order has promoted arrangements thought to advantage those then labeled "white," while a rival order has sought to end many of those advantages.

The three eras thus defined are the *slavery era* from 1789 to 1865, when the maintenance and extension of slavery were the battleground issues; the *Jim Crow era*, consolidated in the mid-1890s after a transition period and lasting officially to 1954, when the maintenance and extension of *de jure* segregation and effective black disfranchisement were the central issues; and the *modern era of race-conscious controversies*, which consolidated after a transition by the mid-1970s and continues today, and in which the defining battles are over whether public policies should be "color blind" or "race conscious" (King and Smith 2008, pp. 686–88).

During the *slavery* and *Jim Crow* eras, the strength of the two contesting racial orders fluctuated over time but culminated in a decisive and enduring victory by one side on the battleground issues of the day. In the subsequent transition eras, coalitions re-formed in support of or opposition to different policies, with each side claiming to accept the positions that ultimately prevailed in the previous period. Thus champions of Jim Crow did not seek to restore legal chattel slavery. They instead advocated "separate but equal policies" that anti-segregation forces saw, convincingly, as efforts to perpetuate white supremacy, but in different forms and through different means.

Similarly, today proponents of color-blind policies do not seek to recreate *de jure* Jim Crow segregation laws. Indeed, both modern advocates of color-blind policies and modern proponents of race-conscious policies see themselves as the true heirs of the triumphant anti-segregation civil rights movement, and both criticize their opponents for betraying its aims. For color-blind alliance members, the civil rights movement centered on Martin Luther King's famed hope that persons would be judged not by the color of their skin but by the content of their character. They believe that race-conscious measures violate that aspiration and perpetuate racial divisions. Race-conscious alliance members believe instead that the central aim of the civil rights movement was to reduce deeply entrenched, unjust, material racial inequalities. They see the color-blind alliance's rejection of race-targeted policies as operating to perpetuate and even exacerbate pervasive inherited white advantages, whether or not that outcome is intended.

We have argued that these two modern alliances emerged initially over issues of affirmative action in employment but that they can be found largely intact in legislative and judicial struggles over a range of other issues, including majority minority districts, census categories, school vouchers, and much more (King and Smith 2008, p. 700n1). Their basic structure is as follows.

Color-Blind Order, 1978–2006

- most Republican Party officeholders and members after 1976
- President, 1980–1992, 2001–2006
- some conservative, neo-conservative Democrats
- majority of Supreme Court after 1980
- most lower federal court judges, many state judges after 1980
- some white-owned businesses and business lobbyists
- conservative think tanks/advocacy groups, e.g. Center for Individual Rights, Cato Institute
- fringe white supremacist groups
- Christian right groups, e.g. Family Research Council
- conservative foundations, e.g. Bradley Foundation.

Race-Conscious Order, 1978–2006

- most Democratic Party officeholders and members
- President (mixed support), 1993–2000
- some liberal, pro-corporate Republicans
- some federal, state judges
- many civil service members of executive agencies
- many large businesses, minority-owned businesses
- most labor unions
- military leadership
- liberal advocacy groups, e.g. ACLU
- most non-white advocacy groups: NAACP, La Raza, Asian American Legal Defense Fund

- liberal religious groups, e.g. National Council of Churches
- liberal foundations: Soros, Ford.

Note that some members of the color-blind order, such as white supremacists, clearly support color-blind policies such as affirmative action strictly tactically, as politically potent means to preserve white advantages, while others undoubtedly do so sincerely. We are unable to judge the proportions or motives, so we presume most proponents of color-blind policies genuinely believe these measures are best for both racial progress and justice.

Note also that these modern coalitions cannot be adequately grasped in class terms: the business sector is divided on race-conscious measures, while most unions, formerly frequent opponents of civil rights reforms, now largely support them. But in sharp contrast to the racial alliances that comprised the Jim Crow era, the modern rival racial institutional orders are much more closely identified with the two major political parties. Whereas both parties before 1954 contained segregationists and anti-segregationists, today Republicans overwhelmingly favor color-blind policies and the great majority of Democrats favor race-conscious measures, as indicated by their party platforms since 1976 (King and Smith 2008, p. 691). This partisan polarization on racial issues is consistent with and may indeed be a significant contributor to the heightened partisan polarization documented by many political scientists (e.g. McCarty, Poole, and Rosenthal 2006). And primarily because most American voters are white and most whites oppose race-conscious policies, the color-blind alliance rose to predominance in the last two decades of the 20th century along with the GOP, although without ever wholly eclipsing race-conscious proponents, institutions, and policies (p. 692).

Modern Racial Orders and the 2008 Election

Consider what this structure of partisan-allied rival racial orders meant for both the McCain and Obama candidacies. First, Senator McCain, as the champion of the color-blind alliance, could not openly express concern about the race of his opponent: after all, the ideology of his coalition was that race should be treated as politically irrelevant. At the same time, simply because Barack Obama appears black to most Americans, his candidacy undoubtedly raised worries among many in the color-blind order that a President Obama would expand pro-black racial preferences in many ways. But unless Obama provided an opening by strongly advocating such policies, which he was careful not to do, the McCain campaign had the challenge of making those concerns salient to voters without explicitly speaking of race. This may account for the McCain ads asking "Who is the real Barack Obama?" and saying that McCain was in contrast "the American President Americans have been waiting for" (Kurtz 2008; Raasch 2008). McCain also accused Obama of pursuing a socialist agenda (Curl 2008). And at its close the McCain campaign spotlighted Joe the Plumber, who repeatedly urged the electorate to "Vote for a real American, John McCain" (Bash 2008). All these tropes represent efforts to arouse doubts and to plant fears about Obama, and for at least some of those who favor color-blind policies, those fears must have included concerns that he would champion racial preferences.

Obama faced complementary strategic challenges when campaigning for the presidency as a black American at a time when most voters leaned toward color-blind policies. Press coverage based on interviews with white working-class voters suggest that it would have been enormously difficult for him to speak extensively about race and racial issues without triggering widespread anxieties that he would indeed support more expansive race-targeted programs, anxieties that might well have insured his defeat (Simkins 2008; Wallsten 2008). At the same time, his racial identity and his background as a civil rights lawyer meant that many proponents of race-conscious measures were willing to presume he would be far more sympathetic to their concerns than his opponent, without Obama's having to articulate a specifically racial agenda. Even so, Obama would have alienated important segments of his core supporters if he had explicitly repudiated race-conscious programs and policies. Hence his best option was to campaign in ways that were largely "race-neutral" in the policies he foregrounded, while retaining in the background indications of constrained but continuing support for race-conscious measures like affirmative action.

Obama made very clear in his book of policy and campaign positions, *The Audacity of Hope*, that he did indeed favor this strategy, for these reasons. In his chapter on "race," Obama offered "a word of caution" about whether "we have arrived at a 'postracial' politics" or "already live in a color-blind society" (Obama 2006, p. 232). He referred briefly to the statistics on persisting racial inequalities we have reviewed, as well as to his own personal experiences of racism. Obama then argued, in accord with moderate race-conscious proponents, that: "Affirmative action programs, when properly structured, can open up opportunities otherwise close to qualified minorities without diminishing opportunities for white students," and he added that "where there's strong evidence of prolonged and systematic discrimination by large corporations, trade unions, or branches of municipal government, goals and timetables for minority hiring may be the only meaningful remedy available" (p. 244). But Obama also stressed his understanding of the arguments of those who favor color-blind measures. He advocated an "emphasis on universal, as opposed to race-specific programs" as not only "good policy" but also as "good politics" (p. 247). He concluded that "proposals that solely benefit minorities and dissect Americans into 'us' and 'them' may generate a few short-term concessions when the costs to whites aren't too high, but they can't serve as the basis for the kinds of sustained, broad-based political coalitions needed to transform America" (p. 248).

In so arguing, Obama in his book and his campaign sought to build a new, broader coalition that blended those Americans who predominantly favor color-blind policies, but who do want to see real material racial progress and can tolerate a few race-conscious measures, with those who think substantial race-conscious measures are needed, but who are willing to see them put on the back burner if progress is indeed being achieved through other means. He did this, for the most part, simply by not talking about race and by minimizing its likely impact on the election, thereby permitting color-blind and race-conscious advocates to interpret his rhetorical emphases on both unity and change in terms congenial to them. But Obama did, of course, feel compelled by the controversy over the racial views of his long-time pastor, Reverend Jeremiah Wright, to address race directly in his National Constitution Center speech on March 18, 2008.

There, in contrast to the dominant approach in his campaign, Obama stated that "race is an issue that I believe this nation cannot afford to ignore right now." He called attention again to persisting material racial "disparities," many of which, he argued, "can be directly traced to inequalities passed on from an earlier generation that suffered under the brutal legacy of slavery and Jim Crow." To the dissatisfaction of some critics, Obama suggested only briefly that "current incidents of discrimination" were also sources of those inequalities. But he did argue, as we have here, that anger "over welfare and affirmative action helped forge the Reagan Coalition"; and he contended that conservative politicians and commentators "exploited fears of crime" and built careers "unmasking bogus claims of racism while dismissing legitimate discussions of racial injustice" (Obama 2008a).

Nonetheless, Obama counseled against labeling "the resentments of white Americans" as "misguided or even racist." Instead, echoing his arguments in *The Audacity of Hope*, Obama urged "the African American community" to bind "our particular grievances" with "the larger aspirations of all Americans" by focusing on "investing in our schools and our communities; by enforcing our civil rights laws and ensuring fairness in our criminal justice system; by providing this generation with ladders of opportunity that were unavailable to previous generations." He urged "all Americans to realize that your dreams do not have to come at the expense of my dreams; that investing in the health, welfare and education of black and brown and white children will ultimately help all of America prosper."

In these ways, Obama adroitly restated the central theme of his campaign, embodied in his own life story, that the nation must continue to strive to achieve the promise of *e pluribus unum*, "that out of many, we are truly one" (Obama 2008a). He did not minimize the persistence of racial inequalities neither did he repudiate all race-conscious measures, but his emphasis remained on programs, principles, and purposes designed to further the shared values and goals of all Americans.

Beyond the 2008 Election

Aided by a not particularly adept opponent representing a party tied to two long-lasting, increasingly unpopular wars, and the worst economic crisis since the Depression, Obama won his historic victory the following November. But he also said in his NCC speech: "I have never been so naïve as to believe that we can get beyond our racial divisions in a single election cycle, or with a single candidacy" (Obama 2008a). And so the question remains: if the structuring of American racial politics via struggles between color-blind and race-conscious racial orders helps explain the ways the major party candidates dealt with race in the 2008 campaign, what does the electoral success of Obama's "foreground universal programs without repudiating all race-conscious measures" strategy suggest for whether an Obama administration will move and should move the nation further toward a post-racial era?

Again, the starting point for any credible answer must be the longstanding and entrenched patterns of material racial inequalities that are present in virtually all spheres of American life. As Obama himself acknowledges, as long as those racial disparities persist, it is a virtual certainty that racial divisions will be visible in American politics as well. The first answer to whether the United States is on its way to a post-racial political future, then, is that it depends on whether Obama's combination of "mostly universal/ partly race-conscious programs" succeeds in improving many of those patterns of material inequality. At this juncture, when much of what Obama will seek to do concretely remains unclear, it is obviously not possible to assess how much success he will have—but the fact that his administration will be trying to reduce severe material racial gaps while at the same time leading the nation to overcome its worst economic crisis in modern times suggests strongly that the prospects for dramatic progress in the foreseeable future are not good. If in Obama's first term the nation's economy appears at least to be moving in the right direction, he may be able to sustain and even broaden his coalition, making a second term and further change possible. But the notion that Americans will make enough advances in reducing racial inequalities to foster a post-racial politics seems utopian.

That conclusion will not seem particularly surprising or controversial to most readers. But there is also a second, somewhat less obvious reason why Obama's election and his program do not signify a post-racial American political future, much less the achievement of a post-racial America in the present. This reason might be termed "the multicultural challenge." It is a challenge that goes to the heart of Obama's core promise: to embrace the diversity of Americans and yet to find ways to "bridge our differences and unite in common effort—black, white, Latino, Asian, Native American; Democrat and Republican, young and old, rich and poor, gay and straight, disabled or not," as he put it in his Ohio "closing statement" near the end of the campaign. All Americans are to come to feel and act politically as "one nation, and one people" who will together "once more choose our better history" (Obama 2008b).

One reason this promise is so challenging is that Americans do not agree on what constitutes their "better history." Some see the spread of religious diversity and considerable secularity, for example, as advances for freedom. Others see those developments as a retreat from America's true calling to be a shining "Christian nation." Some believe their country's "best history" centers on the realization of ideals arising in historically Anglo-American cultural traditions. Others see those cultural traditions as historically responsible for the repression of communities and identities that they regard as most valuable and most their own. Put more broadly, the difficulty is that it may well be impossible both to give any specific content to the putative shared, unifying values and purposes of Americans, without appearing to fail to recognize and accommodate adequately the diversity of values and purposes Americans in fact exhibit.

Obama, of course, presents his own identity as a preeminent example of how unity can be forged from a background encompassing a remarkably broad mix of races, religions, nationalities, geographic residences, educational systems, and economic statuses. But his identity has arguably been forged most of all by his choices to embrace much that characterizes dominant but contested forms of American identity, including Christianity over Islam or secularity, American patriotism over either cosmopolitanism or foreign allegiances, and a stress on unity across the races over racial separatism. Among the race-conscious coalition that forms a substantial part of Obama's political base, there are many who favor a more overtly multi-cultural America. This vision depicts a greater diversity of community identities, both subnational and transnational, which would be not only tolerated but actively assisted in public systems of political representation, public aid programs, educational curriculum, legally recognized group rights, and much more. Even if by some miracle severe racial inequalities were sharply alleviated during an Obama administration, controversies will likely still remain over whether the kind of unity out of diversity that he offers as a shared national ideal really fulfills the aspirations of all or even most of the persons and communities whose differences he seeks to bridge. And because those diverse aspirations include differing visions among members of existing racial groups, it is likely that a United States marked by such controversies will still not be an America whose politics can credibly be deemed post-racial. Neither is it at all clear that it should be: multicultural ideals have force in part because there are good reasons to doubt the propriety of a strongly unified sense of American national identity and purpose.

But even if it is not likely that the United States has entered or will soon enter a post-racial political era, and even if there are legitimate debates over whether that goal is, in fact, desirable, it is also true that the election of 2008 made real a form of racial progress that many of us thought virtually impossible. Because it did, there is a basis for believing that an Obama administration may be able to reduce at least some unjust racial inequalities and to foster among Americans a more broadly shared sense of common values and purposes that embraces legitimate forms of diversity. Admittedly, the difficulties in making such progress increase every day that the current economic crisis deepens; but crises often bring great opportunities as well as great challenges. If that conclusion seems optimistic, we submit that at this historical moment, more than most others, it is permissible to entertain what the new president—following Reverend Wright—has appropriately termed the audacity of hope.

The Policy Agenda

We have argued that the context in which President Obama's engagement with policies aimed at reducing enduring material race inequalities is determined by the macro-level division between advocates of color-blind versus advocates of race-conscious measures (King and Smith 2011). The color-blind approach stresses the end of legal discrimination and the development of legal remedies for victims of racial prejudice. This new legal environment offers, such color-blind advocates believe, the opportunity for individuals to get on with their lives and to build personal wealth through equality of opportunity. For advocates of race-conscious targeting in public policy, the entrenched and to some extent structural nature of racial inequalities—for instance in housing, education, levels of home ownership, employment and completion of university degree programs—remains of such a scale that it demands purposeful public policies aimed at improving the circumstances of African American and other minorities. Race-conscious advocates seek evidence of equality of outcome not just opportunity.

Paradoxically advocates of both color-blind and race-conscious policies claim a shared political and intellectual mantle—the legacy of civil rights reforms orchestrated in the Civil Rights Act 1964 and the Voting Rights Act 1965, and the ideological values expressed by the civil rights leader Dr. Martin Luther King. Where King strongly argued that Americans be judged not by the color of their skin but by their character, so color-blind advocates cite this mantra as a guide to modern policy: individualism and character should guide policy not policies such as affirmative action aimed at remedying historical injustices. Race-conscious advocates also relish King's character-focused values but note that he lobbied equally for material improvements in the circumstances of African Americans—such as fair housing policy and targeted employment and education programs—not just legal defences against discrimination. They argue that without the deliberate and purposeful allocation of funds to dedicated programs in such areas as fair housing and employment enduring material race inequalities will persist and indeed will deepen under the pressures of the current Great Recession (which has had adverse effects on African Americans' employment levels and rates of homeownership).

Two areas of particular significance are employment and high school education. A recent study finds that in the last two decades disparities between the wages and rate of employment of black and white Americans have grown since the 1970s. The authors locate these patterns not in standard accounts of deindustrialization but much more in government policy, unionization, and labour market institutions contending that positive state measures are much more important in improving disparities than cyclical patterns of jobs expansion and contraction. Sites and Parks (2011, p. 61) find that

> broader economic shifts rarely corresponded to changes in racial wage and employment disparities and that ... racial labor-market inequalities have been strongly influenced by political or institutional forces: government policies related to discrimination, wages, employment and incarceration—along with union and social movement activities.

Government policy and state strategy are decisive in shifting entrenched patterns of inequality. A second area of systemic and enduring material racial inequality is found in schools. Because of residential segregation, and despite the illegality of segregated schools in practice, America's elementary and high schools are hugely segregated by race. The empirical evidence from studies over the last half century is pretty unequivocal about what works: getting children from poorer income households into better schools makes a huge difference to their levels of educational attainment (Schwartz 2010). Achieving this more favourable and supportive educational context for children requires integrating schools, which means greater racial and ethnic integration, a process which still provokes "bitter resistance" (Herbert 2011). Improving race equality in both education and employment requires dedicated policies according to these and other studies (Orfield 2011).

President Obama's policy response to this context has been clear. He has embraced and advanced policies universalist in design maintaining that the long-term benefits of improving circumstances for everyone will benefit the most disadvantaged too. This rationale informs his struggle to reform health care provision with the Patient Protection and Affordable Care Act 2010 (Jacobs and Skocpol 2010). The Act fulfils a longstanding ambition of reformers to extend health care coverage to all Americans; and of the close to 40 million previously lacking coverage a disproportionately high number were African Americans and other minority members. But the struggle to enact the health care reform was immense, using up much political capital for the President and helping to contribute to the surge in Republican votes in November 2010 when Tea Party backed candidates galvanized the Republicans to a majority in the House. Like the health care reform act the economic stimulus package passed in spring 2009 to address the Great Recession stressed general solutions—building programs, infrastructure projects, aid to states and cities—rather than specific targeted measures. The same rationale informs the Obama administration's expansion of federal education resources administered by the Education Secretary Arne Duncan under the No Child Left Behind Act.

These measures are fine and the universalist strategy makes electoral and political sense for the President. Obama cannot appear to be an incumbent in the White House seeking preferential treatment for one special group in the electorate, despite the generations of discrimination African Americans have endured and the legacies of which constrain their opportunities. But the dichotomy between colour-blind and race-conscious approaches may limit unnecessarily the policy options appropriate to ameliorating long-term entrenched inequalities. Such limitations mean that by the end of the Obama administration less may have been achieved in reducing race inequality than might have been expected, and this pattern will stir up long-term challenges in America's transition to a post-racist society. Such challenges cannot be ignored indefinitely by policymakers.

Notes

1   The editors are grateful to Cambridge University Press for granting permission to reprint this essay, which was originally published in the *Du Bois Review, Social Science Research on Race* 2009: 6, 1, 25–35.
2   Blame and credit for all our collaborative works should be apportioned equally. The order of the authors' names indicates only which author initiated a particular project. We are grateful to Timothy Weaver for excellent research assistance. All errors are our own.

References

Bash, Dana. "Joe the plumber—a no show!,' 2008, at http://ac360.blogs.cnn. com2008/10/30/joe-the-plumber-a-no-show/

Bobo, Lawrence D. and Dawson Michael C. "The 'work' race does: back to the future," *Du Bois Review* 2008: 5, 1–4.

Center for Responsible Lending. *African American Homes at Risk: predatory mortgage lending* (Durham, NC: Center for Responsible Lending, 2008).

Connerly, Ward. "Obama is no 'post-racial' candidate," *Wall Street Journal* 2008: June 13, A15.

Curl, Joseph. "McCain decries Obama's 'socialism'," 2008, www.washingtontimes. com/news/2008/oct/19/

Danzinger, Sheldon and Danzinger Sandra K. "Poverty, race and antipoverty policy before and after Hurricane Katrina," *Du Bois Review* 2006: 3, 23–36.

Fernandez, Manny. "Study finds disparities in mortgages by race," *New York Times*, 2007, www.nytimes.com/2007/10/15/nyregion/15subprime.html/

Geronimus, Arline T. and Thomson, J. Phillip. "To denigrate, ignore, and/or disrupt: racial inequality in health and the impact of policy-induced breakdown of African American communities," *Du Bois Review* 2004: 2, 247–79.

Herbert, Bob. "Separate and unequal," *New York Times*, March 11, 2011.

Jacobs, Lawrence R. and Skocpol, Theda. *Heath Care Reform and American Politics* (New York: Oxford University Press, 2010).

Katz, Michael B., Stern, Mark J., and Fader. Jamie J. "The new African American inequality," *Journal of American History* 2005: 91, 75–108.

King, Desmond S. and Smith, Rogers M. "Racial orders in American political development," *American Political Science Review* 2005: 99, 75–92.

King, Desmond S. and Smith, Rogers M. "Strange bedfellows? Polarized politics? The quest for racial equity in contemporary America," *Political Research Quarterly* 2008: 61, 4, 686–703.

King, Desmond and Smith, Rogers M. *Still a House Divided: race and politics in Obama's America* (Princeton, NJ: Princeton University Press, 2011).

Kurtz, Howard. "McCain spot asks: 'Who is Barack Obama?'," 2008, voices. washingtonpost.com/the-trail/2008/10/06/

McCarty, Nolan, Poole, Keith T., and Rosenthal, Howard. *Polarized America: the dance of ideology and unequal riches* (Cambridge, MA: MIT Press, 2006).

Obama, Barack. *The Audacity of Hope: thoughts on reclaiming the American dream* (New York: Three Rivers Press, 2006).

Obama, Barack. "Transcript of Obama's speech on race," 2008a, www.msnbc.com /id/23690567/print/1/displaymode/1098/

Obama, Barack. "Closing statement," 2008b, www.nytimes.com/2008/10/27/us/politics /27text-obama/html/

Oliver, Melvin L. and Shapiro, Thomas M. *Black Wealth/White Wealth: a new perspective on racial inequality*, 2nd edn (New York: Routledge, 2006).

Orfield, Gary and Lee, Chungmei. *Racial Transformation and the Changing Nature of Segregation* (Cambridge, MA: Civil Rights Project at Harvard University, 2006).

Orfield, Myron. "Regional strategies for racial integration of schools and housing post-Parents involved," *Law and Inequality* 2011: 29, 149–73.

Raasch, Chuck. "McCain's 'American' claim sparks critics," 2008, www.usatoday.com /news/opinion/columnist/raasch/2008-04-03-raasch_N.htm/

Schlosser, Eric. "The prison industrial complex," *Atlantic Monthly*, December 1998, www.theatlantic.com/doc/199812/prisons

Schwartz, Heather. *Housing Policy is School Policy: economically integrative housing policy promotes academic success in Montgomery County, Maryland* (New York: Century Foundation, 2010).

Shapiro, Thomas M. *The Hidden Cost of Being African American: how wealth perpetuates inequality* (New York: Oxford University Press, 2004).

Simkins, Chris. "US voters offer opinions about Barack Obama, his race, and its impact on the upcoming election," *Voice of America News*, October 14, 2008, www.voanews.com/english/Africa/2008-10/2008-10-14-voa36.cfm

Sinclair-Chapman, Valeria and Price, Melanye. "Black politics, the 2008 election, and the (im)possibility of race transcendence," *PS: Political Science and Politics* 2008: 61, 4, 739–45.

Sites, William and Parks, Virginia. "What do we really know about racial inequality? Labor markets, politics, and the historical basis of black economic fortunes," *Politics and Society* 2011: 9, 40–73.

Street, Paul. "White America lives in vicious racial denial—Obama is making it worse," *Black Agenda Report*, 2008, www.blackagendareport.com

U.S. Census. *Income, poverty, and Health Insurance Coverage in the United States: 2007*, 2008, www.census.gov/prod/2008pubs/p60-235.pdf

U.S. Department for Health and Human Services. *Health, United States, 2007*, National Center for Health Statistics, 2007, www.cdec.gov/nchs/data/hus/hus07.pdf

Wallsten, Peter. "For Obama, an uphill climb in Appalachia," *Los Angeles Times*, October 5, 2008, A-1.

7 "The Final Frontier"

Barack Obama and the Vision of a Post-Racial America

Kevern Verney

It is well known that Barack Obama is a devotee of the original *Star Trek* television series. In a Wyoming campaign speech in March 2008 he stated simply: "I grew up on *Star Trek*. I believe in the final frontier." In 2009 the President reputedly asked Paramount Pictures for a White House screening of the Hollywood reboot of the 1960s' classic. In April 2012 actress Nichelle Nichols, who played Lieutenant Uhura in the original television series, tweeted a photograph of herself with Obama taken during a private meeting in the Oval Office.[1]

The President's enduring admiration for the iconic science fiction program can in part, as he suggested, be attributed to generational factors. Born in 1961, his early life coincided with the television debut and peak years of success for the program. For Obama the mature politician, more calculated reasoning can be found for his decision to periodically remind the American public of this childhood love. In addition to showing an endearing side of his character, it enables the President to establish a rapport with the successive generations of Americans who were themselves brought up on either the original television series or its later incarnations. It enables the President to identify with *Star Trek*'s optimistic vision of the future as an era when scientific and technological progress has resolved many of the present-day problems that beset mankind, from climate change through to economic prosperity and health care. Similarly, it offers a vision of a time when national and racial differences have given way to multicultural harmony, as reflected in the ethnic diversity of the crew on the starship *Enterprise*. A United Nations in microcosm, they provide a reassuring image of a society at ease with itself, free from racial and class divisions.

For many political and media commentators, the election of Obama in 2008 was hailed as an indication that more than three centuries of racial conflict in the United States were finally coming to an end. The country, like the new President himself, was now genuinely post-racial in character and outlook. MSNBC television host David Gregory articulated the hopes of many on election night. "The son of an African father, a Kenyan, and a white mother from Kansas, in a country that was stained by slavery, is now President of the United States," he proclaimed. "The ultimate color line has been crossed."[2]

In his inaugural address, the following January, the president-elect advanced similar views, declaring "our patchwork heritage is a strength, not a weakness." The United States was

> a nation of Christians and Muslims, Jews and Hindus—and non-believers. We are shaped by every language and culture, drawn from every end of this earth; and because we have tasted the bitter swill of civil war and segregation, and emerged from that dark chapter stronger and more united, we cannot hope but believe that the old hatreds shall someday pass.

Echoing the optimism of *Star Trek* creator Gene Roddenberry, he predicted that in the years ahead "the lines of tribe shall soon dissolve," and "that as the world grows smaller, our common humanity shall reveal itself; and that America must play its role in ushering in a new era of peace."[3]

Encapsulating the mood of the occasion, this uplifting rhetoric was testimony to both Obama's ability as a charismatic orator and the historic symbolic importance of his election as the nation's first African American President. It also reflected growing national awareness of the profound and inexorable long-term demographic changes taking place within American society. In 1970 the overwhelming majority of Americans could be categorized in one of two racial groups, a white majority, who made up 87.5 percent of the population, and African Americans, who comprised an 11 percent minority group. By 2000 the proportion of white Americans had fallen to 69 percent, with African Americans at 12 percent, the proportion of Hispanic Americans rising to 12 percent, and Americans of Asian or Pacific Island origins at 4 percent.[4]

The impact of these trends for the future was highlighted by a United States Census Bureau report published in August 2008. This predicted that by the year 2042, if not earlier, African Americans, Hispanic Americans, and Asian Americans would comprise more than 50 percent of the population. By this date Hispanic Americans will comprise almost one-quarter of the total U.S. population and white Americans will no longer be a majority ethnic group. For younger generations, the demographic shift will take place even sooner, with white Americans set to lose their numerical majority among the under-18 age group as early as 2023. In the words of one commentator: "[E]very child born in the United States from here on will belong to the first post-white generation."[5]

Significant as the U.S. Census Bureau report may have been, it only served to confirm demographic change that had been apparent for some time. From the early 1990s growing public awareness about the changing composition of the U.S. population can be seen as being manifested in a variety of ways. A number of Hollywood films examined the anxieties of white Americans about their potential loss of status as the majority ethnic group in the United States. In *Falling Down* (1993), Michael Douglas played a middle-aged white professional in Los Angeles who, in what turns out to be an increasingly nightmarish day, finds himself bemused and threatened by the manifestations of multiculturalism, ranging from Korean shopkeepers to Hispanic street gangs. In *White Man's Burden* (1995), Harry Belafonte and John Travolta starred in a parallel America in which African Americans were the dominant racial group and whites, like Travolta, subject to segregation and discrimination.[6]

In 2001 Tim Burton's re-imagining of the 1960s classic *Planet of the Apes* portrayed a dystopian vision of the future far removed from the optimistic vision of *Star Trek*. Instead of multicultural harmony, time-travelling astronauts from the present find themselves in a future where whiteAmericans are oppressed by the apes that they once exploited as slaves and servants. In 2010 *Fox News* host and Tea Party activist Glenn Beck sought to take advantage of this imagery by comparing Obama's America to the "goddam Planet of the Apes." His televised outburst came only days before he addressed a major Tea Party rally, "Restoring Honor," from the steps of the Lincoln memorial on 28 August. The choice of venue and the date, coinciding with the anniversary of Martin Luther King's "I Have a Dream" speech at the 1963 March on Washington, were heavy with symbolism. In part attempting to counter the racist image of the Tea Party Movement, the rally can also be seen as challenging Obama's well-known admiration for, and self-identification with, Lincoln.[7]

During the 2008 election campaign T-shirts with a picture of Obama's face morphed with that of Lincoln were a common piece of tourist memorabilia. Interestingly, the concluding image of Burton's film, also shot at the Lincoln memorial, depicted the statue of Lincoln, but with the benign face of the martyred president replaced by that of the gorilla General Thade. The descendant of a formerly enslaved group and, by implication, Lincoln's successor, Thade was a repressive dictator rather than an enlightened democrat. This can be seen as echoing similar charges of totalitarianism made against Obama by Tea Party activists such as Beck.

In an earlier film, *Gangs of New York* (2002), director Martin Scorsese preferred to examine ethnic conflict in a historical context rather than entering into the realms of science fiction. Depicting the violent career of a bigoted protestant nativist, "Bill the Butcher" Cutting, played by Daniel Day Lewis, the production was in many ways dark and disturbing. At the same time it did at least seem to finish on a positive note, with the final image of a prosperous present-day New York towering over Cutting's neglected grave. The message appeared to be that the anti-immigrant prejudices and conflicts of the past, like Cutting himself, were now long since buried and forgotten. By way of contrast, *Crash* (2005), set in present-day Los Angeles, highlighted the enduring nature of racial and ethnic prejudice. Exploring the subject from almost every conceivable angle, the film appeared to suggest that even the most seemingly enlightened individuals were capable of bigoted thinking at times of stress or at particular occasions or locations.[8]

Within the academic community white racial anxiety over demographic change can be seen as being manifested in the rise of "whiteness studies", from the early 1990s. In a series of important new works leading scholars such as David Roediger in *The Wages of Whiteness* (1991), Grace Elizabeth

Hale, *Making Whiteness* (1991), and Michelle Brattain, *The Politics of Whiteness* (2001) examined the history and characteristics of white racial and cultural identity. They also highlighted the changing perceptions of whiteness over time, showing how ethnic groups once seen as a threat to dominant white values, such as the Irish and southern and eastern European immigrants, had become absorbed into mainstream white American culture.[9]

Political leaders also displayed growing awareness of the nation's changing population patterns.

> Today, largely because of immigration there is no majority race in Hawaii or Houston or New York City. Within five years there will be no majority race in our largest state, California. In little more than fifty years there will be no majority race in the United States

President Clinton predicted in an oft cited speech at Portland State University. "No other nation in history has gone through demographic change of this magnitude in so short a time," he noted. However, rather than being a source of anxiety such change should be welcomed as "immigrants are energizing our culture and broadening our vision of the world. They are renewing our most basic values and reminding us all of what it truly means to be American."[10]

Not all commentators were so sanguine. In 1995 journalist Peter Brimelow put forward a more pessimistic interpretation in *Alien Nation: common sense about america's immigration disaster*. Ironically, Brimelow, born in the United Kingdom, was himself an immigrant to the United States. Other conservative commentators followed his lead including Republican presidential candidate Patrick Buchanan, Harvard professor and public intellectual Samuel P. Huntington, Colorado congressman Tom Tancredo, and Californian academic Victor Hansen. The recurring themes in all these works were effectively summarized by Buchanan, who warned that not just the United States but "Western civilization" was faced with a crisis that consisted of "three imminent and mortal perils; dying populations, disintegrating cultures and invasions unresisted."[11]

The first of these perils was the result of falling birth rates among white Americans and in western European countries. The contraceptive pill had become "the suicide tablet of the West" and in the United States abortions had "replaced tonsillectomies as the most common surgical procedure." The net result was that whereas in 1960 people of European ancestry comprised 25 percent of the world's population by 2000 this had dropped to around 17 percent and, on future projections, was set to fall to 10 percent by 2050. These were the "statistics of a vanishing race."[12]

The second threat came from the rise of what Tom Tancredo called the "cult of multiculturalism." More than just a "benign philosophy of teaching an appreciation and a tolerance of differences," he lamented, this was a "malignant" force that degrades and debases our uniquely American culture as well as Western civilization in general. It teaches our children that there is no value to who we are and what our country has accomplished ... except that *whatever* we've done has been bad or has had a negative impact on the world.

In similar vein, Samuel Huntington warned that "multiculturalism represented the culmination of a long erosion of the emphasis on national identity in American education." The net result was that in 1999 a survey of seniors at 55 leading U.S. colleges found that 40 percent of respondents could not even say within a half-century the dates of the American Civil War. More students named Ulysses S. Grant as the general who led the American armies to victory in the War of Independence than those who cited George Washington.[13]

The final danger came from the rising levels of immigration into the United States, principally from Mexico. During the 1990s the number of people of Mexican ancestry in the United States increased from 14 million to 21 million, settling mostly in the southwest. By 2006 43 percent of the population of New Mexico and 34 percent of the populations of Texas and California were of Hispanic descent. Moreover, by this time almost 70 percent of all immigrants, both legal and illegal, who arrived in the United States each year came from Mexico. These new immigrants reinforced the move towards multiculturalism, because rather than assimilating mainstream American values they formed ethnic ghettos within U.S. towns and cities, "maintaining their language and identifying with one another not America." Indeed, as their numbers grew Mexican Americans felt "increasingly comfortable with their own culture and often contemptuous of American culture."[14]

A striking feature of conservative critiques of Mexican immigration is the extent to which immigrants themselves are portrayed more as conscripts in an invading army than individuals simply seeking a better way of life or greater economic opportunities. Samuel Huntington thus wrote of Mexican and other Hispanic immigrants as "establishing beachheads" in the United States, evoking much more menacing imagery than that associated with alternative descriptions that he could have used, such as ethnic communities. A recurring theme in right-wing commentaries is the threat of the *Reconquista*. This is based on the belief that Mexican immigrants are seeking to reclaim by demographic invasion the territories ceded to the United States by Mexico as a result of military force during the Mexican American War of 1846–48.[15]

This bold thesis can be seen as problematic in a number of respects. In the first instance, it supposes that Mexican immigrants are motivated by a desire for revenge for a conflict that took place more than one and a half centuries ago. This is in spite of the fact that many of the immigrants come from Indian communities south of the border that suffered from longstanding discrimination and economic deprivation at the hands of successive Mexican governments. Such experiences would appear to constitute less than fertile soil for nurturing patriotic loyalty to the land of their birth. Moreover, the notion of the *Reconquista* credits Mexican immigrants with a clearly better knowledge of, and affinity with, the history of their own country than that enjoyed by their white American counterparts in the 1999 college survey. Paradoxically, the same commentators who attribute such sinister motives to Mexican immigrants also berate them for having much lower levels of educational achievement than other ethnic groups in the United States. The specific objectives of the alleged *Reconquista* movement are also less than clear, ranging from simply the cultural domination of the American southwest to the establishment of an independent republic in the region or political reunification with Mexico.[16]

If the shape of things to come is uncertain, albeit invariably negative, the soothsayers on the right who seek to look into the future are united in appealing to historical precedent to provide justification for their bleak predictions. The dire lessons that can be learnt from the experience of classical antiquity are often cited. For Victor Hansen, a classicist at California State University, the West was "drawing millions to its shores—in the manner that Athens once attracted metics from Asia, and Rome drew Africans, Jews and Armenians." Patrick Buchanan evoked a similar comparison, predicting that by 2050 "America will have become a multiracial, multi-ethnic, multi-lingual, multicultural conglomerate … a replica of the Roman Empire after the Goths and Vandals have passed over." Tom Tancredo advanced a like prognosis. To him, the United States ran the risk of becoming a "nation of the same kind of self-indulgent hedonists that characterized the failed societies of past civilizations." By the time the danger was recognized, "our country may itself be so weakened … that the barbarians at the gate will only need to give a slight push and the emaciated body of Western civilization will collapse in a heap."[17]

Looking to the past to seek a better understanding of the problems of the present is not unreasonable. At the same time, to be a meaningful exercise the historical comparisons that are made must also be appropriate. The fall of the Roman Empire may evoke dramatic images on an epic scale, but it is another matter whether or not it constitutes a suitable case study to understand the challenges faced by the United States at the start of the 21st century. A more obvious line of enquiry would be to start closer to home, looking at the last time that the United States experienced comparable levels of mass immigration and demographic change, in the late 19th and early 20th century.

The prophets of doom are, of course, well aware of this analogy. Unfortunately, it does not easily fit in with the ideological message that they seek to convey. One hundred years on the "Great Wave" of immigration to the United States in the period 1880–1920 does not take on the appearance of a demographic disaster. On the contrary, it can be argued that the mass immigration of those years provided the workforce needed for industrial expansion; the spectacular economic growth that helped propel the United States to the status of a global superpower by the mid-20th century. Similarly, the opponents of that immigration seem to be less than far sighted visionaries, grimly vindicated by the passage of time. Instead, their historical reputation is one of narrow minded nativists out of touch with the forces of modernity and tainted by ethnic and religious bigotry.

For these reasons, the critics of present-day immigration go to great pains to identify reasons why the demographic changes taking place in America now are fundamentally different from those of a century ago. One of the arguments most frequently advanced is that the sheer volume of immigration since the 1990s is vastly greater than anything experienced in the past. In 2006 Patrick Buchanan thus warned that there were "36 million foreign born in the United States," a figure that was "almost three times as many people as the 13.5 million here at the peak of the Great Wave in 1910." Moreover, the "foreign-born population today" was "almost equal to the 42 million who came over the three and a half centuries from 1607 to 1965."[18]

Such claims need to be subjected to careful scrutiny. Elsewhere in the same volume Buchanan qualifies the figure of 36 million "foreign born" by stating that this includes not only immigrants, but also their children, at least some of whom would have been born in the United States. This would suggest there is, at the very least, a degree of uncertainty about the figures cited. Moreover, even if the unqualified estimate of 36 million "foreign born" is accepted as accurate this needs to be viewed in the context of the total population of the nation. In 1910 the population of the United States was just 92.2 million. The 13.5 million "foreign born" inhabitants cited by Buchanan thus made up some 14.5 percent of the national population. By 2011 the total U.S. population had risen to 311 million. The 36 million "foreign born" inhabitants comprised slightly less than 12 percent of the total population, a lower proportion than in 1910, and also smaller than the comparable figure for 1860, when immigrants comprised 13.2 percent of the national population. Indeed at no stage in the history of the United States have immigrants made up more than one-seventh of the nation's population.[19]

Admittedly, the number of people living in America in 2011 was much greater than a century earlier, but the population density of 35 to 50 people per square kilometre in the United States was much lower than that of almost every European country. By comparison the population density in Germany and the United Kingdom was 200 to 300 people per square kilometre, and that of France 150 to 200 people per square kilometre. Even the Republic of Ireland had a higher population density than the United States, at 50 to 75 people per square kilometre. This hardly supports the view of the United States as a country suffering from overpopulation.[20]

Another argument put forward is that the immigrants since the 1990s were of a different calibre and mindset to those of previous generations. "For years I have witnessed a difference in both the kinds of immigration and the kinds of people who are coming to the United States," noted Colorado Congressman Tom Tancredo. "Too many new immigrants continue to be loyal to their native countries. They desire to maintain their own language, customs and culture; yet they seek to exploit the success of America while giving back as little as possible." Patrick Buchanan claimed to observe similar trends. There were "profound differences in attitudes between the immigrants who came from Europe, carrying a burning desire to be part of the American people" and the immigrants of today who were "mostly illegal and mostly from Mexico."[21]

The fact that "at least six million" Mexican immigrants to the United States entered the country illegally only confirmed their suspect motives and character. "They broke the law to get in. They break it every day to stay here," protested the indignant Buchanan. "This wholesale trampling on U.S. law and the constant lies illegals must tell to stay here and to stay employed here engender a contempt for the law and the moral authority of the United States."[22]

In addition to their mode of entry into the United States the geographical origins of the new immigrants was also an issue. "Unlike the immigrants of a century ago, who bade farewell to their native lands forever when they bordered the ships, for Mexicans the mother country is only hours away. Millions have no desire to become American citizens or learn English." Indeed, Mexican immigrant workers in the United States sent $15 billion a year in remittances to their families back home.[23]

A number of observations can be made in respect to such claims. The assertion that the character of present-day immigrants is different from that of their predecessors echoes the arguments put forward by anti-immigrant campaigners at the end of the 19th century. The 41-volume report of the Dillingham Commission set up by Congress in 1907 to study the "new" immigration of that era thus concluded that many immigrants had come to the United States as transients rather than permanent settlers. In part, this view was justified. Rather than possessing a "burning desire to be part of the American people," many immigrants of this time were "birds of passage," who sought employment in America during the spring and summer and then returned to their native country during the winter months. Between 1908 and 1916 U.S. immigration recorded 6.7 million arrivals in the United States, but also just over 2 million departures. This suggests a repatriation rate of around 20–30 percent, although admittedly a significant proportion of those departing may ultimately have taken up long-term residence in the United States.[24]

Moreover, the new arrivals were concentrated in large cities rather than spreading out across the United States. Within these urban centres, they congregated into ethnic enclaves that made it more difficult for them to be assimilated into U.S. culture and society. For Victor Davis Hanson and Patrick Buchanan, it is a source of concern that California today is the destination for 40 percent of all immigrants to the United States and that Hispanics comprise 34 percent of the total population of California and Texas. However, this pattern of settlement is similar to that during the "Great Wave" at the end of the 19th century, when 80 percent of the new immigrants settled in the north eastern United States and two-thirds in New England, New York, Pennsylvania, and New Jersey. Moreover, in the leading urban centres the concentration was even higher. In 1910 75 percent of the populations of New York City, Chicago, Detroit, Cleveland, and Boston were made up of immigrants and their children.[25]

It was also the case that these immigrants retained a sense of loyalty to their own language and culture. Between 1884 and 1920 there were over 3,500 foreign-language newspapers published in the United States. Although it is true that many of these died out over time, as late as 1920 there were still 276 German language newspapers published in the United States, 118 papers in Spanish and Portuguese, 111 in Scandinavian languages, 98 in Italian and 76 in Polish. In 1916 72 percent of the population of San Francisco did not have English as their first language. Yet paradoxically, it is the new arrivals of that era who the anti-immigrant writers of today hail as a successful example of Americanization. In its day the Dillingham Commission also looked back to a nostalgic, mythical, past praising immigrant arrivals before the 1880s for possessing the drive and commitment to build a new life in America that their successors supposedly lacked. In the same way that conservative commentators blame lax border controls and the close proximity of Mexico to the United States for the high levels of immigration today, so concerned social and political leaders in the late 19th and early 20th centuries blamed the cheap fares and mass advertising of the new steamship lines for artificially stimulating mass immigration from Europe.[26]

It is difficult to know quite what to make of the sense of outrage at the current levels of illegal immigration from Mexico. For the great majority of European migrants 100 years ago, this was simply not an issue because of the limited immigration controls then in place. In 1891 the establishment of the Federal Bureau of Immigration was the first of a series of measures designed to tighten up controls on immigrants from Europe. In particular, these sought to turn away groups perceived to be undesirable. These included "idiots, insane persons, paupers or persons likely to become public charges, persons suffering from a loathsome or dangerous contagious disease, persons who have been convicted of a felony or other infamous crime or misdemeanour." In practice, however, the policy of unrestricted immigration, embodied in the phrase the "open door," continued largely unaltered. As late as 1914 only around 2 percent of immigrants arriving at Ellis Island were denied entry into the United States.[27]

In respect to the vast tracts of land appropriated by U.S. settlers during the 19th century from Mexico and Native American peoples the extent to which they can be regarded as lawful is at best a matter of scholarly debate. The 4 million African Americans freed from slavery at the end of the Civil War in 1865 were all descended from ancestors who were captured and taken to the United States against their will. Albeit permissible under international law at the time such acts can hardly be seen as enhancing the "moral authority of the United States." Moreover, for those slaves transported to the United States between the abolition of the international slave trade in 1808 and the end of the Civil War, when the ban on their importation was flagrantly flouted, even the defence of abiding by the law cannot be cited.[28]

For many critics of present day immigrant communities in the United States the principal issue is one of assimilation. By this interpretation in the "Golden Age" of immigration between 1880 and 1920 the United States was a "melting pot" in which, whatever their origins or past experiences, new immigrants, or if not them their children, learned to cherish shared American values. Today, it is argued, this is no longer the case. In part, this is because of the negative mindset of the immigrants themselves. More importantly, it reflects the rise of a multicultural philosophy promoted by liberal politicians and self-serving immigrant leaders.

"In today's America, immigrants are welcomed by a society intoxicated with the idea of multiculturalism," complained Colorado congressman Tom Tancredo. In this new political climate, traditional American values are questioned and derided rather than being honored. This development manifested itself in a variety of different ways, from Hispanic immigrants booing the United States team in a 1998 football match against Mexico in Los Angeles to disrespect for the Christian faith. Similarly, it was the rise of multiculturalism that was responsible for schoolchildren no longer having knowledge of, or pride in, their nation's history. "What many still see as a glorious past others see as shameful history," lamented Pat Buchanan, "Columbus, Washington, Jefferson, Jackson, Lincoln and Lee, heroes of the old America" were "all under attack." Rather than being revered, "the discovery of America by the explorers from Columbus to Captain John Smith, and the winning of the West by pioneers, soldiers, and cowboys" were "no longer seen as heroic events but matters of which Western man should be ashamed."[29]

This line of reasoning can be challenged in a variety of ways. In the first instance, it derives from a romanticized, and highly selective, vision of the nation's past. It presupposes a previous consensus view of American history that never existed. In this vein, Buchanan looked back to the more halcyon days of 1960, a time when 89 percent of the U.S. population were of European ancestry and 10 percent African Americans. "Though of two races, we were of one nationality. We were all Americans," he recalled. "We worshipped the same God, studied the same literature and history, honored the same heroes, celebrated the same holidays, went to the same movies, read the same newspapers and magazines." Admittedly, there was the unfortunate issue of racial segregation, but despite this African Americans "were fully assimilated into American culture."[30]

This is not a view that everyone would share. The fact that native Americans made up less than 1 percent of the nation's population by this time is a poignant reminder that "the winning of the west" during the 19th century was an achievement that not all Americans could celebrate. For the young Malcolm X, his experiences of studying history at school in the 1930s were dominated by memories of the racist anecdotes of his teacher and finding that the section on African American history in the school textbook "was exactly one paragraph long." The successful introduction of network television in 1948 may have been a remarkable technological advance in American popular culture, but it did not bring any immediate improvement in the depiction of African Americans within the new medium. Throughout the 1950s and well into the 1960s African Americans in light entertainment programs on television were overwhelmingly portrayed as comic, servile, characters in shows such as *Amos 'n' Andy* or *Beulah*. More often than not black performers were simply denied the opportunity to appear on television at all.[31]

In a new departure during the 1960 presidential election, the Democratic candidate John F. Kennedy famously debated live on television with his Republican opponent Richard Nixon. During the course of the debates, Kennedy reflected on the respective life opportunities for white and black babies born in the United States that year. He observed that a black baby had "half as much chance to go through high school ... a third as much chance to be a professional ... about half as much chance to own a house" and "about four times as much chance" of being out of work. In Kennedy's own words, "America can do better." This is a less than ringing endorsement for the view that African Americans were "fully assimilated into American culture" at that time.[32]

Ultimately, the view that newcomers and minority groups in the United States must assimilate themselves into mainstream American society is a deeply conservative philosophy. The traditional values, or American creed, eulogized by conservative commentators are predominantly those of the dominant white culture. The writers who advocate these values are careful in their use of language, claiming to be merely seeking to preserve Western culture or Western civilization. In doing so, they come uncomfortably close to evoking the racially charged imagery of pseudoscientific commentators in the early decades of the 20th century.[33]

Openly stating their belief in white racial supremacy writers like T. Lothrop Stoddard and Madison Grant bemoaned what they saw as the threat to the "Nordic race" by mass immigration. In 1921 Stoddard thus envisaged "enduring conquests like migrations which would swamp whole populations and turn countries now white into colored man's lands irretrievably lost to the white world." In the same vein, Grant warned of an impending struggle against

> the dangerous foreign races, whether they advance sword in hand or in the more insidious guise of beggars at our gates, pleading for admittance to share our prosperity. If we continue to allow them to enter they will in time drive us out of our own land by mere force of breeding.[34]

Substitute phrases like the "Nordic race" or the "white world" for terms like "Western man" or "Western civilization" and such claims echo the views put forward by the right-wing opponents of Hispanic immigration today. At times this is something that some present-day critics appear to tacitly acknowledge. In 2006 Patrick Buchanan thus reflected that if racism meant "a belief in the superiority of the white race and its inherent right to rule other peoples," then "American history is full of such men." Paradoxically, Buchanan and the conservative commentators who share his views then berate citizens of the United States who are not white, and often the descendants of those who suffered most as a result of this presumption of white racial superiority, for their refusal to venerate "such men." Indeed, in seeking recognition and respect for alternative cultural traditions the advocates of a more inclusive multicultural philosophy are condemned for trying to undermine the nation's cultural heritage. "We may call our ancestors racists as we trumpet our moral superiority," scolded Buchanan. "But history may yet mark ours as the generation of fools that threw away the last best hope on earth."[35]

The doom-laden conservative predictions of American in 2050 as a "balkanized" or "Third World" nation, a multiracial and multiethnic "Tower of Babel" can be questioned on a number of counts. Sensationalist in tone, they rely on a selective use of evidence and future projections that are not supported by historical precedent. However, this does not mean that the more liberal, optimistic, vision of a multicultural America transcending the racial and ethnic divisions of the past is likely to be any more accurate. Unfortunately, there are a variety of reasons for believing that the arrival of the *Star Trek* generation remains a utopian vision rather than a pending reality.

The projected 2042 tipping point when white Americans will no longer be a majority of the United States population may be of symbolic significance, but what difference, if any, this will make from a practical perspective remains to be seen. White Americans will still, by a wide margin, constitute the single largest ethnic group in the United States, followed by Hispanic Americans at around 24 percent and African Americans at approximately 10 percent. Moreover, if whites and African Americans historically have had a strong sense of collective identity this is not true of other ethnic groups. In the first decade of the 20th century the Dillingham Commission simplistically attributed common traits and characteristics to all immigrants from southern and eastern Europe. Such analysis failed to take account of the inevitable cultural, ethnic and national diversity that existed among immigrants who originated from a range of different countries. In the first decade of the 21st century the unqualified use of the terms Hispanic or Latino risks making the same error. In reality, they are no more than convenient descriptions of a broad and complex ethnic grouping that includes not merely Americans of Mexican ancestry but also those with roots in the Caribbean and Central and Latin America.[36]

There are other lessons that can be learnt from the historical experience of immigration in the United States. By the mid-20th century the immigrants from southern and eastern Europe and their descendants had become successfully assimilated into mainstream American culture. The racial category of white was no longer reserved largely, if not exclusively, for protestant Americans with an ancestry that could be traced back to northern and western Europe. It is not unreasonable to suppose that a similar process of assimilation will take place among Hispanic and Asian immigrant communities in America today. Younger Americans are significantly more likely than their parents or grandparents to marry someone outside their own ethnic or racial group. In this "beigeing" of America, it is likely that at least some of the children from these unions will consider themselves to be white and identify with the values of a mainstream white-dominated culture and society.[37]

Admittedly, the process of assimilation may only serve to delay by a few decadesthe historic moment when the majority of Americans who fill in their census returns no longer perceive themselves as white. At the sametime, the current projected turning point of 2042 is some 30 years away. By 2012 there were also signs of a decline in the levels of migration from Mexico to the United States and of a declining birth rate among Latino Americans. If the projected 2042 transition year should, as a result, recede yet further into the future the potential impact on American society today of this transition also becomes increasingly speculative and far removed. In the long run, as the economist John Maynard Keynes is reputed to have observed, "we are all dead."[38]

More importantly, a focus on the census returns runs the risk of becoming too preoccupied with simple numbers and percentages, however interesting they may be. Ultimately, what matters is not the respective size of different racial and ethnic groupings but their share in the distribution of wealth, power, and influence within American society. Since the introduction of the 20th Amendment to the United States Constitution in August 1920 women have comprised around 50 percent or more of the American electorate. Despite this they have been, and continue to be, greatly under-represented in terms of political office holding at national, state, and local level. Almost 100 years later the nation still awaits the election of its first woman president. During the 2008 primary and election campaigns the two most prominent women contenders, Hillary Clinton and Sarah Palin, both complained about the overtly sexist nature of the political and media coverage that they received. This included media commentaries on their physical appearance, hairstyles, and choice of clothing in a way that would have been inconceivable for any of their male rivals. A Facebook group, "Hillary Clinton: Stop Running for President and Make Me a Sandwich," attracted "tens of thousands of members."[39]

What is true of gender also applies to race. The same year that Barack Obama was inaugurated as President of the United States less than 10 percent of all the nation's elected public officials were of African American, Latino, or Asian ancestry. White voters also continue to exercise disproportionate power at the ballot box. In 2000 they comprised 69 percent of the U.S. population but made up 77 percent and 74 percent respectively of voters in the 2004 and 2008 presidential elections. Hispanic Americans, who comprised 14.4 percent of the population accounted for around only 6 percent of voters. In part, this was because they were less likely to exercise their right to the franchise. It also reflected the number of Hispanic Americans living illegally in the United States and therefore unable to vote in elections. The net result was that in terms of the total population whites outnumbered Hispanic Americans by around five to one, but that at the ballot box the white vote was "thirteen times the size of the Hispanic vote."[40]

In social and economic terms, white Americans also continue to enjoy disproportionate power and influence, a fact acknowledged by Barack Obama himself. "We know the statistics," the future president reflected in *The Audacity of Hope* (2006), in "almost every single socioeconomic indicator, from infant mortality to life expectancy to employment to home ownership, black and Latino Americans in particular continue to lag far behind their white counterparts. In corporate boardrooms across America, minorities are grossly underrepresented." In 2006 the average black and Latino wages were 75 percent and 71 percent of the average white wage. Black medium net worth was around $6,000 and Latino net worth around $8,000 compared to $88,000 for whites. Although growing numbers of African American and Latino families have achieved middle-class status and incomes in recent years, white socioeconomic domination remains unchallenged.[41]

In 1967 the population of the United States surpassed 200 million. By 2006 it reached 300 million and by 2050 is set to grow to around 420 million. In part this is a result of immigration. It also reflects the higher birth rates among immigrant and non-white ethnic groups in the United States. By contrast, the birth rate among white Americans is no longer sufficient to maintain current population levels and the average age profile of whites is increasingly ageing.[42]

At the same time the United States continues to be a white-dominated culture and society. This is likely to remain the case, even if by 2042 whites no longer constitute a majority of the United States population. By that time white Americans will still constitute easily the largest single racial group within the United States and there is no reason to suppose that they will lose their preponderance of wealth and political power simply because they no longer constitute a numerical majority of the population. Paradoxically, rather than undermining this domination the process of demographic change could even reinforce it by increasingly contributing to the pool of younger workers needed to sustain future economic growth. By 2050 the United States may, as a result, be a more multiethnic, multicultural society, but it is also likely to be one in which white Americans still disproportionately enjoy the best opportunities to live long and prosper.[43]

Notes

1 Gavin, Patrick. "Trekkie in chief wants screening," www.politico.com/news/stories/0509/22270.html; "Barack Obama shows off his Vulcan salute," www.nypost.com/p/pagessix/barack_obama_shows_off_his_vulcan_ 9y2k0QG4BMd6 hStyBkZCyH; Simpson, Connor. "Romney and Obama are both big 'Star Trek' fans," www.theatlanticwire.com/entertainment/2012/06/romney-and-obama-are-both-big-star-trek-fans/53093/

2   Marable, Manning. "Introduction: racializing Obama: the enigma of postblack politics and leadership," in Marable, Manning and Clarke, Kristen, eds., *Barack Obama and African American Empowerment: the rise of black America's new leadership* (New York: Palgrave Macmillan, 2009), p. 1; Walker, Clarence E. and Smithers, Gregory D. *The Preacher and the Politician: Jeremiah Wright, Barack Obama and race in America* (Charlottesville: University of Virginia Press, 2009), p. 7; Sugrue, Thomas J. *Not Even Past: Barack Obama and the burden of race* (Princeton, NJ: Princeton University Press, 2010), p. 1; Gregory, David, quoted in White, John Kenneth. *Barack Obama's America: how new conceptions of race, family, and religion ended the Reagan era* (Ann Arbor: University of Michigan Press, 2009), p. 213.

3   "Transcript—Barack Obama's inaugural address—text," www.nytimescom/2009/01/20/us/politics/20text-obama.html?pagewanted = all

4   White, *Barack Obama's America*, pp. 202–203.

5   Hsu, Hua. "State of the Union: the end of White America?," *Atlantic Monthly* January–February 2009: p. 48.

6   *Falling Down* (Director, Joel Schumacher, Alcor Films, 1993); *White Man's Burden* (Director, Desmond Nakamo, A Band Apart Films, 1995).

7   *Planet of the Apes* (Director, Tim Burton, Twentieth Century Fox, 2001); "Glenn Beck Compares Obama's America to 'Planet of the Apes'," www.huffingtonpost.com/2010/08/07glenn-beck-compares-obama_n_674591.html

8   *Gangs of New York* (Director, Martin Scorsese, Miramax Films, 2002); *Crash* (Director, Paul Haggis, Lions Gate Films, 2005).

9   Roediger, David. *The Wages of Whiteness: race and the making of the American working class* (New York: Verso, 1991); Ignatiev, Noel. *How the Irish Became White* (New York: Routledge, 1995); Hale, Grace Elizabeth. *Making Whiteness: the culture of segregation in the South, 1890–1940* (New York: Pantheon Books, 1998); Brattain, Michelle. *The Politics of Whiteness: race, workers and culture in the modern South* (Princeton, NJ: Princeton University Press, 2001); Verney, Kevern. *The Debate on Black Civil Rights in America* (Manchester: Manchester University Press, 2007); Hsu. "State of the Union," pp. 50–1.

10 Bill Clinton, quoted in Hsu. "State of the Union," p. 48.

11 Brimelow, Peter. *Alien Nation: common sense about America's immigration disaster* (New York: Random House, 1995); Buchanan, Patrick J. *The Death of the West: how dying populations and immigrant invasions imperil our country and civilization* (New York: St. Martin's Press, 2002); Hanson, Victor Davis. *Mexifornia: a state of becoming* (New York: Encounter Books, 2003); Huntington, Samuel P. *Who Are We? The challenges to America's national identity* (New York: Simon & Schuster, 2004); Buchanan, Patrick J. *State of Emergency: the third world invasion and conquest of America* (New York: St. Martin's Press, 2006), p. 2; Tancredo, Tom. *In Mortal Danger: the battle for America's border and security* (Nashville, TN: Cumberland House Publishing, Inc., 2006).

12 Buchanan. *Death of the West*, pp. 11–12, 26–7.

13 Tancredo. *In Mortal Danger*, pp. 37–8; Huntington, *Who Are We?* pp. 174, 176.

14 Buchanan. *State of Emergency*, pp. 12, 114, 133, 135; Hanson, Victor Davis. *Mexifornia: a state of becoming*, rev. edn. (New York: Encounter Books, 2007), p. xiii.

15 Huntington. *Who Are We?* pp. 221, 226, 246; Buchanan. *State of Emergency*, pp. 105–7.

16 Hanson. *Mexifornia* (rev. edn.), pp. 6, 30; Huntington. *Who Are We?* pp. 221, 229–30, 234–5; Buchanan. *State of Emergency*, pp. 107–117, 123–8.

17 Hanson. *Mexifornia* (rev. edn.), p. 142; Buchanan. *State of Emergency*, pp. 245–6; Tancredo. *In Mortal Danger*, pp. 23, 51.

18 Huntington. *Who Are We?*, pp. 222–5; Buchanan. *State of Emergency*, pp. 9–10.
19 Buchanan. *State of Emergency*, p. 244; Jones, Maldwyn A. *The Limits of Liberty: American history, 1607–1980* (Oxford: Oxford University Press, 1983), p. 646; http://geography.about.com/od/obtainpopulationdata/a/uspopulation.htm; Jones, Maldwyn A. *American Immigration* (Chicago: University of Chicago Press, 1992), p. 177; Jones, Maldwyn A. *Destination America* (London: Weidenfeld & Nicolson, 1976), p. 11.
20 *The 21st Century World Atlas* (Naples, FL: Trident Press International, 1998), pp. 92–3.
21 Tancredo. *In Mortal Danger*, p. 33; Buchanan. *State of Emergency*, p. 133.
22 Buchanan. *State of Emergency*, p. 135.
23 Ibid.; Hanson, *Mexifornia* (rev. edn.), p. xv.
24 Jones. *American Immigration*, p. 152; Kraut, Alan M. *The Huddled Masses: the immigrant in American society, 1880–1921* (Arlington Heights, IL: Harlan Davidson, Inc., 1982), p. 17.
25 Hanson. *Mexifornia* (rev. edn.), p. 4; Buchanan. *State of Emergency*, p. 12; Kraut. *The Huddled Masses,* pp. 76–7.
26 Jones. *American Immigration*, pp. 156, 195; Kraut. *The Huddled Masses*, p. 77.
27 Kraut. *The Huddled Masses*, pp. 52–3; Jones. *Destination America*, p. 64.
28 Franklin, John Hope and Moss, Jr., Alfred A. *From Slavery to Freedom: a history of negro Americans*, 6th edn. (New York: Alfred A. Knopf, 1988), pp. 86, 201.
29 Tancredo. *In Mortal Danger*, p. 22, 39–41; Huntington. *Who Are We?* p. 5; Palin, Sarah. *America by Heart: reflections on family, faith, and flag* (New York: HarperCollins Publishers, 2010), pp. 209–12; Buchanan. *State of Emergency*, p. 158.
30 Buchanan. *State of Emergency*, pp. 136, 176.
31 Haley Alex, ed. *The Autobiography of Malcolm X* (London: Penguin Books, 1968), pp. 109–10; Verney, Kevern. *African Americans and U.S. Popular Culture* (London and New York: Routledge, 2003), pp. 51–3.
32 Kennedy, quoted in Verney, Kevern. *Black Civil Rights in America* (London and New York: Routledge, 2000), p.117.
33 Hill, Johnny Bernard. *The First Black President: Barack Obama, race, politics and the American dream* (New York: Palgrave Macmillan, 2009), p. 39; Sawyer, Mark. "On black leadership, black politics, and the U.S. immigration debate," in Marable and Clarke, eds. *Barack Obama and African American Empowerment*, p. 75. Walker and Smithers. *The Preacher and the Politician*, p. 36.
34 Grant, Madison. *The Passing of the Great Race; or, the racial basis of European history* (New York: Charles Scribner's Sons, 1916); Stoddard, T. Lothrop. *The Rising Tide of Color Against White World Supremacy* (first published 1921, Burlington, VT: Ostara Publications, 2011 reprint), pp. ii, xiv.
35 Buchanan *State of Emergency*, pp. 85, 92.
36 Jones. *American Immigration*, pp. 154–5; Buchanan. *State of Emergency*, p. 57.
37 Hsu. "State of the Union," pp. 47–8; White. *Barack Obama's America*, p. 63; Nasaw, Daniel. "What will a white-minority US look like?" www.bbc.co.uk/news/magazine-18108845
38 "Non-Hispanic US births now the minority in US," www.bbc.co.uk/news/world-us-canada-18100457; Keynes, quoted in Knowles, Elizabeth, ed. *The Oxford Dictionary of Quotations*, 5th edn. (Oxford: Oxford University Press, 1999), p. 435.
39 Palin, *America by Heart*, p. 130; Nelson, Michael. "The setting: diversifying the presidential talent pool," in Nelson, Michael, ed. *The Elections of 2008* (Washington, DC: CQ Press, 2010), p. 13.
40 Mfume, Kweisi. Keynote address, "The civil rights century: the NAACP at 100," conference, February 6, 2009, Baltimore, Maryland, Johns Hopkins

University; White. *Barack Obama's America*, p. 203; Buchanan. *State of emergency*, p. 65.

41   Obama, Barack. *The Audacity of Hope: thoughts of reclaiming the American dream* (Edinburgh: Canongate, 2007), pp. 232, 242–3.

42   White. *Barack Obama's America*, pp. 1–2; Tancredo. *In mortal danger*, p. 101.

43   Nasaw. "What will a white-minority US look like?".

8　Still Mariachi Politics

Latinos and the Obama Administration

Lisa García Bedolla

The "Great Tamale Incident" occurred in 1976 when Gerald Ford, after touring the Alamo in San Antonio, Texas, bit into a tamale without removing the corn husk. The gaffe made national news, and was seen as representing President Ford's lack of awareness of Latino food, and, by extension, Latino issues. Since this famous presidential gaffe, politicians on both sides of the aisle have become more sophisticated in their outreach to Latino voters. Not only do both parties now spend millions of dollars reaching out to the Latino vote during each campaign, but these appeals have become more sophisticated, including the utterance of a few phrases in Spanish when President Obama makes speeches in front of majority-Latino audiences. Yet, it remains unclear to what extent these overtures translate into substantive policies of benefit to the U.S. Latino community. A review of policy positions of interest to Latinos during President Barack Obama's first term suggests that the administration's approach to Latino issues is, at best, symbolic, and at worst contrary to community interests. I call this a continuation of "mariachi politics"—a politics that includes cultural overtures to Latino voters, but that does not result in a group-relevant focus when it comes to public policy.

Winning the Future

The Obama administration frames its efforts to reach out to the Latino, African American, and Asian American communities as "Winning the future." Each group has a dedicated web page on the whitehouse.gov website. These pages are meant to highlight the administration's policy efforts that are most critical for each group. The web pages for all three groups look identical, with a navigation bar across the top, a group-relevant picture beneath, and under that a set of links to blog posts, videos, and other reports thought to be of interest to each constituency. For the Latino page, the picture shows President Obama being interviewed by Univisión national news anchor Jorge Ramos. The major report available for download is "President Obama's agenda and the Hispanic Community." The highlighted videos are of the President signing the executive order creating the White

House Initiative on Educational Excellence for Hispanic Americans and of Dolores Huerta receiving the Medal of Freedom in 2011.

Looking at the Latino site in comparison with the other two sites, the Latino site contains fewer links to substantive policy content. For example, the African American home page includes five "fact sheets" delineating the administration's efforts on behalf of African Americans overall, with a specific focus on creating jobs and pathways to opportunity for African Americans. Similarly, the Asian American site provides links to the executive order establishing the initiative and the president's advisory commission (which Obama reinstated after its lapse under the Bush administration), the goals of the advisory commission, and its accomplishments since its inception, as well as four fact sheets (including two "infographics") that include detailed background information about the Asian American community in the United States. The Latino page, in contrast, has no fact sheets, no specific information on the status of Latinos in the United States, and no summary documents specifying how President Obama's policies have helped the Latino community. Instead, the home page includes a brief statement about the "integral part" the Latino community plays in "winning the future" for the United States, with little specificity.

The same trend is evident when looking at the "president's agenda" reports that are available on each group's website. These documents are meant to summarize President Obama's agenda in reference to each particular group. The reports vary in length, with a high of 44 pages for African Americans to a low of 14 for Asian Americans. The Latino report falls somewhere in the middle at 31 pages. This may seem a random difference, given these pages are designed, updated, and maintained by the administration staffers charged with running these initiatives. Yet, these websites are meant to serve as the entry portals for each community into the administration's work. As such, they represent the administration's efforts to frame the president's political agenda in the most positive light possible vis-à-vis each subgroup. It is telling that there is so little evidence of any sort of sensitivity to the types of issues (such as language, poverty, nativity, youth) that affect Latinos in ways that vary from other U.S. ethnoracial groups.

Reading these White House documents, what is clear is a lack of any specific focus on Latinos on the part of the administration. Administration programs designed for the general population may affect Latinos, but these impacts are incidental rather than purposeful. It is clear from these documents that Latino issues not only do not drive the Obama administration's agenda, but are not even secondary within the administration's policy-making process. This is not to say that the administration's policies will not be of benefit to community members. Rather, the point is that there is little evidence from the administration's record that there is a desire on the part of policymakers within the executive branch to ensure their policies are sensitive to the particular needs faced by their Latino constituents. The result is a "one size fits all" approach that, by treating all groups equally actually maintains, and at times exacerbates, existing inequalities between Latinos and other ethnoracial groups.

To support this argument, I will explore the administration's efforts across four areas of public policy that are especially important to Latinos in the United States: education, housing, health care, and immigration. These are issue areas that continually top the list of "most important" issues in surveys that include Latino respondents. The administration's approaches to these issue areas, then, provide a snapshot of the degree to which the issues of greatest interest to the Latino community are adequately addressed within the administration's policy program.

Education

Education is a critical issue for Latinos in the United States and is consistently reported as the top issue of concern to Latinos when surveyed. Latinos comprise the fastest growing segment of the U.S. school-age population. According to the Pew Hispanic Center, the number of Latino students in the nation's public schools nearly doubled from 1990 to 2006, accounting for 60 percent of the total growth in public school enrollment over that period (Fry and Gonzales 2008). In 2001 Latino children made up just under 17 percent of U.S. public elementary and secondary school students; by 2008, that number had grown to just over 21 percent (National Center for Education Statistics 2010). There are now approximately 11 million Latino students in America's public schools. In 2010, Latino children became the majority of the school-age population in the country's most populous state, California. The growth in the Latino student population is expected to continue, increasing 166 percent by 2050. Thus, by 2050 there will be more school-age Hispanic children in U.S. schools than school-age non-Latino white students.

Yet, Latino children face significant challenges in terms of their educational attainment. Latino students are increasingly likely to attend racially segregated schools and to live in poor neighborhoods (Orfield and Lee 2007; Suárez Orozco and Suárez Orozco 2009). The national drop-out rate for Latino youth is more than twice the national average (Chapman, Laird, and Ramani 2010). In 12th grade, Latinos average only an 8th grade reading level (Suárez Orozco and Suárez Orozco 2009). It is estimated that almost one in two Latino students currently drops out of high school.[1] Although over 40 percent of Latinos enter some sort of postsecondary educational program, fewer than 20 percent complete a 4-year degree. Because Latino college graduation rates have remained stagnant for almost three decades, Latinos have the lowest college attendance rates of all ethnoracial groups in the United States (Gándara and Contreras 2009; Pérez Huber et al. 2006). Even though second-generation Latino children often achieve greater academic success than their parents (Kasinitz et al. 2009; Portes and Rumbaut 2001), recent longitudinal work suggests a movement toward "third generation decline." In other words, worsening Latino academic success in the third generation and beyond (Telles and Ortiz 2008). As Gándara and Contreras show (2009: 2), these disturbing trends cannot be attributed simply to immigration and Latino immigrants' lower educational levels. Their work, along with that of Telles and Ortiz (2008) and Farkas (2003), strongly suggests that low Latino educational attainment is not simply a matter of difficulties with immigrant integration, but rather structural inequalities in terms of the educational opportunities afforded to Latino students, regardless of nativity.

President Obama's approach to Latino educational issues does not address the specific, and unique, needs of this community. The centerpiece of the administration's plan for addressing Latino education is the White House Initiative on Educational Excellence for Hispanic Americans. Originally established in 1990 by President George H.W. Bush, President Obama renewed the initiative in October 2010 with Executive Order 13555. The initiative includes a presidential advisory committee and interagency working group, along with a national Latino education summit and a series of meetings across the country to address the educational needs of Latino youth. These meetings resulted in an April 2011 White House report entitled "Winning the future: improving education for the Latino community," which lays out the administration's efforts to address the Latino education gap.

A close reading of the report, however, shows that little of the President's education policies are designed to directly address the issues Latino youth face. For example, participation in early education programs has been shown to have a positive effect on children's cognitive development and subsequent educational attainment (Bowman, Donovan, and Burns 2000; Schweinhart et al. 2004). Latino children, however, have the lowest rates of participation in early childhood education. As part of the American Recovery and Reinvestment Act of 2009 (ARRA), the Obama administration invested an additional $5 billion in early learning programs, which the administration claims will address this gap in participation between Latinos and other American children. Yet, without any understanding of *why* Latino families are not participating in these programs, increasing their availability will not necessarily increase Latino participation in them. The administration's approach presumes that the participation gap is a product of availability. It could just as easily reflect cultural or linguistic differences between the service providers and their Latino families. Without a better sense of the underlying problem, and the ability to design policy programs to address those core problems, it is not at all certain that this additional funding will address the early learning gap.

Similarly, a centerpiece of the Obama administration's education policy program has been the "Race to the top" program, which emphasizes the use of standards-based testing to improve educational outcomes for all children. Yet, it is unclear how effective standardized tests are in measuring the outcomes for Latino students, particularly those who are English learners (ELs). In their study of English learners in California, Rumberger and Gándara (2004) find that the state's testing-based accountability system is of little use for monitoring the academic progress of English learners, largely because the only measures of achievement for EL students are tests administered in English. They site the reports of several research and professional organizations stating that "testing students in a language in which they are not yet proficient is both invalid and unethical" (Rumberger and Gándara 2004: 2041). This does little good from the standpoint of accountability or in terms of helping teachers to enhance instruction. Given it is understood to take at least four years for individuals to become English proficient, they argue "the burden is on the state to demonstrate that test scores for English learners who have been in the United States for less than four years are valid, yet the state has not made any attempt to obtain information to shed light on this question" (Rumberger and Gándara 2004: 2042). The same is true for the Obama administration, which has not developed an approach to standardized testing that addresses the needs of English learners. As a result, Menken (2008) argues our testing regime comprises the United States' current language policy, a policy that does not meet the needs of immigrant students. On testing policy, then, we see that the Obama administration's approach does not incorporate Latinos' unique needs into its design.

Housing

According to the Pew Hispanic Center, Latino wealth has fallen by 66 percent since 2005, compared to 53 percent for African Americans and 16 percent for whites (Taylor et al. 2011). Much of this loss may be attributed to decreases in housing values because two-thirds of Latino net worth was derived from home equity and their households tended to be concentrated in the states hit hardest by the housing crash: California, Florida, Nevada, and Arizona. As a result, about one-quarter of Latino households in 2009 had no wealth other than a vehicle, compared to just 6 percent of white households. And, the crisis is nowhere near its end. According to a recent study by the Center for Responsible Lending, we are only halfway through the foreclosure crisis; millions more families can be expected to lose their homes (Bocian et al. 2011). A disproportionate number of those families will be Latino, given 24 percent Latino and African American borrowers have lost their homes compared to 12 percent of white borrowers.

Thus, addressing the housing crisis would have a disproportionate impact on the wealth and well-being of Latino households. Yet, a recent watchdog report on the Hardest Hit Fund, the program designed to help homeowners in the communities worst hit by the housing crisis, found that the program had spent only 3 percent of its budget since its inception in 2010 (Lowrey 2012). Similarly, the administration's Home Affordable Modification Program (HAMP), the centerpiece of the president's efforts to address the housing crisis, has, as of January 2012, provided permanent loan modifications to less than 1 million homeowners—significantly fewer than needed given the scope and depth of the crisis. In 2012 the Obama administration announced changes to the program designed to increase the number of homeowners eligible for assistance under the program. But, given the structural problems with HAMP laid out by former Special Inspector Neil Barofsky in his 2012 book *Bailout*, none of which is addressed by the new policy, it is unlikely HAMP will be able to provide relief to a significant number of distressed homeowners, many of whom are Latino. In addition, an exploration of the HAMP website makes clear that the needs of Spanish-speaking Latino homeowners, or other immigrant homeowners, was not a central concern for the program. None of the information on the HAMP website is translated into Spanish or any other language, neither is there information about how non-English speakers can receive information. Thus, again, we see an administration policy program that is not sensitive to the needs of the Latino community.

Health Care

Latinos make up just over 30 percent of the U.S. uninsured population, a rate almost double their proportion of the population overall (which is 16 percent). This is significantly higher than African Americans, who comprise 21 percent of the uninsured, and whites, who make up about 12 percent (Department of Health and Human Services 2011). The expansion of health care coverage through the Affordable Care Act (ACA), then, will have a significant impact on Latinos. But, studies have shown that citizenship status, English-language proficiency, and socioeconomic status all affect access to health care (Capps, Kenney, and Fix 2003; Fremstad and Cox 2004). Forty-six percent of noncitizens lack health insurance, compared to 14.1 percent of the native-born population and 19 percent of the naturalized population (Siskin 2011: 12). Noncitizens also have the lowest rate of Medicare coverage. Noncitizen children who are Spanish speaking also are four times more likely (72 percent to 17 percent) than white children to lack health insurance (Ku and Waidman 2003: 1).

In many cases, these noncitizens and children, particularly those with limited English skills, are eligible for health coverage, but do not access the programs for which they are eligible. U.S. citizen children with noncitizen parents also are less likely to access the care they are eligible for, even if they are English speaking. States that have attempted to broaden coverage to include undocumented immigrants or children from mixed-status families, such as California, have found many eligible immigrant children do not sign up for benefits. For this reason, Dorn and Kenney (2006) suggest auto-enrolling children into health care programs for which they are eligible. Nativity, language, and poverty then, have important implications for health insurance coverage, even for those currently eligible for insurance.

Since 40 percent of Latinos are foreign born and one in 10 families in the United States is of mixed status,[2] these findings have important implications for Latino access to quality health care (Fix and Zimmerman 1999). The

Affordable Care Act, unfortunately, does not adequately address these issues. The law expressly exempts unauthorized aliens from the mandate to have health coverage and bars them from a health insurance exchange. Unauthorized aliens are not eligible for the federal premium credits or cost-sharing subsidies. Unauthorized aliens are also barred from participating in the temporary high-risk pools (Siskin 2011: 10). Unauthorized immigrants would still be able to find treatment in emergency rooms, but hospitals fear that other cuts in federal support mandated by the ACA will put financial pressure on those hospitals that provide care to large numbers of unauthorized immigrants. The federal government currently spends $20 billion a year reimbursing hospitals for providing those services. The ACA is expected to cut that amount in half, based on the expectation that there will be fewer uninsured people seeking treatment after the law takes effect (Bernstein 2012). Clearly, this aspect of the law does not take into consideration those individuals, such as the unauthorized, who will be barred from participating in the new system.

Even when Latinos are eligible for health care, California's experience shows that many mixed status families do not enroll their children for the care because they fear bringing themselves to the attention of government authorities. This is critically important, since about 4.5 million U.S.-born children have at least one unauthorized parent (Passel and Cohn 2011). In addition, the lack of interpreters and other culturally relevant programs within health care providers also limits these patients' ability to access quality care when they do access their benefits (Ku and Waidman 2003). With the ACA, we see the Obama administration passing a law that will, on its face, be of benefit to the Latino community because it addresses a serious social problem—the large number of Latinos who are currently uninsured. Yet, the law does not take into consideration the factors that affect Latinos' access to quality health care—nativity, language use, and poverty. Without specific policies designed to address these issues, it is unlikely Latinos will be able to take full advantage of the benefits of the ACA. In addition, its exclusion of the unauthorized makes it possible the law will make health access even worse for the community's most vulnerable members.

Immigration

According to Immigration and Customs Enforcement (ICE), the Obama administration has deported just under 1.5 million immigrants.[3] The levels of deportation under this administration have been significantly higher than those of George W. Bush. Much of this increase is due to the expansion of the Secure Communities program under the Obama administration. Recent studies have shown that Latinos are disproportionately the targets for arrest and deportation under this program. Mexican nationals, in particular, are overrepresented among deportees. Although it is estimated that 59 percent of unauthorized immigrants are of Mexican origin, Mexican immigrants made up 73 percent of removals in 2010 (López, González-Barrera, and Motel 2011: 12). These deportations have led to widespread anxiety and fear within Latino communities. Scholars studying the 2006 immigration marches, in follow-up interviews with activists, have found that the Obama deportation regime has had a chilling effect on these activists' subsequent political engagement.

The administration's deportation policies are important because, even though not all Latinos are immigrants, about 40 percent of Latinos are foreign born. In addition, policies designed to address unauthorized immigration have been shown to have a negative effect on native-born Latinos as well. For example, UC Berkeley's Warren Institute's study of arrest data related to an ICE-local law enforcement partnership in Irving, Texas, showed that arrests of Latinos (citizen and noncitizen) for petty offenses increased dramatically after the implementation of the program, strongly suggesting that the Irving police engaged in racial profiling of Latinos after the partnership was implemented (Gardner and Kohli 2009). Similarly, a study of the Secure Communities program found ICE arrested 3,600 U.S. citizens through the Secure Communities Program and that about 88,000 U.S. citizen families had been affected by deportation under Secure Communities as well (Kohli, Markowitz, and Chávez 2011). These studies, along with others criticizing the Criminal Alien and Secure Communities (or 287g) programs, led the Obama administration to announce on June 25, 2012 that it would suspend the 287g/Secure Communities program indefinitely. This decision is expected to decrease administration deportations since many observers believe the increases under Obama have been largely driven by immigrants being deported for petty offenses under this program.

Obama's deportation record has surprised advocates because the president campaigned on a promise to champion comprehensive immigration reform (CIR). Many pundits claim he increased border enforcement in order to secure Republican support for CIR. Yet, even after CIR failed in 2010, the high rates of deportation remained until the administration's recent commitment to end Secure Communities. The Obama administration had an additional reversal of its immigration policy in June 2012. On June 15, the president announced a deferred action program for unauthorized youth. Under this executive order, eligible immigrants must have arrived in the U.S. before their 16th birthday, be 30 or younger, have been living in the United States at least five years, be in school or have graduated or have served in the military. Applicants also must not have a criminal record or otherwise pose a safety threat. Eligible immigrants can apply to stay in the country and be granted a work permit for two years, but they would not be granted citizenship. It is estimated that 1.4 million youth will be eligible to apply for deferred action under this program.

This effort on the part of the administration is meant to help the population called "DREAMers"—unauthorized youth eligible for the DREAM Act. The DREAM Act, first introduced in Congress in 2001, would create a pathway to citizenship to youth who meet the same eligibility criteria as those required for the president's deferred action, in addition to maintaining good moral character. The bill, originally embraced by Republicans and Democrats, failed to pass the Senate in 2010. There are no plans to bring it back to the floor of either chamber of Congress.

Together, the deferred action program and suspension of Secure Communities are important policy changes that can be expected to reduce the pressure felt by immigrant communities under the current deportation regime. Yet, both remain temporary solutions to the problem. The deferred action only lasts two years and can be overturned by executive order. The Secure Communities program has been suspended but not permanently ended. It, too, could be reinstated at any time. These policy changes are important moves forward for the administration in terms of addressing the complex problems embedded in the U.S. immigration system. But, short of comprehensive immigration reform and the passage of the DREAM Act, they remain stop-gap measures that fail to address the core problem: the United States' broken immigration system.

Conclusion

In her comprehensive study of Spanish-language media advertising to Latinos, Marisa Abrajano (2010) finds that most political campaigns make symbolic appeals, rather than substantive ones. Ironically, she finds that those candidates that make substantive appeals actually are successful with the Latino electorate. Her findings are relevant to political science research exploring Latino descriptive versus substantive representation. Looking at the substantive representation of Latino interests by U.S. House members, Hero and Tolbert (1995) find little evidence of direct, substantive representation. They argue, however, that since Latino-relevant legislation was enacted, Latinos received indirect representation from the Democratic Party overall. Knoll (2009) updates and reaffirms these findings. Yet, little scholarship has considered Latino representation and policy influence in the executive branch. This analysis suggests that, within the Obama administration, Latino influence remains largely symbolic—the equivalent of having a mariachi band play at a rally. For that impact to be considered substantive, the administration would have to incorporate the particular needs of its Latino constituents into its policymaking process in a systematic fashion. Although the administration seems to have taken some steps in that direction with regard to immigration policy, the changes are temporary and do not address the underlying structural problems within the U.S. immigration system.

As Iris Young (1990) so cogently pointed out, treating everyone equally when groups are unequal to begin with is not a route to social justice. Quite the contrary, equal treatment of this sort will only reify and normalize established inequalities. In political discourse around the significance of the election of our first African American president, there was an underlying assumption that Barack Obama, because he was African American, would somehow govern differently and, perhaps, more inclusively. This discussion suggests that, at least with regard to Latino issues, this administration does not constitute a significant departure from previous Democratic administrations. Latinos are seen as an important voting bloc that must receive some outreach. But, that outreach does not necessarily translate into the substantive incorporation of a Latino focus into the development and implementation of public policy. Until that happens, the administration will continue to play mariachi politics—symbolically relevant but lacking the policy substance necessary to address Latino community needs.

Notes

1 These results are based on a 4-year cohort analysis.
2 "Mixed status" refers to the situation when a U.S.-born child has one or more parents who are unauthorized.
3 These numbers include deportations beginning in fiscal year 2009 through June 16, 2012. www.google.com/url?sa=t&rct=j&q=&esrc=s&source=web&cd=1&ved= 0CFQQFjAA&url=http%3A%2F%2Fwww.ice.gov%2Fdoclib%2Fabout%2Fof-fices%2Fero%2Fpdf%2Fero-removals1.pdf&ei=9S4XUPCVGJGlqQGZ64 AY&usg=AFQjCNGiO9lS34y2FFpQg1FcIZVQZ37HpQ

References

Abrajano, Marisa. *Campaigning to the New American Electorate: advertising to Latino voters* (Palo Alto, CA: Stanford University Press, 2010).

Barofsky, Neil. *Bailout: an inside account of how Washington abandoned Main Street while rescuing Wall Street* (New York: Free Press, 2012).

Bernstein, Nina. "Hospitals fear cuts in aid for care to illegal immigrants," *New York Times*, July 26, 2012, www.nytimes.com/2012/07/27/nyregion/affordable-care-act-reduces-a-fund-for-the-uninsured.html?pagewanted=all

Bocian, Debbie Gruenstein, Reid, Carolina, Li, Wei, and Quericia, Roberto G. *Lost Ground, 2011: disparities in mortgage lending and doreclosures* (Durham, NC: Center for Responsible Lending, 2011).

Bowman, B., Donovan, M.S., and Burns, M.S. *Eager to Learn: educating our pre-schoolers* (Washington, DC: National Academy Press for the National Research Council, 2000).

Capps, Randy, Kenney, Genevieve, and Fix, Michael. *Health Insurance coverage of children in mixed-status immigrant families* (Washington, DC: Urban Institute, 2003).

Chapman, C., Laird, J., and Ramani, A. Kewal. *Trends in High School Dropout and Completion Rates in the United States, 1972–2008, Compendium Report* (Washington, DC: U.S. Department of Education, National Center for Education Statistics, 2010).

Dorn, Stan and Kenney, Genevieve M. *Automatically Enrolling Eligible Children and Families into Medicaid and SCHIP: opportunities, obstacles, and options for federal policymakers* (New York: Commonwealth Fund, 2006).

Farkas, G. "Racial disparities and discrimination in education: what do we know, how do we know it, and what do we need to know?," *Teachers College Record* 2003: 105, 1119–46.

Fix, Michael and Zimmerman, Wendy. "All under one roof: mixed-status families in an era of reform," paper presented at the annual meeting of the Population Association of America, New York, 1999.

Fremstad, Shawn and Cox, Laura. *Covering New Americans: a review of federal and state policies related to immigrants' eligibility and access to publicly funded health insurance* (Washington, DC: Center on Budget and Policy Priorities, 2004).

Fry, R. and Gonzales, F. *One-in-Five and Growing Fast: a profile of Hispanic public school students* (Washington, DC: Pew Hispanic Center, 2008).

Gándara, P. and Contreras, F. *The Latino Education Crisis: the consequences of failed social policies* (Cambridge, MA: Harvard University Press, 2009).

Gardner, Trevor and Kohli, Aarti. *The C.A.P. Effect: racial profiling in the ICE Criminal Alien Program* (Berkeley, CA: Chief Justice Earl Warren Institute on Law and Social Policy, 2009).

Hero, Rodney E. and Tolbert, Caroline J. "Latinos and substantive representation in the U.S. House of Representatives: direct, indirect, or nonexistent?" *American Journal of Political Science* 1995: 39, 3, 640–52.

Kasinitz, P., Waters, M., Mollenkopf, J.H., and Holdaway, J. *Inheriting the City: the children of immigrants come of age* (New York: Russell Sage, 2009).

Kohli, Aarti, Markowitz, Peter L., and Chávez, Lisa. *Secure Communities by the Numbers: an analysis of demographics and due process* (Berkeley, CA: Chief Justice Earl Warren Institute on Law and Social Policy, 2011)

Knoll, Benjamin. "Amigo de la raza? Reexamining determinants of Latino support in the U.S. Congress," *Social Science Quarterly* 2009: 90, 1, 79–195.

Ku, Leighton and Waidman, Timothy. *How Race/Ethnicity, Immigration Status and Language Affect Health Insurance Coverage, Access to Care and Quality of Care Among the Low-Income Population* (Washington, DC: Kaiser Family Foundation, 2003).

López, Mark Hugo, González-Barrera, Ana, and Motel, Seth. *As Deportations Rise to Record Levels, Most Latinos Oppose Obama's Policy* (Washington, DC: Pew Hispanic Center, 2011).

Lowrey, Annie. "Treasury faulted in effort to relieve homeowners," *New York Times*, April 12, 2012, www.nytimes.com/2012/04/12/business/economy/treasury-department-faulted-in-effort-to-relieve-homeowners.html?_r=1&adxnnl=1&adxnnlx=1343678080-PJFezgNx90vOfbdGFrji0A

Menken, Kate. *English Learners Left Behind: testing as language policy* (Tonawanda, NY: Multilingual Matters, 2008).

Orfield, G. and Lee, C. *Historic Reversals, Accelerating Resegregation, and the Need for New Integration Strategies* (Los Angeles: UCLA Civil Rights Project/Proyecto Derechos Civiles, 2007).

Passel, Jeffrey and Cohn, D'Vera. *Unauthorized Immigrant Population: national and state trends* (Washington, DC: Pew Hispanic Center, 2011).

Pérez Huber, L., Huidor, O., Malagon, M., Sanchez, G., and Solorzano, D. *Falling Through the Cracks: critical transitions in the Latina/o educational pipeline, rep. no. 7* (Los Angeles: UCLA Chicano Studies Research Center, 2006).

Portes, A. and Rumbaut, R. *Legacies: the story of the immigrant second generation* (Berkeley: University of California Press, 2001).

Rumberger, R.W. and Gándara, P. "Seeking equity in the education of California's English learners," *Teachers College Record* 2004: 106, 2032–56.

Schweinhart, L.J., Montie, J., Xiang, Z., Barnett, W.S., Belfield, C.R., and Nores, M. *Lifetime Effects: the High Scope/Perry Preschool Project through age 40* (Ypsilanti, MI: High/Scope Press, 2004).

Siskin, Alison. *Treatment of Noncitizens Under the Patient Protection and Affordable Care Act* (Washington, DC: Congressional Research Service, 2011).

Suárez Orozco, M. and Suárez Orozco, C. "Educating Latino immigrant students in the twenty-first century: principles for the Obama administration," *Harvard Educational Review* 2009: 79, 327–40.

Taylor, Paul, Kochhar, Rakesh, Fry, Richard, Velasco, Gabriel, and Motel, Seth. *Wealth Gaps Rise to Record Highs Between Whites, Blacks, Hispanics* (Washington, DC: Pew Research Center, 2011).

Telles, E.E. and Ortiz, V. *Generations of Exclusion: Mexican Americans, assimilation, and race* (New York: Russell Sage, 2008).

Young, Iris Marion. *Justice and the Politics of Difference* (Princeton, NJ: Princeton University Press, 1990).

9 You Say Obama, I Say Osama, Let's Call the Whole Thing Off

Race and U.S. Foreign Policy Today

Lee Marsden

The 2008 American presidential election returned the first African American president to the world's most powerful nation, a result that reverberated around the globe. Obama's victory was hailed as the ultimate expression of the American dream that a black man with a Kenyan father could rise to the very highest position in the land of the free. It appeared that years of racism, which existed from slavery and kept African Americans and people of color from positions of power and influence within U.S. polity, had been set aside and that America might truly be entering into a post-racial era. The candidate of "change we can believe in" offered little in the way of campaign promises but presented himself as the non-Bush candidate who would heal America's divisions, restore America's reputation in the world, and bring hope to a nation in the midst of financial crisis. In this chapter, we concern ourselves with the role race has played in U.S. foreign policy and the extent to which the election of the first African American president has changed U.S. foreign policy and perceptions of the United States in the world.

We begin with some historical background on the role of race in U.S. foreign policy before analyzing the Obama phenomenon and whether given the nature of the election campaign, subsequent criticism of the image of a post-racial America is accurate. There follows an examination of Obama's foreign policy challenges and ambitions at the start of his presidency and the impact his racial background was expected by many commentators to play in improving bilateral relations with other countries and regions. The essay progresses with an evaluation of Obama's foreign policy over the first three years of his premiership and the extent to which those hopes have been realized before concluding that, for all its symbolism, Obama's race has made little difference to the actual delivery of U.S. foreign policy. The essay argues that Obama has continued to conduct a foreign policy that is indistinct from that pursued by his white Anglo-Saxon protestant predecessors. Rather than introducing a post-racial era, racism remains a significant factor within the formation and delivery of U.S. foreign policy.

Race and U.S. Foreign Policy

The emergence of Barack Obama as president and commander-in-chief in the first decade of the 21st century has led to a revival of interest in the phenomenon of race and U.S. foreign policy. The British scholar Mark Ledwidge argues that race has always been an under-acknowledged and integral feature of U.S. foreign policy (Ledwidge 2009, 2011). The under-acknowledgement is reflected in a domestic U.S. polity that effectively limited African American involvement in the political process until the 1960s. The assumption, however, that the struggle for emancipation and civil rights consumed African American political energy and resources on domestic politics rather than foreign policy is overstated. Such a judgment negates the active organization and participation in foreign affairs by African Americans dating from the 19th century by ambassadors, diplomats, civil and human rights leaders, and activists (see Krenn 1988, 1999; Ledwidge 2011; Plummer 1996). Journalist Christopher Williams argues that African Americans' domestic battles often ran parallel with an interest in foreign affairs: "In many cases, the domestic fight for civil rights found an extended ally in the effort to articulate a foreign policy voice for African-Americans" (Williams 2007: 135). African Americans, drawing on their experience of injustice and discrimination approached foreign affairs in the latter half of the 20th century from two distinct perspectives, namely the concern as citizens to be engaged in all aspects of the U.S. polity and as diasporic communities, albeit many generations removed, with an interest in pan-African affairs (Williams 2007: 137).

Distinctive African American approaches to foreign affairs have focused attention on Africa, particularly sub-Saharan Africa, the Caribbean, Vietnam, the United Nations, and human rights. African Americans were heavily involved in support of anticolonial struggles in Africa including opposition to apartheid in South Africa. Opposition to the Vietnam War featured many prominent African Americans including Martin Luther King and Muhammad Ali. The National Association for the Advancement of Colored People, Congressional Black Caucus, Nation of Islam, and Malcolm X's Organization of African American Unity have pursued foreign policy objectives that have often been at odds with the foreign policy pursued by successive U.S. administrations (see Copsey 2003). The prioritization of civil and human rights issues has been highlighted within African American churches and with an identification with Islam as a symbol of returning to the Muslim roots of those brought to America as slaves, identification with Africa, identifying with oppressed peoples, and as part of an international community not identified by white oppression. Foreign affairs positions emerge from a religious imperative that identifies with the poor and oppressed against the powerful and mighty, a position made problematic by the emergence of the American Empire where "national interests" invariably trump concerns of fairness and justice. Clemens suggests that the history of African Americans makes them more likely than other racial groups to "assume foreign affairs interpretations and positions that are antithetical to the stance maintained by the U.S. foreign policy establishment"(Clemens 2010: 148).

In contrast to African American foreign policy priorities, U.S. foreign policy has been inherently racist, centered on "white Anglo-Saxon Protestant" (WASP) elites from the ethnic cleansing of the Native American population, territorial expansion into Mexico and Pacific Islands, to the "civilizing mission" to the rest of the world bringing American values of free enterprise and liberal democracy.

> Our foreign policy posture is alarmingly colored by the racial complexions of the countries with which we are involved. We do, indeed, have a bipartisan and racial and ethnic foreign policy; one which operates positively towards countries most similar to us—predominantly white, and another which operates negatively for countries whose inhabitants are predominantly non-white.
>
> (Moss 1970: 80)

U.S. Professor Samuel Huntington laments that towards the end of the last century WASP culture and creed was increasingly affected by multiculturalism, diversity, and multiethnic immigration, which undermined national identity and skewed U.S. foreign policy in new directions favored by diasporic communities (Huntington 1997, 2004a, 2004b). Although Huntington's target group was Hispanics, the same racist attitudes have prevailed to exclude African Americans from foreign policy decision-making processes. Racism has been institutionalized within the foreign policy process by developing and maintaining structures that exclude or subordinate other ideologies or personnel who do not reflect the dominant paradigm.

> Racism is a structural relationship based on the subordination of one racial group by another. Given this perspective the determining features of race relations is not prejudice towards blacks but rather the superior position of whites and the institutions—ideological as well as structural—which maintain it.
>
> (Wellman 1977: 35)

In suggesting that U.S. foreign policy is institutionally racist how is it then possible to explain the emergence of African Americans Andrew Young, Donald McHenry, Colin Powell, Condoleezza Rice, and Susan Rice to key positions withinthe higher echelons of the foreign policymaking establishment as ambassadors to the United Nations, national security advisors and secretaries of state? In the first George W. Bush administration in 2001, the incoming president appointed Colin Powell as the first black U.S. Secretary of State and Condoleezza Rice as the first black National Security Advisor. Rice succeeded Powell during the administration's second term. As leading figures within the administration, they both featured prominently in the policymaking processes that determined America's response to 9/11 and the subsequent War on Terror.

In the Secretary of State Confirmation hearings before the Senate Committee on Foreign Relations race played an insignificant role in both 2001 and 2005, despite the committee comprising only one African American senator in the 2005 hearing—the Junior Senator for Illinois, Barack Obama. Under the de facto chairmanship of Jesse Helms (Joseph Biden having handed over responsibility to Helms) the senator overcame his noted antipathy towards African Americans in politics to welcome Colin Powell's nomination on the grounds of his service record and Republican ideology. Powell pointed to his nomination being a credit to his race and making a rite of passage while four years later Rice, despite Obama's leading, ascribed her nomination to her own abilities and the drive of her parents. Both nominations were confirmed on the same day, with little controversy and only positive comments about race as an issue. Powell believed that his race would lead to George Bush paying attention to Africa during his first term (Allen, Tillery, and Haynes 2010; Lasane 2006). Although Bush certainly paid far more attention to Africa than did his predecessors, Powell's role was somewhat incidental with the Christian right being far more significant in persuading Bush to launch his President's Emergency Plan for AIDs Relief (see Marsden 2008).

Lasane argues that Powell and Rice adopted a "strategic racial affinity," which enabled them to use their racial identity and experiences to "argue and defend Bush administration policies" while not being substantially influenced by that identity (Lasane 2006: 3). Republican and Democratic liberals use the appointments of Powell and Rice as evidence that U.S. foreign policy has embarked on a post-racial era. The Achilles' heel of U.S. Cold War foreign policy was always its treatment of its African American citizens and the ability of Powell and Rice to be appointed to lead the U.S. foreign policy apparatus on merit was hailed as laying this particular problem to rest (Dudziak 2000: Lasane 2006). Ledwidge, by way of contrast, disparages the idea of a "race-neutral meritocratic analysis" because it fails to account for Euro-American institutional hegemony, which excludes African Americans from most positions of influence and limits access to political networks. Rather than having influence to direct U.S. foreign policy in the direction advocated by African American networks in order to enter the foreign policy elite "they must conform to the WASP worldview" (Ledwidge 2009: 158).

The Obama Phenomenon

If Powell and Rice represented a breakthrough for African Americans in terms of foreign policy influence, the election campaign and subsequent victory of Barack Obama should be considered transformational. Obama's autobiography (1995) reveals a search for identity that is reflected in the stories of America's multiethnic population. He was born in Hawaii to a white mother and black Kenyan father, and lived for some of his childhood in Indonesia when his mother remarried an Indonesian Muslim. For the most part, he was brought up by his white grandparents and was conscious of his different skin color. Understandably, Obama's search for identity and belonging was to become an integral part of who he is today and how he came to be president. The journey from biracial child to a man comfortable with his African American ethnicity took Obama through the writings of Malcolm X, Frederick Douglass, and Martin Luther King, and to acceptance as a community organizer and member of Trinity United Church of Christ.

Obama and media commentators sought to play down the question of race within the campaign, and, for the most part, it remained an unspoken issue. The campaign was fought most significantly over which male candidate was deemed better equipped to pull the United States out of economic crisis. Foreign policy figured to the extent to which Obama had made the right call on the Iraq War and the ability of the respective candidates to defend the nation against terrorist attack. Obama promised to provide a new beginning in terms of relations with the Middle East, to share the security burden in terms of blood and treasure with allies. Obama's campaign slogans of "hope" and "change we can believe in" resonated with the electorate without the need to put forward a substantive policy platform. The story of the election turned into the story about Obama and America in the 21st century. Could the country overcome its racist past and elect an African American to the highest office in the land? Was the country prepared to put its divisions behind it and in electing Obama rise to the ideals of its higher self?

Obama presented himself as variously the multiracial candidate or post-racial candidate more concerned with issues confronting "ordinary Americans" than issues surrounding race. He may have had a funny name but that reflected the stories of America's diverse population. His Muslim stepfather and his time spent in Indonesia as a boy were assets to be utilized in undo-ing the damage to America's international relations caused by Bush's wars and the failing Israel–Palestine peace process. As a born-again Christian he had bone fide credentials and had led moves in the Democratic Party to re-engage with religion (Marsden 2011). Obama the metropolitan candidate enjoyed incredible popularity in Europe and Africa and at home, the electorate opted for the charismatic and youthful Obama over the elderly maverick McCain. In the dying days of the campaign, Colin Powell hailed Obama as an internationally "transformational figure" who could restore the tarnished reputation of the American government after eight years of the Bush administration of which he had been an early member (Prosser 2009).

Obama's election victory was historic, but far from heralding a new post-racial era the campaign revealed an underlying racism in the American polity and a clear separation from the ideological outlook of the African

American candidate and African American foreign policy aspirations. Obama presented no threat to WASP foreign policy orthodoxy but rather sought to deliver the same objectives more effectively than his predecessor. Rather than marking a radical departure from all previous presidents because of the color of his skin, Obama represented continuity in ascribing to views of America exceptionalism and its role in the world. Unlike the unsuccessful orthodox African American campaigns of Jesse Jackson, Obama presented no challenge to the existing order and as a good-looking and charismatic figure had an appeal that crossed racial barriers. Senate Leader Harry Reid felt that Obama's race would actually help his candidacy believing that the country was ready to embrace a black candidate, especially a "light-skinned" African American "with no Negro dialect, unless he wanted to have one" (Heilemann and Halperin 2010: 35).

Many republicans, however, were dismayed at the prospect of a non-white president and sought to undermine Obama's credibility as a suitable candidate. Rather than attack him directly on the grounds of his race, opponents found surrogates for racial attacks. Obama was characterized at various stages in the campaign as being unpatriotic, un-American or worse still non-American, a Marxist, a black Christian nationalist, and a Muslim. Obama was presented by his opponents as the Manchurian candidate and decidedly "other"—someone who was not to be trusted. A well-orchestrated smear campaign was greatly assisted by Obama's autobiography and, in the context of presidential elections, unusual name. At the extreme end of the smears was the accusation by some apocalyptic conservative evangelicals that Obama was the anti-Christ even claiming that, if played backwards, the campaign slogan "yes we can" sounded like "thank you Satan." The same group claimed that the Democratic candidate represented the fulfillment of Islamic prophecy that one would rise in the west to lead people to faith in Allah (Obama Antichrist.org 2008).

Republican opponents pointed to his friendship with William Ayres and Bernardine Dohr, founding members of the Weather Underground, as evidence that Obama was a Marxist or at least a fellow traveler (Murdock 2008). Obama's well-documented religious conversion and outreach to evangelical voters starting from the Democratic convention in 2004 was used against him as YouTube clips emerged of his pastor Jeremiah Wright's sermons denouncing U.S. foreign policy and race relations within the United States. Wright and the First Trinity United Church of Christ in Chicago are part of a long tradition of black activism, black Christian nationalism, and black theology of liberation that rejects white interpretations of Christianity in favor of overcoming a sense of racial inferiority and empowering African Americans (Walker and Smithers 2009: 32). The church describes itself thus:

> We are a congregation which is Unashamedly Black and Unapologetically Christian.... Our roots in the Black religious experience and tradition are

deep, lasting and permanent. We are an African people, and remain 'true to our native land', the mother continent, the cradle of civilization. God has superintended our pilgrimage through the days of slavery, the days of segregation, and the long night of racism. It is God who gives us strength to continuously address injustice as a people, and as a congregation. We constantly affirm our trust in God through cultural expression of a Black worship service and ministries which address the black Community.

(Trinity 2011)

Barack Obama was converted in the church and remained a member for 20 years from 1988 until he resigned during the election campaign in a bid to disassociate himself from his friend and pastor Jeremiah Wright when his campaign faced derailment. Obama's opponents played the race card by distinguishing between "good" blacks and the scary ones such as Al Sharpton, Jeremiah Wright, and his friend Louis Farrakhan of the Nation of Islam. Wright's sermons were accused of being anti-American and Obama, having sat in the church for two decades listening to such sermons, was guilty by association. Wright's sermon on "Confusing God and government" delivered on April 13, 2003 contained the following: "'God Bless America.' No, no, no. Not 'God Bless America'; God Damn America!," which was played over and over by news channels led by *Fox News*. Wright's comments were taken out of context and when the sermon is examined it provides a black theological understanding and conceptualization of U.S. foreign policy. Wright's complaint was that, in its foreign policy, America sought to play the part of God and that being human was fallible and it would therefore fail. The congregation needed to place their trust in God who will not fail them:

Military might does not make for peace; war does not make for peace. Occupying somebody else's country doesn't make for peace. Killing those that fought to protect their own homes does not make for peace. Press conferences claiming victory do not make for peace. Regime change, substituting one tyrant for another tyrant with the biggest tyrant pulling the puppet strings of all the tyrants, that does not make for peace! Colonizing a country does not make for peace!

Where Governments lie, God does not lie. Where Governments change, God does not change.

Governments fail. And the United States of America government, when it came to treating her citizens of Indian decent fairly, she failed. She put them on reservations. When it came to treating her citizens of Japanese descent fairly, she failed. She put them in internment prison camps. When it came to treating her citizens of African descent fairly, America failed. She put them in chains. The government put them in slave quarters, put them on auction blocks, put them in cotton fields, put them in inferior schools, put them in substandard housing, put them in scientific experiments, put them in the lowest paying jobs, put them outside the equal protection of the law, kept them out of their racist bastions of higher education and locked them into positions of hopelessness and helplessness. The government gives them the drugs, builds bigger prisons, passes a three-strike law, and then wants us to sing "God Bless America." No, no, no. Not "God Bless America"; God Damn America! That's in the Bible, for killing innocent people. God Damn America for treating her citizen as less than human. God Damn America as long as she keeps trying to act like she is God and she is supreme!

(Wright, 2003)

Obama initially sought to portray Wright as an embarrassing elderly uncle who represented the past whereas Obama represented the future. Racism was a part of U.S. history but he emphasized in his race speech "A More Perfect Union" in Philadelphia on March 18, 2008 that Wright's "mistake" was to portray America as static whereas his campaign had demonstrated that "America can change. That is the true genius of this nation. What we have already achieved gives us hope—the audacity of hope—for what we can and must achieve tomorrow" (Obama 2008). Pundits and academics alike have described the race speech as one of the finest speeches on that subject, although Wright remained unrepentant and accused Obama of saying what was necessary to get elected leading to the candidate's resignation from the church.

If black liberation theology and Wright's sermons opened up the issue of race in the campaign the underlying issue of Obama's American credentials did not go away. Wright's close association with black Muslim leader Louis Farrakhan and the candidate's Kenyan Muslim father and Indonesian Muslim stepfather aroused suspicion that Obama was not, in fact, a Christian but a Muslim, and he would reveal his true allegiance after the election. Television commentators and political opponents tripped over his name to conflate Barack Obama with Barack Osama. His middle name of Hussein was used to emphasize his difference from previous presidents and his opponent. Glen Beck of *Fox News* led a campaign that extended beyond the election, casting doubt on whether Obama had been born in Hawaii, obliging the President three years into his presidency to produce his birth certificate. Obama's boyhood attendance in an Indonesian Muslim school provided further evidence to opponents that the Democratic candidate with the funny name was "other." It was more politically acceptable to be prejudiced against Obama's Muslim pedigree than the color of his skin, especially as the nation was at war with al-Qaeda led by Osama bin Laden and had fought a controversial war with Saddam Hussein in the War on Terror. Muslims are portrayed as suspect communities by media and counterterrorism experts and Barack Hussein Obama was also cast as suspicious.

Far from a post-racial society the Obama campaign reveals that racism is alive and well in the U.S. polity. Despite irrefutable evidence that Obama is neither Muslim nor a foreigner, according to a *Time Magazine*/ABT SRBI survey on August 16–17, 2010, 24 percent of Americans believed that Obama is a Muslim and 43 percent had unfavorable views about Muslims. Although Obama won a clear electoral victory with 52.9 percent of the popular vote to McCain's 47 percent, he only attracted 42 percent of the white vote. In the most racially divisive states, he only received 26 percent of the white vote and the size of his victory, despite the unpopularity of the previous Republican administration and his opponent's inability to articulate a coherent economic strategy, was small (Lewis-Beck, Tien, and Nadeau 2010). Despite racism in the campaign, Obama emerged triumphant as the victorious candidate and promised a new approach to foreign policy that would restore America's international reputation and enable the country to continue leading the world.

Change We Can Believe In

Barack Obama entered office with considerable goodwill around the world after the somewhat chequered presidency of George W. Bush. Favorability ratings towards the United States were at very low levels across the Middle East. Zogby International polling revealed 26 percent of Moroccans had a favorable attitude towards the United States compared with 9 percent of Egyptians, 16 percent of Jordanians, and 13 percent in Saudi Arabia. On taking office, favorability ratings in each country rose to 55 percent in Morocco, 30 percent in Egypt, 25 percent in Jordan, and 41 percent in Saudi Arabia (Zogby 2011). Obama introduced a new spirit of cooperation and respect for other traditions and spoke the language of a common humanity. In his inaugural address, he described the United States as a "nation of Christians and Muslims, Jews and Hindus—and non-believers" and specifically addressed the Muslim majority world:

> To the Muslim world, we seek a new way forward, based on mutual interest and mutual respect. To those leaders around the globe who seek to sow conflict, or blame their society's ills on the West—know that your people will judge you on what you can build, not what you destroy. To those who cling to power through corruption and deceit and the silencing of dissent, know that you are on the wrong side of history; but that we will extend a hand if you are willing to unclench your fist.
>
> (Obama 2009a)

Obama's desire to reach out to Muslim leaders around the world reflected the nature of the foreign policy problems he inherited from his predecessor. America was actively engaged in a war on terror againstal-Qaeda and associated groupings around the world, and still had troops on active service in Iraq and was at war in Afghanistan. The previous administration failed to bring the Israel–Palestinian peace talks to a successful conclusion and the incoming administration was determined to give the peace process the highest priority. Indeed, the final weeks of the Bush presidency witnessed a military assault by the Israeli Defense Forces on Gaza resulting in the death of 1,100 Palestinians in an asymmetric conflict that lasted three weeks. Obama remained silent during the worst violence seen in the region since the 2006 Israeli assault on southern Lebanon. Iran was still pursuing a nuclear program despite U.S.-led sanctions against the regime. The excesses of the War on Terror led to human rights abuses, extraordinary rendition, and torture. Guantanamo Bay still housed hundreds of captives, described by the Bush administration as "enemy combatants," outside of the U.S. legal process. All of which diminished America's international reputation. Obama made clear promises to change perceptions of U.S. foreign policy by committing the U.S. not to use torture, including waterboarding, to close down Guantanamo within a year, to withdraw U.S. combat troops from Iraq and draw down all U.S. troops there by the end of 2011. He declared his intention to defeat al-Qaeda and leave behind a stable Afghanistan after the withdrawal of U.S. forces. No longer would America act unilaterally, expecting allies to follow its lead, but there would be an active consultation process and allies would act in multilateral partnership.

Obama set about pursuing these objectives by actively engaging with leaders in Muslim majority countries. Early in his presidency he visited Turkey and Saudi Arabia and then most spectacularly at Cairo University in June 2009 when he outlined his hopes for a new relationship with countries in the Middle East.

> I've come here to Cairo to seek a new beginning between the United States and based upon the truth that America and Islam are not exclusive and need not be in competition. Instead, they overlap, and share common principles—principles of justice and progress; tolerance and the dignity of all human beings.
>
> (Obama 2009b)

Although mindful of prevailing accusations sustained by the domestic right-wing media about being a Muslim, Obama sought to sow seeds for fruitful relationships in the future with Muslim majority counties facilitated by knowledge of his Kenyan and Indonesian heritage. The Nobel Peace Prize committee was sufficiently impressed with Obama's transformative potential to award him the annual prize at a ceremony in Oslo in December 2009. Obama, who at that stage was arguably the least qualified recipient in the history of the award, was aware of the irony of awarding a peace prize to the commander-in-chief of a nation fighting two wars. At this most historic of occasions Obama used the opportunity to distance himself from his African American lineage and embrace the pragmatic foreign policy position adopted by his white predecessors:

As someone who stands here as a direct consequence of Dr. King's life work, I am living testimony to the moral force of non-violence. I know there's nothing weak—nothing passive—nothing naïve—in the creed and lives of Gandhi and King.

But as a head of state sworn to protect and defend my nation, I cannot be guided by their examples alone. I face the world as it is, and cannot stand idle in the face of threats to the American people. For make no mistake: Evil does exist in the world. A non-violent movement could not have halted Hitler's armies. Negotiations cannot convince al Qaeda's leaders to lay down their arms. To say that force may sometimes be necessary is not a call to cynicism—it is a recognition of history; the imperfections of man and the limits of reason.

(Obama, 2009c)

Anyone Still Believing?

Obama's Nobel Prize speech, as with many of the president's speeches, was an impressive rhetorical feat with the capacity to inspire but delivered very few changes in foreign policy. The expectations brought about by campaign promises and slogans of change and hope were inevitably going to be disappointed in the harsh realities of an economic downturn and a president who is noted for caution and pragmatism. In relation to Israel–Palestine, the President has continued U.S. support for Israel, protecting it in the United Nations Security Council by vetoing critical resolutions following Operation Cast Lead and the storming of a flotilla bound for Gaza. Although Obama enabled both parties to re-start peace talks, he failed to persuade the Israelis to halt settlement building in the occupied territories of the West Bank and East Jerusalem resulting in the collapse of talks. Although critical of Israeli Prime Minister, Benjamin Netanyahu, Obama has, like his predecessor, sought to isolate the radical Palestinian organization, Hamas, from any involvement in the peace process and to apply extraordinary pressure to persuade the Palestine Authority not to seek UN recognition of statehood in September 2011. Rather than representing African American foreign policy positions of support for the Palestinian position, Obama has been more mindful of the strength of the domestic Israel lobby and pursued the same pro-Israeli foreign policy undertaken by every U.S. president since 1967. The Palestine papers released in 2010 revealed the extent of Israel–U.S. cooperation and the impotence of the Palestinian leadership in being able to reach a settlement when realities on the ground enable Israel to gain further land (Palestine Papers 2010).

The Obama administration abandoned the terminology of the War on Terror replacing it with the term "'overseas contingency operations" (Burkeman 2009). Despite the new terminology, the modus operandi remains the same, with targeted assassinations of key personnel and increasing use of drone attacks. Obama has been more successful than Bush in downgrading al-Qaeda's capability, in particular through the execution of Osama bin Laden. Obama was persuaded by the Defense Department and military leaders on the ground to adopt the Petraeus strategy of troop surge and winning over local insurgents deployed in Iraq to the Afghan theatre (Woodward 2010). Obama significantly increased troop numbers while increasing drone and Special Forces attacks in the adjoining Pakistan provinces. The campaign has effectively been extended to incorporate Yemen and Somalia. The distinguished American journalist Bob Woodward has revealed how the president was bounced into a particular course of action over troop increases in Afghanistan, while simultaneously drawing troops down in Iraq, but race does not figure in his narrative. Indeed, had Clinton or McCain been elected, it is difficult to envisage an alternative strategy being adopted.

Two years after Obama promised to close down Guantanamo the camp still houses several hundred prisoners held without charge for over a decade. Orders have been given to end extraordinary rendition and all forms of torture and yet few believe that when conducting counterterrorism operations such ideals are upheld. Despite offering the hand of friendship, there has been little attempt to engage with Iran over the issue of its nuclear program. The previous administration's policy of punitive sanctions and threats has remained while cooperating or coordinating sabotage efforts with Israel on the nuclear program through the assassination of Iranian scientists and introducing the stuxnet computer virus (Jaseb 2011; Williams 2011). In this, there has been little departure from the policy of the previous administration. The policy to withdraw troops from Iraq and hand over responsibility to Iraqi government forces remains on track. As with the previous administration, however, a longer term presence in terms of some form of military base to protect U.S. interests in the region remains an objective despite agreements requiring all U.S. troops to leave the country by the end of 2011.

The Arab Spring of 2011 has brought about a significant shift in U.S. policy to differentiate the Obama administration from its predecessors, although this again represents a pragmatic rather than an ideological shift. Where the Bush administration encouraged democracy promotion while supporting despots to protect U.S. oil and other strategic and security interests, after initially continuing the policy, the Obama administration had to respond to the popular democratic awakenings across the region. While initially supporting allies in the region including despotic leaders in Tunisia, Saudi Arabia, Bahrain, Egypt, Yemen, and Algeria, who pointed to threats of domestic Islamists seizing power, Obama belatedly supported Mubarak's stepping down from office in Egypt and the overthrow of the Gaddafi regime in Libya achieved with air support from NATO, including U.S. drones. In a rapidly changing environment in which protestors have taken to the streets seeking democracy, the balance of power has shifted away from America's traditional allies and the Americans having been peripheral to events have been obliged to reconfigure their strategy and establish good relations with whoever looks the most likely winners in very different national struggles.

As an African American president, Obama, like Colin Powell, would have been expected to spend greater energy on sub-Saharan African issues. As the sonof a Kenyan, Obama enjoyed celebrity status on the continent since being elected as Junior Senator for Illinois in 2004. A Ghanaian journalist on the eve of the president's first visit to Africa contextualized the visit. "[T]he election of the first black president, a man with a Kenyan father who came on a scholarship in Hawaii, has been celebrated as a kind of second coming throughout Africa. The symbolism is obvious. President Obama arrives with enormous expectations that he will do more and care more" (Washington 2010: 4).

In his first speech in Africa, rather than launching a new initiative or seeking to develop closer relations with African countries, he used the opportunity to urge Africa to take responsibility for its own economic problems through good governance and democracy. The continent should work towards the peaceful resolution of conflict and, in return, the United States would offer some food assistance and the continuation of President Bush's PEPFAR initiative. Rather than embracing a distinctive African American approach to Africa, Obama produced an endorsement of neoliberal solutions to African problems (Washington 2010: 8). The enormous expectations of Africans have not been realized.

The Obama presidency has disappointed many as unrealistic expectations were raised based on a catch-all message of hope and believable change. African Americans joined with others in projecting their own image on the green screen presented by the metropolitan candidate. What they failed to appreciate is that Obama convinced the Democratic establishment and its corporate sponsors that he was reliable and would not depart from the white Anglo-Saxon orthodoxy that persisted in domestic and foreign policy. The structure of the foreign policy decision-making process limits the ability of an agency to institute change, even when that agency is the president. Obama was different to look at and had an unorthodox background but his neoliberal message was the same as that of his white predecessors and his foreign policy premised on maintaining America's status as the most powerful nation in the world intent on promoting American values.

The surge in goodwill towards the United States dissipated as the hoped for change in foreign policy failed to materialize. By the middle of 2011 during the Arab Spring, favorable attitudes towards the United States declined in Morocco to 12 percent, Egypt to just 5 percent, Jordan to 10 percent, and 30 percent in Saudi Arabia (Zogby 2011). In Pakistan and Turkey, key allies in the War on Terror and the latter a member of NATO, favorable attitudes to the United States were shared by only 12 and 10 percent of the population respectively (Pew, 2011). In the United States, presidential approval ratings by September 2011 had fallen from 69 percent to a mere 42 percent, with a 49 percent disapproval rating (Gallup 2011). Dissatisfaction centered on Obama's policies rather than his race.

Conclusion

Barack Obama encountered a great deal of racism during the 2008 election campaign, often disguised as enquiries or challenges about his religion, place of birth, political beliefs, schooling, and friendships with Marxist revolutionaries and black Christian nationalists. Following the attacks of 9/11, Islamophobia has never been far below the surface as the media, neo-conservatives, and conservative evangelicals continue to portray Muslims as being a suspect community and potential supporters of Islamist terror. The name Barack Hussein Obama sounded similar to the Bush administration's prime enemies Osama bin Laden and Saddam Hussein. Obama's political opponents could not resist positioning him as "other," not a "real" American. And yet Obama was able to overcome these obstacles, and residual racism, to win the election by seeking to avoid race as an issue and convincing Democrat apparatchiks and voters that he was dependable, and represented continuity in a Democratic tradition, rather than someone who would use the opportunity of incumbency to overturn racial injustice at home and abroad. In foreign policy terms, Obama had demonstrated during his short time on the Senate foreign relations committee that he was not about to rock the boat. In office, he surrounded himself with white foreign policy specialists, largely from the Clinton administration, representing continuity rather than change. Traditional African American foreign policy concerns including Africa and Palestine were pursued in much the same way as that of the previous administration and not as the African American foreign affairs networks would wish.

The ability of any president to affect U.S. foreign policy is limited by the constraints imposed by foreign policy structures. In terms of structure and agency, U.S. foreign policy has been premised on WASP structures and agents with agents from different racial and religious backgrounds being assimilatedwithin the dominant organization structure. Contingency provides agents with the opportunity to substantively affect structures and policy but the emerging contingency of the Arab Spring caught the president off guard and unable to make the necessary adjustments from supporting despots, who protected U.S. geostrategic interests in the region, to the Arab street seeking the democracy encouraged by successive US administrations. Obama does not represent the dawn of a new post-racial era because, in order to be selected and receive the billion dollars necessary to win the presidential election, he had to convince supporters and donors that he represented no challenge to the existing white order. Obama, as an African American brought up by white grandparents, was never fully of the African American community and paid little attention to African American foreign policy positions, conducting his foreign policy as commander-in-chief with the same values and power maximizing objectives as successive white presidents. Race remains an issue in both U.S. domestic and foreign policy—although Obama killed Osama, his political opponents have no intention of calling the whole thing off—and race and Islamophobia remain part of the American polity and foreign policy continues to be white not post-racial.

Bibliography

Allen, J., Tillery, A., and Haynes, W. "The making of African American foreign policy makers: Senate confirmation hearings on Secretaries of State Colin Powell and Condoleezza Rice," in Clemens, M., ed. *African Americans and Global Affairs: contemporary perspectives* (Lebanon, NH: Northeastern University Press, 2010).

Burkeman, O. "Obama administration says goodbye to 'war on terror'," *Guardian*, March 25, 2009, www.guardian.co.uk/world/2009/mar/25/obama-war-terror-overseas-contingency-operations>

Clemens, M., ed. *African Americans and Global Affairs: contemporary perspectives* (Lebanon, NH: Northeastern University Press, 2010).

Copsey, R. *The Congressional Black Caucus and Foreign Policy 1971–2002* (Hauppauge, NY: Novinka Books, 2003).

Dudziak, M. *Cold War Civil Rights: race and the image of American democracy* (Princeton, NJ: Princeton University Press, 2000).

Gallup, "Presidential approval ratings," *Gallup*, www.gallup.com/poll/113980/Gallup-Barack-Obama-Job-Approval.aspx

Heilemann, J. and Halperin, M. *Game Change: Obama and the Clintons, McCain and Palin, and the race of a lifetime* (New York: HarperCollins, 2010).

Huntington, S. "The erosion of America national interests," *Foreign Affairs* 1997: 76, 5, 28–49.

Huntington, S. "The Hispanic challenge," *Foreign Policy* 2004a, www.civicamericana.org/HispanicChallenge.pdf

Huntington, S. *Who We Are: the challenge to American national identity.* (New York: Simon & Schuster, 2004b).

Jaseb, H. "Iranian nuclear scientist killed in Tehran," *Reuters News Agency*, July 23, 2011, www.reuters.com/article/2011/07/23/us-iran-assassination-idUSTRE76M1WI 20110723

Krenn, M., ed. *Race and US Foreign Policy from the Colonial Period to the Present: a collection of essays* (New York: Garland Publishing, 1988).

Krenn, M. *Black Diplomacy: African Americans and the State Department, 1945–1969* (Armonk, NY: M.E. Sharpe, 1999).

Lasane, C. *Colin Powell and Condoleezza Rice: foreign policy, race and the new American century* (Westport, CN: Praeger, 2006).

Ledwidge, M. "Race, African-Americans and US foreign policy," in Parmar, I., Millar, L.B., and Ledwidge, M., eds. *New Directions in US Foreign Policy* (Abingdon, UK: Routledge, 2009).

Ledwidge, M. *Race and US Foreign Policy: the African-American foreign affairs network* (Abingdonk, UK: Routledge, 2011).

Lewis-Beck, M., Tien, C., and Nadeau, R. "Obama's missed landslide: a racial cost?," *PS: Political Science & Politics* January, 2010: 69–76.

Marsden, L. *For God's Sake: the Christian right and US foreign policy* (London: Zed Books, 2008).

Marsden, L. "Religion, identity and American power in the age of Obama," *International Politics* 2011: 48, 326–43.

Moss, J. "The civil rights movement and American foreign policy," in Shepherd, G., ed. *Racial Influences on America Foreign Policy* (New York: Basic Books, 1970).

Murdock, D. "Obama's weathermen pals should worry you," *National Review Online*, October 13, 2008, www.nationalreview.com/articles/225952/obamas-weathermen-pals-should-worry-you/deroy-murdock#

Obama Antichrist.org. "Obama antichrist: the evidence," 2008, www.obamaantichr ist.org/category/obama-antichrist-evidence

Obama, B. *Dreams from my Father: a story of race and inheritance* (New York: Three River Press, 1995).

Obama, B. "A more perfect union," speech given in Philadelphia on March 18, 2008, www.huffingtonpost.com/2008/03/18/obama-race-speech-read-th_n_92077.html

Obama, B. "Inaugural address," January 20, 2009a, ObamaSpeeches.com, http://obamaspeeches.com/

Obama, B. "Cairo speech," delivered Cairo University, *New York Times*, June 4, 2009b, www.nytimes.com/2009/06/04/us/politics/04obama.text.html?pagewanted=all

Obama, B. "Nobel Prize acceptance speech," delivered Oslo, MSBNC, December 10, 2009c, www.msnbc.msn.com/id/34360743/ns/politics-white_house/t/full-text-obamas-nobel-peace-prize-speech/

Palestine Papers. "Palestine papers," at al Jazeera, 2010, http://english.aljazeera.net/palestinepapers/

Pew Forum. "Pew Global Attitudes Project report," *Pew Forum*, 2011, www.pew-global.org

Plummer, B. *Rising Wind: black Americans and U.S. foreign affairs 1935–1960* (Chapel Hill: University of North Carolina Press, 1996).

Prosser, M. "Obama's culturally transformational identities and accommodations toward the Middle East and Islam," *Journal of Middle Eastern and Islamic Studies (in Asia)* 2009: 3, 3, 1–13.

Trinity United Church of Christ. "About us," Trinity United Church of Christ Chicago, 2011, www.trinitychicago.org/index.php?option=com_content&task=view& id = 12& Itemid = 27

Walker, C. and Smithers, G. *The Preacher and the Politician: Jeremiah Wright, Barack Obama, and race in America* (Charlottesville, VA: University of Virginia Press, 2009).

Washington, R. "Obama and Africa," in Cunnigen, D. and Bruce, M., eds. *Race in the age of Obama* (Bingley, UK: Emerald Publishing Ltd, 2010).

Wellman, D.T. *Portraits of White Racism* (New York: Cambridge University Press, 1977).

Williams, C. "Stuxnet virus: U.S. refuses to deny involvement," *Daily Telegraph*, May 27, 2011, www.telegraph.co.uk/technology/news/8541587/Stuxnet-virus-US-refuses-to-deny-involvement.html

Woodward, B. *Obama's Wars* (New York: Simon & Schuster, 2010).

Wright, J. "Confusing God with government," sermon delivered by Senior Pastor Jeremiah Wright, Trinity United Church of Christ Chicago, 2003, www.blackpast.org/?q=2008-rev-jeremiah-wright-confusing-god-and-government

Zogby, J. "Arab attitudes, 2011," poll conducted by Zogby International for Arab American Institute Foundation, 2011, http://aai.3cdn.net/5d2b8344e3b3b7ef19_xkm6ba4r9.pdf

10 The Color of Obama's World

Race and Diplomacy during the Barack Obama Administration

Michael L. Krenn

The election of Barack Obama as President of the United States in 2008 was a landmark in the often disturbing history of racism and bigotry in America. Many hoped that his election would galvanize the nation into not only facing its racist past, but recognizing that racism was still alive and working its destructive powers in our society. Many went so far as to proclaim that his election marked the beginning of a "post-racial" era in the history of the United States. Yet, at home and abroad, President Obama has often seemed reluctant to delve into the uglier side of American racism, preferring to address incidents and issues involving race with comments about "teachable moments" and the holding of "beer summits."

This chapter examines the Obama administration's attitudes toward race and American foreign policy by first looking at the initial optimism around the globe and in the United States that Obama's election would mean a substantially different relationship between America and the world. By 2012, however, most of that early enthusiasm was dead or dying and there were scathing criticisms of Obama's diplomacy. Underlying many of these criticisms were deep resentments that had their historical basis in centuries of exploitation and brutality at the hands of white Europeans and Americans who embraced the theory of white racial supremacy. This chapter briefly examines the record of U.S. racism and its foreign relations and also explains how Obama tends to minimize, ignore, or misinterpret that history. In an attempt to close the circle, it will also look at the contemporary domestic implications that may arise from the American nation's continuing reluctance to fully confront its history of racism and the impact of that on its relations with the world. In doing so, I hope to locate the Obama administration's approach toward the international implications of race in an historical framework in which we may examine the divergences and continuities with the past. And this will allow us to address the central and crucial question: Does the foreign policy of the Obama presidency reflect a break with the racist past, as the stirring rhetoric in his March 2008 "A More Perfect Union" speech suggested it might? Or has such optimism been misplaced and the hopes for a "post-racial" America dashed against the seemingly adamantine shoals of American racism and discrimination?

In the wake of Barack Obama's victory in the 2008 presidential election, more than one observer declared that America had now entered the "post-racial" phase of its history.[1] The basic premise of the argument was that with the election of America's first black president, the old racial issues that previously divided the nation had been put aside. No one, of course, suggested that every vestige of racism had been eradicated from American society, but the standard interpretation of Obama's election was that no longer would racism be a matter of national concern. The old civil rights movement, once venerated, was brought into question with some writers suggesting that the protests, angry speeches, and constant referrals to the pernicious effects of racism on American society had, in some ways, set back the movement for racial equality. With the rise of Obama to national prominence, the nation could now talk about race in a less confrontational, more rational way. Even before taking office, the rise of Barack Obama during the presidential campaign of 2008 was being heralded as the dawning of a post-racial society in the United States. Journalist Daniel Schorr declared: "The post-racial era, as embodied by Obama, is the era where civil rights veterans of the past century are consigned to history and Americans begin to make race-free judgments on who should lead them." Once Obama secured victory in the November 2008 presidential election, the pundits sounded even louder, arguing that "race matters much less than it used to, that the boundaries of race have been overcome, that racism is no longer a big problem." Professor John McWhorter put it even more bluntly when he announced that, "Racism is not Black people's main problem anymore. To say that is like saying the earth is flat."[2]

To be sure, there were those who also sounded a note of caution. Even Schorr admitted that: "It may be too early to speak of a generation of colorblind voters, but maybe color blurred?" Fellow journalist Deborah Mathis was more skeptical about the presumed end of American racism when she wrote: "One leap forward—even a gigantic leap like the emergence of the first black president—does not a cure make for this universally human, but quintessentially American, disease." According to Professor Christopher Metzler of Georgetown University, the election of Obama was indeed a "sea change," but needed to be put into historical perspective. After all, he argued, the 1954 Supreme Court decision in the case of *Brown v. Board of Education* was also heralded as a sea change. Yet, decades later large numbers of American schools remained as segregated as ever. The real issue, Metzler argued, was "not whether race exists; it is whether it matters," and Americans needed to push beyond the media rhetoric about a post-racial society and discuss how race continues to matter and why.[3]

A few months before his election, in March 2008, Obama discovered just how much race continued to matter when a public relations storm erupted over comments made by Reverend Jeremiah Wright, the pastor at the soon-to-be-president's Chicago church. In a series of sermons given in early 2008, Reverend Wright repeatedly used the term "God damn America" to criticize domestic actions by the U.S. government, and then went on to suggest that

America was at least partially to blame for the 9/11 attacks, asserting that: "America's chickens are coming home to roost." The media frenzy put Obama on the defensive and the nation watched and waited for his response. This came on March 18, 2008 in what turned out to be Obama's most passionate speech on the topic of race in America. He decried much of what Reverend Wright said as "not only wrong but divisive." Yet, he also tried to explain the basis of Wright's anger by admitting that race was still a problem in the "America I love." Very quickly, however, Obama changed gear and talked about moving "beyond some of our old racial wounds," arguing that black Americans needed to embrace the "burdens of our past without becoming victims of our present." He noted the tremendous progress that had been made and then, having buried most of America's racial problems in the distant past, he moved on to discuss the other issues confronting America: "war, the economy, jobs."[4]

Just months after taking office in January 2009, President Obama was faced with yet another occasion to discuss with his fellow Americans how and why race still matters. On July 16, 2009 Harvard professor Henry Louis Gates was arrested for disorderly conduct outside his home in Cambridge. Gates, an African American, charged that his arrest was racially motivated and the incident soon became a cause célèbre for civil rights activists. President Obama originally expressed his disappointment at the police handling of the matter, then backtracked soon after. Finally, the President did an extraordinary thing: He invited Gates and the arresting officer to join him over beers at the White House and discuss the event. It was in some ways a touching gesture and it certainly made a great photo opportunity. But, for many, it was also disappointing. Certainly Obama did not need to talk to Gates about racism; and certainly the policeman was already embarrassed enough about what he had done. The president needed to use the opportunity to talk to the American people about racism—and he didn't. In many ways, this lack of desire to confront the issue of racism has also seeped into the foreign affairs side of the Obama presidency. The president simply seems unwilling to pick up the issue of race, perhaps preferring to believe—as many Americans do— that it is something from the past that no one wants to dig up once again.

None of this was particularly new for Obama. He had been making the same points for years, perhaps most famously in his March 2007 speech in Selma, Alabama. He paid homage to the struggles of the past and to the violence that scarred Selma in the 1960s. He told his audience:

> [W]e are in the presence today of a lot of Moseses. We're in the presence today of giants whose shoulders we stand on, people who battled, not just on behalf of African Americans but on behalf of all of America; that battled for America's soul, that shed blood, that endured taunts and torment and in some cases gave the full measure of their devotion.

Yet, all of his discussion of the civil rights struggle had the decided tone of a history lesson, as if somehow the civil rights movement—as important as it might have been—was now something for careful and dispassionate study. After all, Obama optimistically told his listeners, those "Moses" of Selma and 100 other civil rights battles of the 1950s and 1960s, "took us 90 percent of the way there. We still got that 10 percent in order to cross over to the other side."[5]

As reluctant as Obama has been to directly confront the issue of race in America, his nearly absolute silence on the international implications of race is perhaps equally troubling. In his famous March 2008 speech on race, Obama barely addressed Reverend Wright's most controversial statements concerning America's foreign policy. In his long rebuttal to Wright's views, Obama declared that those opinions presented a "profoundly distorted view of this country ... a view that sees the conflicts in the Middle East as rooted primarily in the actions of stalwart allies like Israel, instead of emanating from the perverse and hateful ideologies of radical Islam." As he began to list the problems still facing America in the battle against racism, any mention of how that battle has been translated to the international realm disappeared.[6]

Barack Obama's foreign policy was supposed to bring in an era of new beginnings, as it was with his domestic policies. For many of his supporters, simply the fact that a man of African American heritage would be the spokesperson for the United States on the international scene was enough to suggest that walls would come tumbling down and that America could once again take its place as a respected world leader. Particularly in the underdeveloped world in Africa, Asia, and Latin America, the idea that a black man had risen to the position of president of the most powerful nation on earth would render old suspicions about America's intentions and integrity moot. During his presidential campaign in 2008, Obama set the tone of what many hoped would be a sea change in America's relationship with the rest of the world. Speaking in Berlin, he began with an obvious, but important, point: "'I know that I don't look like the Americans who've previously spoken in this great city." He went on to call for closer cooperation between Europe and America and then declared that the "walls" separating humanity must fall. These included those standing "between races and tribes; natives and immigrants; Christian and Muslim and Jew"; all were obstacles that "we must tear down." He then surprised his audience by making an admission that Americans as a whole had been loathe to utter:

> I know that my country has not perfected itself. At times, we've struggled to keep the promise of liberty and equality for all of our people. We've made our share of mistakes, and there are times when our actions around the world have not lived up to our best intentions.

And just a few months after taking office, President Obama maintained those themes in a series of speeches in Europe, admitting that America had sometimes been "arrogant ... dismissive, even derisive." Critics back home labeled Obama's speeches part of his "apology tour," but his admirers (and even some Europeans) felt a new sense of optimism.[7]

That early momentum carried over into Obama's visits to Africa, Asia, and Latin America. Perhaps not surprisingly, many of the highest hopes for a new relationship with America following Obama's ascension to the presidency were expressed in Africa. And when Obama made Ghana the site of one of his first official foreign visits as president the expectations skyrocketed. The President's speech in Accra on July 11, 2009 stressed the importance of Africa to the world community: "I have come here, to Ghana, for a simple reason: the 21st century will be shaped by what happens not just in Rome or Moscow or Washington, but by what happens in Accra as well." While noting the need for a better "partnership" with Africa, Obama also made it clear that "Africa's future is up to Africans." He then proceeded to call on all African nations to respect the democratic process and strive for what he believed was the key ingredient for African prosperity and peace: "good governance." Of course, presidents prior to Obama had often spouted the same rhetoric about partnerships, democracy, and the need for African nations to get their own houses in order. But many people sensed the difference this time around. Kenyan journalist Salim Amin best captured this feeling when he wrote: "For the first time ever an American president can talk tough to African leaders and not be accused of being racist, and not be accused of being imperialist, colonialist."[8]

Expectations were somewhat more subdued in Latin America, which was hardly surprising considering the long and often adversarial relationship with the United States. As one scholar noted: "Barack Obama's rise to the U.S. presidency has left most Latin Americans suspended between skepticism and hope." The new president tried to assuage the skepticism at the Fifth Summit of the Americas in April 2009. During his address to the attendees, Obama declared that: "I know that promises of partnership have gone unfulfilled in the past, and that trust has to be earned over time. While the United States has done much to promote peace and prosperity in the hemisphere, we have at times been disengaged, and at times we sought to dictate our terms. But I pledge to you that we seek an equal partnership." Two years later he traveled to Chile, site of one of the more egregious examples of U.S. interference in Latin America. Here, he attempted to accentuate what he referred to as the "shared values" and "common history" of the two regions, such as the battles to "expand our nations' promise to all people—men and women, white, black, and brown."[9]

For the Asian audience, Obama began by stressing his personal ties to the region: born in Hawaii and raised for much of his youth in Indonesia. As with his visits to Africa and Latin America he also focused on the deep connections between Asia and the United States—what he called "common values" during a speech in Japan in November 2009. Both Japan and America, President Obama announced, shared

> a belief in the democratic right of free people to choose their own leaders and realize their own dreams; a belief that made possible the

election of both Prime Minister Hatoyama and myself on the promise of change. And together, we are committed to providing a new generation of leadership for our people and our alliance.[10]

Despite all the promising rhetoric, by 2012 American policy toward Africa, Asia, and Latin America seemed to have changed very little from the patterns of the past. Obama's policies toward Africa have received the heaviest amount of criticism, perhaps due, in part, to the fact that expectations were so high. Nearly three years after the President's stirring speech in Ghana one African observer expressed the feelings of many when he said: "Wonderful words, but very much unfilled. Those words have to be lived in terms of U.S. foreign policy and we are still waiting for them to be realized." Instead of a new spirit of cooperation, actual policy toward Africa remained relatively unchanged with "too much attention ... placed on U.S. military aid in resource rich countries, without regard to a government's record or how elections are conducted." One journalist summed up the prevailing sense of disappointment when she declared that: "[M]uch of U.S. policy toward Africa remains the same as it was under George W. Bush's administration." Obama's Latin American policy engendered even more frustration over the lack of real and positive change. A *Time* report concluded that: "[W]hen it comes to U.S. policy in Latin America ... it's often hard to tell if George W. Bush isn't still president." It went on to argue that Obama had "ceded Latin American strategy to right-wing Cold Warriors." Another commentator suggested that Obama was missing an important "teachable moment" in terms of U.S. relations with Latin America. But instead of taking advantage of the early positive reception to the new president, the Obama administration had instead blundered into Honduran politics, acted to increase its military presence in Colombia (ostensibly to fight drug trafficking), and steadfastly maintained the nearly 50-year-old (and resoundingly ineffective) trade embargo against Cuba.[11]

For Asia, the Obama administration created an initial surge of optimism followed by the announcement of a "pivot" of U.S. policy toward the region encompassing newer and stronger economic and political relations between the United States and the nations of the Far East. As a Congressional Research Service report in 2012 revealed, however, the "new" approach was simply more of the same under the guise of a catchy new word. As the report concluded, the "pivot" was hardly an earth-shattering change:

The Obama Administration follows a long line of U.S. governments that, since the end of World War II, has sought to underpin stability and security in the Asia-Pacific by maintaining a large troop presence in East Asia and by involving the United States in most major diplomatic developments in the region.

Indeed, despite Obama's talk about mutual interests in building democracies and flourishing economies aside, the "pivot" basically relied on what has historically been the most important tool in dealing with non-European nations:

> The most high-profile and concrete elements of the Administration's announced 'rebalancing' toward the Asia-Pacific have come in the military realm ... President Obama, Secretary of Defense Leon Panetta and other Administration officials have stated that, notwithstanding reductions in planned levels of U.S. defense spending ... the United States intends to maintain and strengthen its military presence in the region.[12]

What can account for such a dramatic turn of events? What began in 2008–09 with Obama's promises of a new American relationship with the world, particularly the world's nations of color, ended in frustration, disappointment, recrimination, and a distinct feeling that little had changed with the election of America's first African American president. There are many factors that might have had an impact on what eventually became Obama's foreign policy. The dramatic economic downturn in America certainly heightened interests in developing (and protecting) U.S. markets overseas. The surging Chinese nation might have raised fears of a new (but still communist) enemy of the United States. Turmoil and drugs might have been seen as the most immediate problem facing U.S. policy toward Latin America.

And yet, American foreign policy under a particular American president—even the first black president—never occurs in a vacuum. For all the talk of change that characterizes the start of every U.S. president's administration, there are always lines of continuity into which the nation's diplomacy also must fit. There are treaties, trade agreements, resolutions, military necessities, alliances, enemies, wars, and a bewildering array of political, economic, and military goals and challenges that confront every president when they enter office. So many of these things, however, are relatively transitory. Treaties, agreements, and resolutions are broken or forgotten; military necessities evolve, as enemies become allies and vice versa. Less apparent, but just as powerful, are the ideological threads that run through America's foreign policy that form the "mental maps" that overlay the geopolitical maps in the White House briefing rooms and Pentagon war rooms. Historian Michael Hunt defines ideology as "an interrelated set of convictions or assumptions that reduces the complexities of a particular slice of reality to easily comprehensible terms and suggests appropriate ways of dealing with that reality." Hunt does admit that these ideological constructs do evolve over time to accommodate the changes in America and the world. However, some ideological threads are stronger than others and, in a strange and sometimes frightening way, force the changing world to accommodate to meet the needs of the particular ideological pressure.[13]

One of the most powerful of these ideological lenses, and certainly the most frightening, through which America views the world, is racism. While many Americans are aware of the historical examples of America's dealings with people of color—the slaughter and concentration of the Native American population throughout the 19th and early 20th centuries, and the enslavement of millions of African natives to serve the demands of both the cotton-growing plantations of the South and the textile mills of the North prior to the Civil War—and have seen the stirring documentaries about the civil rights movement that swept through the United States in the post-World War II period, few are aware of the ways in which this American racism also worked its way into the nation's relations with the people of color around the world.

There is no need here to try to summarize the history of race and U.S. foreign affairs. A substantial literature on the topic has appeared in the last three decades or so, making new and exciting contributions to the history of U.S. diplomacy.[14] Unfortunately, a significant part of Obama's problem in shaping his new foreign policy is that he has been reluctant to address both that history and the continuing impact of race and racism in the realm of international affairs. Perhaps he hopes, as he seems to in dealing with the domestic issue of race and civil rights, that his election signifies not simply a post-racial America, but a post-racial world. After all, if 90 percent of the battle against bigotry and racism at home has been won then the same must surely hold true for the foreign realm. If this is, indeed, the President's thinking on the matter then he is overlooking two critical aspects. First, unlike at home where leaders such as Martin Luther King, Jesse Jackson, and Walter White served to help lead the nation to the promised land of racial harmony, no such "Moseses" ever had the power or the inclination to simultaneously break down the deadly mixture of racism, imperialism, and exploitation that has been one of the saddest and most regrettable aspects of America's foreign policy since the nation's inception. Isolated voices, such as W.E.B. Du Bois tried to raise the alarm, and African American newspapers and magazines during the 1940s and 1950s devoted articles here and there about particular foreign policy issues where race was an obvious factor: South Africa's brutal apartheid system or America's support of continued European colonialism, for example. And, as isolated voices often are, these arguments and criticisms went virtually unheard by the American foreign policy bureaucracy. Second, Obama's failure to directly face the history of American racism leads him again and again to some serious misinterpretations and misunderstandings about race and U.S diplomacy. As the following evaluations of Obama's policies toward Africa, Latin America, and Asia indicate, that failure virtually insures that old wounds will remain open and that new opportunities for closer relations with people of color around the world will continue to take place in an atmosphere that is anything but post-racial.

Obama is certainly no racist and his personal writings seemed to reveal an understanding of the impact of colonialism and imperialism. In his poignant book, *Dreams from my Father*, Obama wrote about a train ride in Kenya and produced the following beautiful and powerful passage that illuminated the two sides of the colonial coin:

> It seemed like ancient history. And yet I know that 1895, the year that the first beams were laid, had also been the year of my grandfather's birth. It was the lands of that same man, Hussein Onyango, to which we were now traveling. The thought made the history of the train come alive for me, and I tried to imagine the sensations some nameless British officer might have felt on the train's maiden voyage, as he sat in his gas-lit compartment and looked out over miles of receding bush. Would he have felt a sense of triumph, a confidence that the guiding light of Western civilization had finally penetrated the African darkness? Or did he feel a sense of foreboding, a sudden realization that the entire enter-prise was an act of folly, that this land and its people would outlast imperial dreams? I tried to imagine the African on the other side of the glass window, watching this snake of steel and black smoke passing his village for the first time. Would he have looked at this train with envy, imagining himself one day sitting in the car where the Englishman sat, the load of his days somehow eased? Or would he have shuddered with visions of ruin and war?[15]

Yet, in his 2009 speech in Ghana, Obama seemed quick to consign European imperialism in Africa to the dustbin of history:

> It is easy to point fingers, and to pin the blame for these problems on others. Yes, a colonial map that made little sense bred conflict, and the West has often approached Africa as a patron, rather than a partner. But the West is not responsible for the destruction of the Zimbabwean economy over the last decade, or wars in which children are enlisted as combatants. In my father's life, it was partly tribalism and patronage in an indepen-dent Kenya that for a long stretch derailed his career, and we know that this kind of corruption is a daily fact of life for far too many.[16]

Obama grasped only a portion of that sad colonial history of Africa. He missed one of those "teachable moments" by leaving race out of the ques-tion, merely noting that the West has treated Africa as a "patron." True enough, but it hardly suffices to explain the often brutal racism exhibited by the West—and America in particular—in its dealings with Africa.

For much of the nation's history, the United States virtually ignored the existence of Africa, save as a source for slaves in the early 19th century or as a setting for tales of an exotic land full of danger, superstition, cruelty, and lethal natives in the late 19th and early 20th centuries. This lack of official attention, however, did not forestall the American public from creating clearly racist stereotypes of the peoples of Africa. Fed by a steady stream of travelers' accounts and Tarzan stories, Americans around the turn of the

20th century learned of the blood-curdling cannibalism, horrific human sacrifices, and other inhuman practices of the black inhabitants of what came to be known as the Dark Continent. Most of Africa was at that time carved into colonial enclaves by the British, French, Germans, and other European imperialists. And for most Americans, that was probably as it should be. Theodore Roosevelt, following his excursions into Africa, proclaimed the black civilizations he encountered to be stuck somewhere back in the prehistoric era and obviously needed the help of their white conquerors in order to achieve even minimal progress.[17]

World War II and the Cold War changed the American strategic interest in Africa, but made no appreciable impact on American perceptions of the continent's inhabitants. Faced with a rising tide of revolution against the old colonial regimes on one side and the threat of communist political gains on the other, U.S. policymakers could not shake their old images of the Africans as uncivilized and virtually helpless when it came to self-government and economic development. Independence for the former colonies, if discussed at all, was usually done so in torturously labored language about the dangers of "premature independence" and the necessity for a slow but sure (with the emphasis on slow) "evolutionary development" of the African nations.

When the Africans obstinately refused to heed U.S. suggestions for how they should determine their own futures, American policymakers clung to the only example of real development on the continent: the white regime of South Africa. The apartheid system in South Africa, which reduced the majority black population of the nation to less than second-class citizenship through a labyrinth of laws designed to promote strict and unbending racial segregation, came in for heated international denunciations throughout the Cold War years. African American civil rights leaders, politicians, and newspapers and magazines were especially critical of the brutal South African government— and the lack of any substantial reaction from the U.S. government.

Aside from occasional slaps on the wrist via withholding economic or military assistance, American presidents and diplomats maintained a stately silence on the issue of apartheid. After all, more than one official noted, those who live in glass houses (built on the firm foundation of Jim Crow) should not throw diplomatic stones. By the 1960s and 1970s the U.S. government threw out all pretense and began the famous Nixon–Kissinger "tilt" toward the white South African government. It was hardly surprising. National Security Council meetings often erupted in riotous laughter when African issues came on the agenda amid jokes about "apes" and the sounds of tom-toms. As President Nixon himself so eloquently put it when discussing Africa with his national security advisor Henry Kissinger: "Henry, let's leave the niggers to Bill [Secretary of State William Rogers] and we'll take care of the rest of the world." This was the ugly racial background that Obama glossed over with talk about how the West often treated Africa as a patron. The humiliating and vicious racial stereotypes, deep reservations about Africans' abilities to govern themselves, and a legacy of support for a brutally oppressive white-minority government in South Africa bespeaks more than a simple case of "patronizing" the African people. It is symptomatic of considering Africa and its peoples utilizing a hierarchy of race in which whites occupy the top rungs while blacks are consigned to the lower levels of the ladder.[18]

In terms of his policy toward Latin America, Obama has consistently stressed the "common history" and "shared values" of the United States and its neighbors to the south. As with his proclamations about Africa and colonialism, Obama was partially correct. The two regions do share much: A history of having started out as European colonial outposts and their revolutions against British, French, Spanish, and Portuguese imperialists. Yet, he has also tended to overstate that common heritage. In his 2008 speech in Berlin, he waxed eloquent about the American adherence to the unity of mankind: "Our allegiance has never been to any particular tribe or kingdom—indeed, every language is spoken in our country; every culture has left its imprint on ours; every point of view is represented in our public squares." Once again, Obama missed an opportunity for one of his famous "teachable moments." For if he had honestly reviewed his nation's history he would surely have found that from the very beginning white Americans had developed a strong and powerful allegiance to a "tribe": the Anglo-Saxons.[19]

The history of race and America's foreign relations go back to the nation's very beginnings—and even beyond—when stories of the Anglo-Saxon heritage of the British people circulated widely among politicians, theologians, and scientists. The Anglo-Saxons, so the mythology went, were a race unto themselves: fiercely independent, dedicated to the ideals of democratic rule, and (perhaps most important) unwilling to mix with other, different, people. Migrating from the forests of what is present-day Germany, they swept westward, finally ending up in Britain. But their progress did not stop there. A hardy few crossed the Atlantic to set up Anglo-Saxon outposts in the New World. And when a new nation was born out of these outposts so, too, was a new people: the Anglo-Americans. They carried with them a deep sense of racial destiny—what came to be known by the mid-1800s as "Manifest Destiny." That destiny drove them, first, to uproot and decimate the Native American population: The "few thousand savages" that, according to President Andrew Jackson, stood in the way of white America's search for the "blessings of liberty, civilization, and religion."[20]

It also inevitably led to a clash with Latin Americans who, unfortunately for them, were the owners of territory and resources that had been promised to the white inhabitants of the United States via the prophecy of "Manifest Destiny." For most Americans, the Latin Americans were always a suspect people. Their lax tolerance toward racial mixing was perhaps most troubling, creating what scientists and laymen alike in the United States referred to as a "mongrel race," consisting of mixtures of Spanish, black, and Native American blood. For Sam Houston, one of the colonists invited by the Mexican government to live in and settle land in its Texas territory, the thought of the "vigor of the descendants of the sturdy north" mixing with the "phlegm of the indolent Mexicans," was reason enough to decide that the Americans living in Texas would be better off as an independent people. The "apes" and "brutes" who made up the vast majority of the Mexican population would, like the Native Americans before them, have to give way to the march of Anglo-Saxon progress. From such thinking, the Texas Revolution, then the Mexican War, proceeded with a certain smug sense of inevitability on the part of the Anglo-Saxon Americans.[21]

The seizing of territory would come to an end by the time of the Civil War, but in the years after "Manifest Destiny" had run its course the United States never lost that sense of superiority over its southern neighbors. Through the Spanish-American War (and the occupations of Cuba and Puerto Rico), numerous military interventions, and often applied economic leverage, there always remained the idea that the Latin Americans were simply a few steps behind the Anglo-Saxons and needed (even if they sometimes did not know it or appreciate it) U.S. leadership in how to run their own affairs. Perhaps President Woodrow Wilson put it most succinctly when he bluntly declared that he was going to "teach the South American republics to elect good men." And so he did. Marines landed in Haiti in 1915 and began an occupation that lasted until 1934; the same occurred in the Dominican Republic, which was occupied from 1916–24. United States troops twice intervened in the Mexican revolution, seizing the port city of Tampico for a time and chasing the "bandit" Pancho Villa deep into Mexican territory.[22]

Relations between the United States and Latin America hit rock bottom by the 1930s and President Franklin Roosevelt proudly announced his "Good Neighbor Policy." Even then, he could not avoid lacing his talk about a new relationship with Latin America based on mutual respect with hints of the old racist paternalism. In describing his view of the new economic relationship with the Latin American nations, he declared: "Give them a share. They think they are just as good as we are, and many of them are." It was nice, of course, to consider giving the Latin Americans a share of their own wealth and touching to think that "many" Latin Americans were "just as good" as North Americans.[23]

Even this "new" view of the Latin Americans did not last long. By the time of the Cold War, U.S. officials were back to their old habits of classifying their southern neighbors as more problem children than hemispheric partners. The Latin Americans, by and large, were childish, obstinate, lacking an elementary understanding of basic economic concepts, and incapable of building democratic governments. There were, of course, exceptions, as a 1949 Department of State report made clear in its comparison of eight major differences between the United States and the nations of Latin America. One glaring difference was in "percentage white population." The Anglo-Saxon mindset was probably not surprised to learn that the least developed Latin American nations were also those with the lowest percentage of white population. Uruguay, Argentina, and Costa Rica—the three nations that scored the highest in this regard—were the most developed. Numbers do not lie, and so American policymakers remained skeptical when Latin American nations pleaded for economic and technical assistance. According to one high-ranking U.S. official, these were people "just out of the palm trees," and the "closer to the palm tree a subject of American aid is, the less likely it is to utilize American assistance to his or our advantage." Despite Obama's optimistic appraisal of the "common heritage" of Latin America and the United States, the lines between the "tribes" had been in place for over 200 years—and rhetoric, no matter how stirring, could not erase the memories of the racism that served as a cornerstone of U.S. policy toward the region.[24]

For Asia, Obama's speech in Japan about partnerships and working together through international organizations must be taken in the context of the President's words on one of the biggest world stages. For even during one of his finest moments in the international limelight, his acceptance speech for the Nobel Peace Prize in 2009, Obama could not escape his predilection for muddying the history of race and America's foreign relations. Particularly for his Asian audience, the speech raised some uncomfortable memories. He recounted the history of America's struggle to insure the international application of the recognition of basic human rights, beginning with the failed, but noble, experiment after World War I: "And so, a quarter century after the United States Senate rejected the League of Nations—an idea for which Woodrow Wilson received this prize—America led the world in constructing an architecture to keep the peace: a Marshall Plan and a United Nations, mechanisms to govern the waging of war, treaties to protect human rights, prevent genocide, restrict the most dangerous weapons." In doing so, he neatly skirted over the fact that, for Wilson, the definition of human rights was circumscribed by definitions of race. He showed this on the domestic side when one of his first official acts as president was to segregate federal offices in Washington, DC. On the international front, he made an even stronger statement. During the Paris Peace talks following World War I, the Japanese delegation proposed what amounted to a racial equality clause for inclusion in the final treaty. Wilson's own bigotry combined with the strong opposition to the clause from the British delegation to form an implacable wall of racism. When the resolution actually passed by a majority vote, Wilson simply declared that an issue of such importance demanded a unanimous vote and killed the Japanese proposal.[25]

For America and Asia, human rights had always been a prickly issue. During the 1870s and 1880s, the Chinese became the first (and only) foreigners banned from immigration into the United States. Those already in America faced a daily barrage of violence and humiliating racial epithets. The Japanese got off a bit easier, with a "gentlemen's agreement" in 1907 in which the United States promised not to pass the same sort of legislation that banned the Chinese if Japan would simply stop issuing passports for Japanese workers seeking entry into America. With the outbreak of World War II, all restraints were off. On the domestic front, the U.S. government acted quickly to herd Japanese-American citizens into concentration camps since they were deemed to be national security risks. (Somehow, those citizens with an Italian or German background were considered less threatening.) For the battlefront, the Japanese were depicted in magazines, newspapers, and films as buck-toothed, emotionless murderers; they were lice, rats, cockroaches or other vermin—and, as with vermin, the only solution was extermination. The savagery of the Japanese troops during the war has been well documented, but the equally brutal actions of their American counterparts have received far less attention. John Dower, in his book *War Without Mercy*, writes about the atrocities committed by U.S. troops: the killings of unarmed prisoners and the desecration of enemy bodies through the collection of gold teeth, ears, skulls, and other bones as gruesome souvenirs. And Obama's talk about "restricting dangerous weapons" must have seemed ironic to his Japanese listeners since, as they well knew, the most dangerous weapons—atomic bombs—had been used just twice in world history. Mere words about partnerships and human rights, it would seem, are hardly likely to erase a history of racially charged anti-Asian sentiments of the past century and longer.[26]

Obama's inability to understand the racial undertones of America's commitment to "human rights," has also led him to trumpet the immense value of the United Nation's Universal Declaration of Human Rights, stating that the

> drafters of the Universal Declaration of Human Rights after the Second World War ... recognized that if human rights are not protected, peace is a hollow promise. ... So even as we respect the unique culture and traditions of different countries, America will always be a voice for those aspirations that are universal.

Well, to a degree. Prior to the passage of the declaration by the UN in 1948, the leading African American voice for equal rights, W.E.B. Du Bois, and other officials from the National Association for the Advancement of Colored People, argued that there was one glaring omission from the ongoing discussions about human rights: the horrible situation faced by African Americans in the United States. Du Bois and others put together a fiery document entitled *An Appeal to the World*, which outlined in stark language the violence, indignities, and lack of basic human rights faced by millions of black Americans each and every day. It called for the United Nations to formally investigate these human rights abuses. The U.S. delegation to the UN's Human Rights Commission squashed the petition and it was never formally submitted to the international body for consideration. The final declaration on human rights uses the word "race" just two times, and nowhere in the document is there any substantial discussion of the power to either investigate or enforce the human rights enumerated in the document. This was largely the work of the U.S. members of the Human Rights Commission who wished to avoid at all costs any document that would allow for the international investigation into the horrendous civil rights record of the United States.[27]

Finally, it seems odd that a man who would point to the long history of international efforts to protect human rights would sidestep the one venue at which racism—one of the most brutal violations of human rights—would be the issue. Just months after taking office, President Obama announced that the United States would boycott the upcoming UN World Conference against Racism in Geneva. Law professor and author on civil rights issues Randall Kennedy noted that: "The administration claimed that the conference was clearly going to be openly and wrongly hostile to Israel." In some ways, this was hardly surprising, given the fact that the U.S. delegation walked out of the first World Conference against Racism held in Durban, South Africa, in 2001 using the same excuse. What made the 2009 action particularly unsettling, however, was the fact that while there were indeed the expected denunciations of Israeli policies, the final declaration from the conference barely mentioned the Israeli–Palestinian issue. In the United States, the Obama administration came under heavy fire for not attending the meeting. The Congressional Black Caucus called the decision to boycott one that "does not advance the cause of combating racism and intolerance, but rather sets the cause back," and blamed right wingers in the White House for pushing Obama to take the step of boycotting the conference. A spokesperson for the Human Rights Watch organization lamented that it was "a missed opportunity, really, for the United States."[28]

But was it just a misguided effort to protect Israel from international condemnation (which it would receive it any case) that caused the Obama administration to stay away from the meeting in Geneva? Professor Michael Janis argues that while that was the public explanation for America's no-show, another factor was also at play. At the 2001 conference, the American representatives did indeed walk out, but one of the most important reasons for that dramatic action was the push by a coalition of African nations to more directly confront the legacy of slavery for the modern world. Encapsulated in what was known as the New African Initiative, this call for a discussion of slavery had the intent of:

> Inviting the international community to honor the memory of the victims of these tragedies. ... Concerning compensation and reparations by so-called 'concerned States' for slavery, the slave trade and other historical injustices, the Conference recognizes that those historical injustices have undeniably contributed to poverty, underdevelopment, marginalization, social exclusion, economic disparities, instability and insecurity that affect many people in different parts of the world, particularly in developing countries.

The United States has been less than receptive to that invitation. As Dr. Janis notes, while some of Obama's predecessors have "admitted to the role of the

U.S. in the evil perpetrated during the slave trade, there has been no official apology or discussion of reparations by the U.S. government." As for Obama himself, he "has remained guarded on his view of reparations, reiterating what he has written in *Dreams from my Father* at the Unity '08 Convention in Chicago: "The best reparations we can provide are good schools in the inner city and jobs for people who are unemployed." Clearly, more than a reflexive right-wing defense of anything related to Israel is at play in the Obama administration's very clear reluctance to have a larger debate about race, racism, and U.S. foreign policy. He does not want an international discussion of either America's racist past or the question of what is justice in terms of compensation for the horrors of slavery.[29]

So, where does this leave Barack Obama and the issue of race and U.S. foreign policy? He can remain with his current mode of approaching the issue of race, which relies on mostly silence interrupted occasionally with "teachable moments" and "beer summits." On the international front, it has been even more silence and a refusal to engage in UN efforts to address the worldwide impacts of racism. Such an approach has already proved to be unsuccessful and even harmful to U.S. foreign relations. In the wake of World War II, the United States laid claim to be leader of the free world. The Soviets, however, were quick to point out that while American officials shed crocodile tears over the lack of democracy in Poland and East Germany, they seemed less interested in the fact that millions of African Americans were denied even the most fundamental right to vote in South Carolina, Alabama, and elsewhere in the South. The basic response of the United States to this propaganda disaster was to either ignore or gloss over the civil rights problems in America. Pamphlets, books, and movies were sent around the world claiming that African Americans were progressing very nicely, thank you, and in any case were better off than people behind the Iron Curtain. When this proved less than effective, the U.S. began a program of "token diplomacy": Sending black entertainers, sports figures, and writers overseas to provide living proof that African Americans were doing just fine. Even the notoriously "lily-white" Department of State and Foreign Service began to appoint a few African Americans here and there as evidence of America's commitment to equal rights. The highlight of all this puffery was the establishment of the "Unfinished business" exhibit at the U.S. pavilion at the 1958 World's Fair in Brussels. Here, America would unflinchingly face the race problem. In three separate rooms, visitors saw the newspaper and magazine headlines and stories that blared out the horrific racial violence in the United States; the evidence that slow by steady progress was taking place; and, in the finale, a large picture of black and white children playing together, symbolizing the equality desired by all Americans. As it turned out, however, the exhibit was a bit too premature. Southern congressmen lashed out at the show in Brussels, demanding that it be closed. President Dwight Eisenhower, who harbored strong misgivings about government action in the civil rights field, caved in to these demands and America's unfinished business remained unfinished. Little wonder that a 1950s report from the Psychological Warfare School called the civil rights problem America's "Achilles' heel" in dealing with the rest of the world.[30]

And so it remains, in different forms for these different times. As Obama so often announces with pride, America is a nation made up of people from so many different backgrounds. Increasingly, however, people from non-European origins are dominating that background. According to the 2010 census, Asians are the fastest growing group of immigrants, with the very fastest growing groups coming from India, Pakistan, Bangladesh, and Sri Lanka. The census data indicate that Asians have now overtaken Hispanics, in terms of rates of growth, although Hispanic Americans continue to be the largest minority group in the United States. What will these changing demographics mean for U.S. foreign policy? Will these groups form vocal and powerful pressure groups, as African Americans attempted to do in the 1950s and 1960s, to try and foment change in America's diplomacy with Asia and Latin America? And if crises that seem to threaten Americans develop in those regions, what will the reaction be in the United States? The recent events involving Americans with Middle Eastern backgrounds provide a helpful, if not particularly uplifting, example. In the wake of the 9/11 terrorist attacks, a wave of violence and intimidation was unleashed against Middle Eastern Americans. The FBI noted that there were nearly 500 hates crimes against people from that group in 2001, most coming after the September attacks. There had been only 28 the year before. Individuals were murdered, beaten, or humiliated. Mosques were desecrated, and dozens of people removed from U.S. aircraft simply because they looked Middle Eastern. One U.S. official even suggested that detention camps for Middle Eastern Americans might be an acceptable reaction to the 9/11 attacks. The recent assault by an individual associated with racist groups on a Sikh temple in Wisconsin in which he killed six people is sobering evidence that the racial hatred engendered by 9/11 continues to reverberate in the United States. As these groups continue to grow in their presence in America, history suggests that so too will grow the racist reactions, particularly in periods of stress and international tensions.[31]

Given this kind of historical and contemporary environment, what would be the results of taking a more aggressive stand today, attempting to engage the people of the United States and the world in a meaningful discussion of race and its devastating history of destruction and bigotry? Pessimists would point to the recent experience of President Bill Clinton as a disappointing example of what happens when a president tries to force the American people to talk about race. On June 14, 1997, Clinton spoke to America and asked for a "candid conversation on the state of race relations today." What came to be known as Clinton's "One America initiative" involved the establishment of the President's Advisory Board on Race. But after that early explosion of rhetoric and activity, what happened? E.J. Dionne, Jr., of the Brookings Institute suggested that Clinton's initiative ran into the "classic problem of American ventures in brotherhood and sisterhood: We can be nice or we can be honest, but we rarely manage both." In short, while the plan sounded wonderful on paper, in practice, no one was really willing to ask the hardest questions for fear of making someone else angry or resentful. The advisory board met infrequently and the meetings were always public, which often limited the honesty with which certain issues were faced. As the head of the advisory board, John Hope Franklin, lamented:"We have learned how difficult it is to hold productive discussions about race under the glare of television lights and cameras in large meetings among relative strangers, and among people who expect more than an advisory board can reasonably deliver." In September 1998 the advisory board handed President Clinton its final report, *One America in the 21st Century: forging a new future.* And, as is the fate of so many reports from so many blue-ribbon panels, it silently sank from public notice.[32]

There was, however, one extraordinarily important observation made in the report:

> [T]he absence of both knowledge and understanding about the role race has played in our collective history continues to make it difficult to find solutions that will improve race relations, eliminate disparities, and create equal opportunities in all areas of American life.

It is a conclusion that is perhaps self-evident to scholars of U.S. race relations, but it does highlight the need for "knowledge and understanding" about race and its impact as an essential first step toward change. The same might be said with at least as much force (although the report does not deal with any international ramifications of race aside from immigration policies) about the role of race in America's foreign relations, an area in which there is even less knowledge and understanding.

And as much as Clinton's initiative might have failed in achieving its grand goals, it might also serve as a spark for Obama's willingness to grapple with race and U.S. diplomacy. For someone who often claims to be a keen student of history, and makes much of his experience of being raised in Indonesia, Barack Obama seems to have let the Bandung Conference of 1955 slip under his intellectual radar. On April 18, 1955 representatives of 29 nations from Asia, Africa, and the Middle East met in Bandung, Indonesia, to discuss common problems and discuss the difficulties of trying to remain neutral and non-aligned in a world that was hardening into east and west camps. Politics and economics were high on the agenda, but so too was an analysis of the historical background of the nations in attendance; a history comprised of degrading and exploitative colonialism for many. Not surprisingly, the racial component of imperialism, always a significant undergirding for white dominance over people of color, was also a topic for discussion. Americans in attendance at the conference (all unofficial attendees, since the United States was not invited) listened to speaker after speaker denounce colonialism and its brutal consequences around the world. They must have been somewhat surprised when the chief of the Philippines delegation rose to address the crowd. The Philippines had been an American colony (in fact, if not in name) for nearly 50 years after the Spanish–American War of 1898. A vicious war between Filipino rebels and U.S. troops resulted in the deaths of tens of thousands of Filipinos from combat and starvation due to the Americans' slash and burn tactics. However, in 1946 the United States formally granted the Philippines independence, although a substantial U.S. military presence remained on the islands. Perhaps Carlos Romulo was thinking of that history when he told the audience at Bandung: "We have known, and some of us still know, the searing experience of being demeaned in our own lands. ... Western white man assumed that his superiority lay in his very genes, in the color of his skin." His blistering conclusion was also an eloquent warning:

> [W]e can only hope that this conference serves as a sober and yet jolting reminder to them that the day of Western racism is passing along with the day of Western power over non-Western peoples. Its survival in any form can only hang like an albatross around the necks of those many people in the West who sincerely seek to build a freer and better world.[33]

People such as Barack Obama, who does seem sincerely committed to building a better world, with America at the forefront of that effort. With all of his prestige, and speaking as a black American, he could certainly step forward and call another Bandung to openly discuss the impacts of race, the lingering reminders of its continuing power, and the best and just ways to deal with the damage that has been inflicted. But until he, like Romulo, can stand before the international audience and deal forthrightly and sympathetically with the historical and contemporary impacts of race on America's dealings with the world, then he—and the United States—will continue to carry the ghastly remains of the albatross of racism.

Notes

1 Wise, Tim. *Colorblind: the rise of post-racial politics and the retreat from racial equity* (San Francisco: City Lights Publishers, 2010); Tesler, Michael and Sears, David O. *Obama's Race: the 2008 election and the dream of a post-racial America* (Chicago: University of Chicago Press, 2010); Parks, Gregory and Hughes, Matthew, eds. *The Obamas and a (Post) Racial America?* (New York: Oxford University Press, 2011); Cose, Ellis. *The End of Anger: a new generation's take on race and rage* (New York: Ecco, 2011). These are just a few of the books released since Obama's election that discuss a "post-racial" America.

2 Schorr, Daniel. "A new, 'post-racial' political era in America," January 28, 2008, www.npr.org/templates/story.php?storyid=18489466; Lum, Lydia. "The Obama era: a post-racial society?," February 5, 2009, http://diverseeducation.com/cache/print.php?articleid=12238

3 Schorr. "A new 'post-racial'"; Mathis, Deborah. "A post-racial era? Let's not be so quick to forget the past," February 2, 2009, www.blackamericaweb.com/

?q=articles/news/baw_commentary_news/6305; Metzler, Christopher J. "The myth of post-racial America: a global perspective," December 10, 2008, http://diverseeducation.wordpress.com/2008/12/10/the-myth-of-a-post-racial-america-a-global-perspective/

4   ABC News. "Obama's pastor: God damn America, U.S. to blame for 9/11," March 13, 2008, abcnews.go.com/Blotter/story?id=4443788#.UCOr90L3BFI; "Transcript: Barack Obama's speech on race," www.npr.org/templates/story .php?storyId=88478467

5   "Barack Obama, Selma speech, March 4, 2007," www.bobmccaughey.com /post1865/?page_id=2144

6   "Transcript".

7   "Obama's Berlin speech: 'A world that stands as one'," www.spiegel.de/ international/germany/obama-s-berlin-speech-a-world-that-stands-as-one-a-567920-druck.html. For a good analysis of the "apology tour" critics and the validity of their arguments, see Kessler, Glenn. "Obama's 'apology tour'," February 22, 2011, http://voices.washingtonpost.com/fact-checker/2011/02/obamas_apology_ tour.html

8   Full text of Obama speech in Ghana, www.huffingtonpost.com/2009/07/11/ obama-ghana-speech-full-t_n_230009.html; Hanson, Stephanie. "Imagining Obama's Africa policy," December 22, 2008, www.cfr.org/africa/imagining -obama-africa-policy/p18006

9   Perez-Rocha, Manuel. "Empire and Latin America in the Obama era," April 1, 2009, www.fpif.org/articles/empire_and_latin_america_in_the_obama_era; "Official remarks of United States President Barack Obama at the opening ceremony of the Fifth Summit of the Americas," April 17, 2009, www.summit-americas. org/V_Summit/remarks_usa_en.pdf; "Remarks by President Obama on Latin America in Santiago, Chile," March 21, 2011, www.whitehouse.gov/the-press-office/2011/03/21/remarks-president-obama-latin-america-santiago-chile

10   "Remarks by President Barack Obama at Suntory Hall," November 14, 2009, www. whitehouse.gov/the-press-office/remarks-president-barack-obama-suntory-hall

11   Colombant, Nico. "Africa policy watchers lose hope in President Obama," January 27, 2012, http://voanews.com/articleprintview/151281.html; Conway-Smith, Erin. "Michelle Obama begins solo Africa tour," June 20, 2011, www. globalpost.com/print/5652431; Padgett, Tim. "Obama's Latin American policy looks like Bush's," *Time*, December 3, 2009, www.time.com/time/printout/ 0,8816,1945440,00.html; People's World. "Obama and Latin America: will policy go beyond small changes?" August 6, 2009, www.peoplesworld.org/ obama-and-latin-america-will-policy-go-beyond-small-changes/

12   Congressional Research Service. "Pivot to the Pacific? The Obama administration's 'rebalancing' toward Asia," March 28, 2012, www.fas.org/sgp/crs/natsec/ R42448.pdf

13   Hunt, Michael H. *Ideology and U.S. Foreign Policy* (New Haven, NJ: Yale University Press, 1987), p. xi.

14   For a good, brief summary of the recent literature on the impact of race on U. S. diplomacy see, Krenn, Michael L. *The Color of Empire: race and American foreign relations* (Washington, DC: Potomac Books, Inc., 2006).

15   Obama, Barack. *Dreams from my Father: a story of race and inheritance* (New York: Three Rivers Press, 2004), p. 368.

16   See n.8, Obama speech in Ghana.

17   For good studies of early U.S.–African relations, see Hickey, Dennis and Wylie, Kenneth C. *An Enchanting Darkness: the American vision of Africa in the twentieth century* (East Lansing, MI: Michigan State University Press, 1993); Duignan, Peter and Gann, L.H. *The United States and Africa: a history* (Cambridge: Cambridge University Press, 1984).

18　There are several fine studies of U.S.–African relations following World War II, many of which focus specifically on the American attitude toward South Africa and apartheid: Noer, Thomas J. *Cold War and Black Liberation: the United States and white rule in Africa, 1948–1968* (Columbia: University of Missouri Press, 1985); Borstelmann, Thomas. *Apartheid's Reluctant Uncle: the United States and South Africa in the early Cold War* (New York: Oxford University Press, 1993); Thomas, Gerald E. "The black revolt: the United States and Africa in the 1960s," in Kunz, Diane B., ed. *The Diplomacy of the Crucial Decade: American foreign relations in the 1960s* (New York: Columbia University Press, 1994), pp. 363–78; Noer. "New frontiers and old priorities in Africa," in Paterson, Thomas J., ed. *Kennedy's Quest for Victory: American foreign policy, 1961–1963* (New York: Oxford University Press, 1989), pp. 253–83; Lyons, Terrence. "Keeping Africa off the agenda," in Cohen, Warren I. and Tucker, Nancy Bernkopf, eds. *Lyndon Johnson Confronts the World: American foreign policy, 1963–1968* (Cambridge: Cambridge University Press, 1994), pp. 245–78; Mahoney, Richard D. *JFK: ordeal in Africa* (New York: Oxford University Press, 1983); Metz, Stephen. "Congress, the anti-apartheid movement, and Nixon," *Diplomatic History* 1988: 12, 165–85. The quote about Africa's need for "evolutionary development" is found in Byroade, Henry. "The world's colonies and ex-colonies: a challenge to America," *State Department Bulletin* November 16, 1953: 29, 655–60. For the Nixon–Kissinger episodes, see Hersh, Seymour M. *The Price of Power: Kissinger in the Nixon White House* (New York: Summit Books, 1983), pp. 110–11.

19　See n.7, Obama speech in Berlin.

20　The best account of the development of Anglo-Saxon thinking in early America is Horsman, Reginald. *Race and Manifest Destiny: the origins of American racial Anglo-Saxonism* (Cambridge, MA: Harvard University Press, 1981). Also see Jordan, Winthrop D. *The White Man's Burden: historical origins of racism in the United States* (London: Oxford University Press, 1974); Hunt, *Ideology and U.S. Foreign Policy*; Gossett, Thomas F. *Race: the history of an idea in America* (Dallas, TX: Southern Methodist University Press, 1963); Drinnon, Richard. *Facing West: the metaphysics of Indian-hating and empire building* (Norman, OK: University of Oklahoma Press, 1997). Jackson quote from Andrew Jackson, "Second annual message," December 6, 1830, in Richardson, James D. *A Compilation of the Messages and Papers of the Presidents 1789–1897, vol. 2, 1817–1833* (Washington, DC: Government Printing Office, 1896), pp. 519–23.

21　Houston quote is found in de Leon, Arnoldo. *They Called Them Greasers: Anglo attitudes toward Mexicans in Texas, 1821–1900* (Austin, TX: University of Texas Press, 1983), p. 7. Also see Weber, David J. "'Scarce more than apes': historical roots of Anglo American stereotypes of Mexicans in the border region," in *New Spain's Far Northern Frontier: essays on Spain in the new west, 1540–1821* (Albuquerque: University of New Mexico Press, 1979); Pike, Fredrick B. *The United States and Latin America: myths and stereotypes of civilization and nature* (Austin, TX: University of Texas Press, 1992); Weinberg, Albert K. *Manifest Destiny: a study of national expansionism in American history* (Baltimore, MD: Johns Hopkins University Press, 1935); Paredes, Raymund A. "The origins of anti-Mexican sentiment in the United States," in Romo, Ricardo and Paredes, Raymund A., eds. *New Directions in Chicano Scholarship* (La Jolla, CA: University of California at San Diego Press, 1978); Hietala, Thomas R. *Manifest Destiny: anxious aggrandizement in late Jacksonian American* (Ithaca, NY: Cornell University Press, 1985); Johnson, John J. *A Hemisphere Apart: the foundations of United States policy toward Latin America* (Baltimore, MD: Johns Hopkins University Press, 1990). Johnson has also written an insightful look at how stereotypes of Latin America and its people were immortalized in editorial cartoons in U.S. newspapers: *Latin America in Caricature* (Austin, TX: University of Texas Press, 1980).

22 Park, James William. *Latin American Underdevelopment: a history of perspectives in the United States, 1870–1965* (Baton Rouge, LA: Louisiana State University Press, 1995) offers a fascinating study of how U.S. views on the racial makeup of Latin Americans, climate, and Spanish colonial heritage combined to create an ideological perspective on how and why Latin America lagged so seriously behind the United States in its political, economic, and social development.

23 For a good study of how the old stereotypes about Latin America withstood even the best intentions of the "good neighbour" policy, see Green, David. *The Containment of Latin America: a history of myths and realities of the good neighbor policy* (Chicago, IL: Quadrangle Press, 1971).

24 Some representative studies of U.S. policy toward Latin America in the Cold War period are Haines, Gerald K. *The Americanization of Brazil: a Study of U. S. Cold War diplomacy in the third world, 1945–1954* (Wilmington, DE: Scholarly Resources, Inc., 1989); Krenn, Michael L. *The Chains of Interdependence: U.S. policy toward Central America, 1945–1954* (Armonk, NY: M. E. Sharpe, 1996); Rabe, Stephen G. *Eisenhower and Latin America: the foreign policy of anticommunism* (Chapel Hill, NC: University of North Carolina Press, 1988); Immerman, Richard H. *The CIA in Guatemala: the foreign policy of intervention* (Austin, TX: University of Texas Press, 1982). Report on the '"percentage white population" is in "Problem Paper," July 5, 1949, Record Group 59, Office Files of the Assistant Secretary of State for Inter-American Affairs (Edward G. Miller), 1949–1953, Box 10, National Archives and Records Administration, College Park, MD. The "palm trees" quotes are from Ellis Briggs, Oral History, June 19, 1970, and October 15, 1972, Dwight D. Eisenhower Presidential Library, Abilene, KS.

25 "Remarks by the President at the acceptance of the Nobel Peace Prize," December 10, 2009, www.whitehouse.gov/the-press-office/remarks-president-acceptance-nobel-peace-prize. For Wilson's actions at the 1919 conference, see Lauren, Paul Gordon. "Human rights in history: diplomacy and racial equality at the Paris Peace Conference," *Diplomatic History* 1978: 2, 257–78.

26 Miller, Stuart Creighton. *The Unwelcome Immigrant: the American image of the Chinese, 1785–1882* (Berkeley, CA: University of California Press, 1969); Hunt, *Ideology and U.S. Foreign Policy*; Thorne, Christopher. "Racial aspects of the Far Eastern War of 1941–1945," *Proceedings of the British Academy* 1980: 66, 329–77; Minear, Richard H. "Cross-cultural perceptions and World War II: American Japanists of the 1940s and their images of Japan," *International Studies Quarterly* 1980: 24, 555–80; Dower, John W. *War Without Mercy: race and power in the Pacific War* (New York: Pantheon Books, 1986).

27 See n.25, Obama speech at acceptance of the Nobel Peace Prize. National Association for the Advancement of Colored People. *An appeal to the world! A statement on the denial of human rights to minorities in the case of citizens of negro descent in the United States of America and an appeal to the United Nations for redress* (New York:NAACP, 1947); Rosenberg, Jonathan. *How far the promised land? World affairs and the American Civil Rights Movement from the First World War to Vietnam* (Princeton, NJ: Princeton University Press, 2006); Anderson, Carol. *Eyes off the Prize: the United Nations and the African American struggle for human rights, 1944–1955* (Cambridge: Cambridge University Press, 2003); Dudziak, Mary L. *Cold War Civil Rights: race and the image of American democracy* (Princeton: Princeton University Press, 2000, 2011).

28 Kennedy, Randall. *The Persistence of the Color Line: racial politics and the Obama presidency* (New York: Pantheon Books, 2011), p. 260; Zunes, Stephen. "Missing an anti-racism moment," April 22, 2009, www.fpif.org/articles/missing_an_anti-racism_moment

29 Janis, Michael. "Obama, Africa, and the post-racial," *CLCWeb: Comparative Literature and Culture*, 2009, http://docs.lib.purdue.edu/clcweb/vol11/iss2/2

30 Some of the best studies of the American dilemma in dealing with the international repercussions of its civil rights problems are Plummer, Brenda Gayle. *Rising Wind: black Americans and U.S. foreign affairs, 1935–1960* (Chapel Hill, NC: University of North Carolina Press, 1996); von Eschen, Penny M. *Race Against Empire: black Americans and anticolonialism, 1937–1957* (Ithaca, NY: Cornell University Press, 1996); von Eschen, *Satchmo Blows up the World: jazz ambassadors play the Cold War* (Cambridge, MA: Harvard University Press, 2004); Borstelmann, Thomas. *The Cold War and the Color Line: American race relations in the global arena* (Cambridge, MA: Harvard University Press); Dudziak. *Cold War Civil Rights*; Fraser, Cary. "Crossing the color line in Little Rock: the Eisenhower administration and the dilemma of race for U.S. foreign policy," *Diplomatic History* 2000: 24, 2, 233–64; Krenn, Michael L. *Black Diplomacy: African-Americans and the State Department, 1945–1969* (Armonk, NY: M.E. Sharpe, 1999); Krenn, "'Unfinished business': segregation and U.S. diplomacy at the 1958 World's Fair," *Diplomatic History* 1996: 20, 4, 591–612.

31 Pew Research Center. "The rise of Asian Americans," June 19, 2012, www.pewsocialtrends.org/2012/06/19/the-rise-of-asian-americans/; Krenn, Michael L. "'America's face to the world': the Department of State, Arab-Americans, and diversity in the wake of 9/11," *Journal of Gender, Race & Justice* 2003: 7, 1, 150–52.

32 "Clinton on race: 'We must break down the barriers'," http://www.cnn.com/all politics/1997/06/14/clinton.race.two; Dionne, Jr., E.J. "Affirmative action—President Bill Clinton's initiative on race—brief article," September 12, 1997, www.highbeam.com/doc/1G1-58400708.html; Smith, Renee M. "The public presidency hits the wall: Clinton's presidential initiative on race," September 22, 1998, www.thefreelibrary.com/The+Public+ Presidency+Hits+the+Wall% 3a+Clinton%27s+Presidential.-a053409264

33 Wright, Richard. *The Color Curtain: a report on the Bandung Conference* (Jackson, MI: University Press of Mississippi, 1994); Lee, Christopher J. *Making a World After Empire: the Bandung moment and its political afterlives* (Miami, OH: Ohio University Press, 2010). Romulo speech found in Romulo, Carlos P. *The Meaning of Bandung* (Chapel Hill, NC: University of North Carolina Press, 1956), pp. 68–9.

11 President Obama's Establishment

Inderjeet Parmar

As President Barack Obama embarks on his second term of office, attention turns again to the (now very) old question: Why has Obama maintained the principal planks of the foreign and national security policies of the George W. Bush administrations, despite promised radical change?

In their haste to explain, most commentators cling to what are now "old favorites": Obama's legacy of wars and financial crises; his lack of experience in foreign affairs; his personal insecurities as commander-in-chief but having served in no wars. None of those arguments is without its merit but they all remain wedded to arguments suggesting had this or that been different, Obama would have transformed U.S. policy and power. This is patently problematic.

The argument pursued here, in assertive and preliminary rather than fully substantiated form, is that President Obama represents the fruition of decades of post-civil rights era political and social development, of the "new" black politics of incorporation, of working from the inside. He is a fully assimilated black elite member of the American establishment who is practically indistinguishable in office from his presidential predecessors.

An article in a pre-election issue of *Foreign Affairs*, house organ of the U.S. foreign policy establishment, unwittingly (almost) hit the nail on the head: "Obama is the Republican candidate," it declared. Actually, Obama was the establishment candidate—and the real establishment is bipartisan, welcoming millionaires from both its wings in the Democratic and Republican parties.

Obama's appointment to defense secretary of former Republican senator, Chuck Hagel, illustrates this perfectly: Variously described as a liberal realist or internationalist, or a Republican realist, Hagel was endorsed by the big guns of the establishment: Colin Powell, Robert Gates, Brent Scowcroft, Zbigniew Brzezinski, and others, who rushed to defend him against neoconservatives' charges of anti-semitism and weakness on Iran, Syria, etc. Hagel supported the Iraq war. He supports full-blooded aid to Israel. He just thinks military power is not always the answer to every problem (this made him, to neoconservatives, weak on national security).

Obama's pick for secretary of state was Senator John Kerry—another pro-Iraq war advocate, as was former secretary of state, Hillary Clinton, the hardline and hawkish state department head; and current vice president, Joe Biden, known as the quarterback of Democratic foreign policy politics, was similarly hawkish.

Withdrawn from nomination for head of the CIA in 2008, John Brennan is Obama's choice for that role from 2013. Brennan's complicity in use of torture, in supporting the Guantanamo facility and the secret prisons program, and escalated drone strikes, i.e., illegal assassinations with plenty of civilian casualties, is well known or widely suspected, but hardly thoroughly investigated. He sailed through Senate confirmation hearings.

Obama promotes those who backed the most pointless American war since Vietnam not because he is insecure, inexperienced, lacking knowledge of foreign affairs, or because he inherited a mess. He is a member of the establishment, fully bought into American global power concepts, and who sees all problems through the prism of U.S. establishment interests. It is not public opinion that drives U.S. foreign policy: it is the establishment and myriad think tanks, foundations, and other experts and financial backers from Wall Street and other prestigious addresses, who are responsible for the global financial crisis and the aggressive character of U.S. power (dressed up as exporting U.S. core values).

What is the "establishment"? Long ago, Godfrey Hodgson, one of the keenest British observers of American political life, provided an excellent definition: The establishment, he argued, is the power behind the throne, the people who know the right people who get things done, those operating outside U.S. Congress and mainly as appointees in the executive branch, whose power is often exercised outside of the constitutional forms. They have the power to block the people who do not belong and to promote those who do. Wall Street, not Main Street, runs America. When it is said that "millions stand behind me" by White House incumbents, they are referring to donations from Wall Street banks and American multinationals such as Lockheed Martin, arms firms at the heart of the military–industrial complex that continues to wield massive influence in the United States.

The Center for Responsive Politics has shown, with excellent data over many years, that Wall Street money has long influenced election outcomes, including Obama's victory in 2008, when he raised $15 million from "big finance." Even in the most recent campaign, Obama raised over $8 million from Wall Street, a sector that his administration did so much to shore up and bail out. Up to June 2012, the Obama and Republican Mitt Romney campaigns had raised $1.2 billion between them from various sources, although Romney outflanked Obama on Wall Street. Overall, however, by election day–November 6, 2012—some estimated that a total of $6 billion had been spent on presidential and congressional races. In British politics, it is said, "money talks"; in the USA, money *screams*.

But the Obama administration outflanked Romney on another bipartisan non-issue in U.S. politics: the military budget. Obama's first administration increased military spending by $200 billion over that of President Bush in

2008; Romney's plans projected spending to increase 38 percent higher than Obama's, including an increase of 100,000 soldiers in the military, from five to nine navy ships built annually, stationing two aircraft carriers off Iran's coast (Obama had ramped up such pressure on Iran, too), and installing a missile defence system in Europe. At the same time, Romney advocated cutting taxes by 20 percent; in 2010, Obama, it may be recalled, retained President Bush's planned tax cuts to the wealthiest Americans. The Obama administration's militarism pushed Romney's to even greater, politically less credible, extremes.

The institutional sources of bipartisan establishment thinking and politics further muddies the ideo-political waters: despite the neoconservatives in his foreign policy team, the single most popular think tank for Romney advisors, *and those of Barack Obama*, was the Council on Foreign Relations, the very heart of the U.S. foreign policy establishment. This suggests that there is a good deal more agreement on the nature and purposes of American power than public utterances might indicate and that, as Lenin said a century ago, there is more than a touch of political theatre—heat—than there is daylight between the two main political parties.

Candidate Obama went on the offensive against Romney on national security: Why did Obama feel he could do that? The Nobel Peace Prize laureate ordered the successful killing of Osama bin Laden; authorized the launch of more drone attacks, i.e., targeted assassinations, than Bush; retained rendition, i.e., kidnapping, as a practice; prevented the U.S. Supreme Court from extending constitutional protections to Bagram inmates; retained the Guantanamo Bay torture facility; extended antiterror surveillance on a massive scale to the "homeland"; ordered and maintained the military surge in Afghanistan, and in July 2012, committed the United States to arms sales to President Karzai's corrupt and warlordist regime after the U.S./NATO withdrawal; continued to defend, finance and arm Israel's aggressions against Palestinians; ramped up the rhetoric of inevitable military strikes against Iran to limit its power in the region which, itself, gained impetus from the war of aggression against Iraq; ordered coercive regime change in Libya; maintained U.S. support for corrupt and bankrupt regimes in the Arab world; and so on. President Obama has ordered the stationing of thousands of U.S. troops in Australia, is concluding military treaties with China's border states, and securing cooperation—cultural, military and other—between India, Japan and Australia: from Beijing, this could look a bit like encirclement. So militaristic is Obama's foreign policy program that he outflanked the neoconservative-backed Mitt Romney and gave him no place to go to but increased rhetorical stridency.

In this, his second term, Obama should have been able to break free from anxiety and inexperience and speak with his own voice, if the usual critics had it right. That he is not doing so is not because he is obtuse: it is because he buys the program. And that program is a bipartisan establishment program that Obama bought into bit by bit over the many decades from his private school education in Hawaii, in California, at Columbia and Harvard universities.

Obama's record in dealing with issues that were *not* inherited legacies gave the game away long ago: the president who would not do coercive regime change supported it in Libya; who professed friendship to the people of the Middle East provided record levels of aid to Israel; who won the Nobel Peace Prize dramatically increased drone strikes across the world and escalated the war in Afghanistan; who believed in democracy backed Hosni Mubarak's oppressive regime in Egypt until it was clear that he was yesterday's man; who backed Saudi military intervention in Bahrain against citizens fighting for their democratic rights; and so on.

Despite the great achievement that President Obama represents as the first African American chief executive, it is important to bear in mind the myth that he represents: He is half-white; not a man of the people, let alone of black people; has dropped any pretence of dealing with the structural and historically rooted problems of racial and social inequality; and has paid his dues to the establishment that placed him in the White House in 2008 to pick up the pieces of crisis-ridden American power after eight years of George W. Bush. The election to the White House of Barack Obama in 2008 was hailed by many as symptomatic of a new era of "post-racial" society and politics. Whether or not this turns out to be the case domestically, U.S. foreign policy *has* an under-appreciated and largely unacknowledged racial dimension, and not principally due to the stewardship of President Obama. Its racialized character is, and has long been, evident in the racial characteristics of the overwhelming majority of members of the U.S. foreign policy establishment, and even more so in their shared mindsets. It is the latter shared mindsets that are and will continue to be fundamentally important, especially over the coming decades as the U.S. evolves into a "majority–minority" nation. Yet, any changes that occur must be understood in a context in which white Anglo-Saxon Protestant (WASP) racial–ethnic *and* class factors combine to produce continuity or rather managed change through sophisticated and deep forms of socialization in an attenuated meritocratic order. Such a system tends to produce evolutionary change in the membership of the establishment in order to adapt to new political environments, especially challenges to elite dominance at home and threats from abroad. It is argued here that Barack Obama is the epitome of the greatest strengths of this system in its racialized context: A system that is able to absorb and incorporate new, rising talent from the "wrong" background, without fundamentally altering broader patterns of power and inequality.

The indirect impacts of race on policy culture or climate of policy opinion do not "cause" policy outcomes but condition the environment within which policy is thought about and formulated. The impact of "race," especially in an era in which racism is popularly denied as a personal or societal trait, consists of deep structures of intergenerationally transmitted but evolving thought, acting as a powerful socializer and conditioner of the policy environment. The greatest success of such a system would be the integration and assimilation of the most elite minority individuals and groups, even though the bulk of those groups' members might continue to experience gross inequality and discrimination. Such success would be compounded by election to the highest office of a minority U.S. president extolling the virtues of color-blind or post-racial politics, and broad continuities in U.S. foreign policy.

I argue here that President Barack Obama is the embodiment of that form of "racial" impact in U.S. foreign policy: that he represents a "wasp-ified" black elite, assimilated into the extant structures of power that remain wedded to a more secular, non-biologically racial, version of Anglo-Saxonism, i.e., Anglospherism, or more broadly *liberal internationalism*. Given the malleable, evolutionary, incorporative, and "inclusive" character of postwar Anglo-Saxonism and its latter-day variants, it should occasion little surprise that, despite Barack Obama's stewardship, there has been so little change in the character and content of U.S. foreign and national security policies.

Clearly, however, there are several specific racial issues raised by the fact that Obama is black. It was largely due to this that Zbigniew Brzezinski called Obama "the new face of American power" that would restore its global reputation. And Obama's race is also the reason that his loyalty and "American-ness" have been challenged by several on the American right, including Republican hopeful, Newt Gingrich, who referred to Obama as having "a Kenyan anti-colonial attitude."

In addition, it is well-known that Obama struggled over many years over his own identity, and it is likely that such "status anxieties" continue to play an important if intangible role during his tenure of the White House. Not only is he a black man at the pinnacle of a mainly white power structure, he is financial-crisis-hit America's CEO without any previous governing experience, and commander-in-chief without a military background who inherited two long-drawn-out wars. Hence, there are several sources of status anxiety for any White House incumbent. But does Obama's racial identity and status anxiety trump all other sources? That is difficult to discern and, given the incendiary character of U.S. racial politics, we will need to wait for release of post-administration memoirs, diaries, and other records to hazard a judgment. It is increasingly clear, however, that class or elite status trumps race as individuals of minority origin climb up the greasy pole of American power.

12 The Im/Possibility of Barack Hussein Obama

Nirmal Puwar and Sanjay Sharma

I am like a Rorschach test. Even if people find me disappointing ultimately, they might gain something.

(Obama, cited in Baker 2008)

Inevitably, Barack Hussein Obama was going to disappoint. Coming into political office at a time of financial meltdown, amid speculation-driven global capitalism, would be a challenge to any U.S. presidential incumbent. "Hope" from the 2008 election turned into doubt and disappointment during his presidency. In the lead up to the 2012 election, as Obama asked for more time, "Hope," although hugely muted this time round, was still in the wings of the new slogan, "Forward." Political gridlock, war and the economy were presented as the challenges to the hope produced in the 2008 election campaign (Obama 2012).[1] The crowds of 2012 were far smaller, as were the iconic artworks that symbolized a global Obama mania. Nonetheless, in campaign materials and re-election speeches, the attempt was made to once again re-invigorate hope to fuel new projected imaginative horizons for the future. Fantasies of the nation—the "we" of "God bless America"—continue to be mirrored back by Obama to the desires of the electorate. Obama reiterates stories from his own biography as well as the lives of other Americans, by way of allegory, to furnish the drama of his speeches to tap into, as well as further fuel, specific imaginations of the nation existing in the democratic body politic of the U.S. The rhetorical weight is on "national building" through education, manufacturing and health, supported by an image of America as a global conductor of freedom and liberty (rather than power).

Obama remains an enigmatic figure. His oblique self-reference to a Rorschach (ink-blot) test in the last election, is as revealing as it is confounding. This test presents structureless and ambiguous entities which we interpret by projecting our own deep-seated feelings and needs. Obama has been cognisant of his broad appeal resting on a capacity to embody the desires of diverse sets of national and global constituencies. Yet, this test also purportedly lays bare our latent pathologies and injurious traits. Peculiarly, Obama has likened himself to a dubious and discredited psychological test.

According to many commentators and critics alike, Obama self-fashioned as an "empty vessel" (Cupp 2009) that can be filled by the political desires of his divergent supporters, is both his strength *and* his weakness.

This essay highlights the irreducible tensions Obama embodies by being both an outsider who is simultaneously an *insider*. Being the President even as he stood for election in 2012 as an insider, he was at the same time at risk of being again positioned as an outsider. Amid the attempts to locate Obama as inauthentic, un-American and associated with "other" places, it can also be argued that vis-à-vis his racial agency, he has been able to make performative use of an otherness. This chapter confronts the complexity and tensions of biography, history and performativity in the arrival of a racialized neoliberal figure in privileged positions historically and conceptually reserved for white men, who have been the somatic norm (Mills 1997; Pateman 1988; Puwar 2004). In other words, it will be argued that the immutable tensions embodied by Obama are a symptom of his im/possibility as a figure of leadership that demands the (unattainable) transcendence of race.

Attachments: The Face of Money

After Obama's election to President, Zygmunt Bauman remarked in *Thesis Eleven*: "Everyone agrees that 40 years ago the stunning life itinerary of Obama would not only be implausible, it would be downright inconceivable!" (Battiston 2009: 143). The impossibility of what is possible as embodied by Obama is constitutive of a *tension*: The reminder and remainder (Amin 2010) of the troubled past as well as an optimistic future, operating as an antagonism that produces political attachments that make obama simultaneously a compelling and ambiguous figure of global leadership. Looking back to his selection as the first black president of the *Harvard Law Review*, Obama noted in his book, *Audacity of Hope*, that the burst of publicity following his initial success testified to what he termed as "America's hunger for an optimistic sign from the racial front—a morsel of proof that after all, some progress has been made" (Obama 2006: xiii). This public hunger continued throughout his presidential election campaign, declined during his term in office and was resuscitated during the 2012 election campaign in the switch in the political slogan from "Yes we can" in 2008 to "Forward" in 2012.

The ambivalent loyalties that Obama has engendered have waxed and waned throughout his career. In 2008 Obama's national and global appeal, especially to subjugated groups, rested on the promise of making the world a better place for all. After enduring the imperious and war-mongering Bush administration, Obama appeared as a beacon of light to many across the U.S. and the world. Yet we find that Obama's promise of hope and change was caught in what Lauren Berlant has termed in her general analysis of state and fantasy, a "cruel optimism." This is "a relation of attachment to compromised conditions of possibility" (2007: 33). Berlant contends that an object of desire embodies a cluster of promises we want to be made possible. Moreover, she writes "all attachments are optimistic," although they do not necessarily all feel optimistic. A cruel optimism is the realisation that this kind of attachment "is discovered to be impossible, sheer fantasy, or too possible, and toxic. [It] is the condition of maintaining an attachment to a problematic object" (p. 33). Obama as our problematic object of desire is thus not merely a figure who will inevitably disappoint. For those on the left, Obama after all is a neoliberal president par excellence. His controversial award of the Nobel Peace Prize in 2009 was ironic to say the least, given his continued commitment to the U.S. corporate–military machine (Ali 2010). Obama has failed to address the indefinite detention of prisoners of Guantanamo; and the normalization of authorized "extrajudicial killings" via the use of drone technology in Afghanistan, Pakistan, and Yemen is deeply disturbing.[2] It is not difficult to agree with Tariq Ali's characterization of Obama, which charges liberals and those on the left to have been deluded for ever hoping that Obama was ever going to be a real force of progress. Ali maintains:

> In reality, Barack Obama is a skillful and gifted machine politician who rapidly rose to the top. Once that is understood there is little about him that should surprise anyone: to talk of betrayal is foolish, for nothing has been betrayed but one's own illusions.
>
> (Ali 2010: 33)

However, Ali does not fully countenance that the desire for political change as embodied by Obama is entrapped by a cruel optimism that is governed by an impossibility of Obama to deliver. Berlant states that within the condition of cruel optimism "the risk of attachment taken in its throes manifests an intelligence beyond rational calculation" (2011: 2). In the rather brief analysis of Obama, in her book *Cruel Optimism* (2011) published after the election of Obama, Berlant inquires: "What is the effect of Obama's optimization of political optimism against the political depression of the historically disappointed, especially given any President's limited sovereignty as a transformative agent in ordinary life?" (2011: 228). Speaking more generally, she notes that

> the *affective* structure of an optimistic attachment involves a sustaining inclination to return to the scene of fantasy that enables you to expect that *this* time, nearness to *this* thing will help you or a world to become different in just the right way.
>
> (2011: 2)

In this regard, the attachments produced in the 2012 election can be seen to be a remanifestation, operating through a nostalgic layering of the fantasy scenes of the 2008 election. The 2012 election was partly a simulacrum of the previous momentous election. In speeches and film productions, Obama himself mentions that moment to reactivate a remembrance of the emotive highs of that specific political time, for the purposes of now. The timeline of "Forward" is thus intimately tied to the large-scale active support provided in 2008, at a time when the active participation was reduced and muted in 2012.

We can read local and global attachments toward Obama as being organized by both the *potential* as well as the *limits* of his racial agency. There is the coexistence of pasts and *speculative political futures*. During the 2008 US pre-election rallies and especially abroad, Obama often smiled when he remarked: "I don't look like the faces on dollar bills." As he paused, knowingly and expectedly, crowds would roar after this remark. Obama frequently capitalized on statements that played on his outsiderness, as he did at one of his most famous speeches—the key note address at the July 27, 2004 Democratic National Convention—"Tonight is a particular honor to me because, let's face it, my presence on this stage is pretty unlikely." Being an unknown, freshman senator, who in his own words was an "improbable front-runner," his newness was in one respect a huge liability but in another sense a virtue, a capacity that allowed him to be seen to be what he declared to be, the face of *hope* and *change*.

It is no simple coincidence that Obama makes reference to the dollar bill. National myth-making is forged in the stories that are told through the figures and landscapes which appear on money (Helleiner 1998). Heritage is thus made on paper and metal in the co-production of nations and transnational commodification. The designs embedded in money are an incorporating and inscribed practice of memory, rather like monuments (Connerton 1989). But more so, money is handled and touched by vast populations everyday as it undergoes constantly shifting exchange value. Since the early part of the 20th century, the faces of the presidents including George Washington, Thomas Jefferson, Abraham Lincoln (as well as treasury statesmen) have all featured on American dollar bills. The history of colonization is central to the imagery that has been embalmed on the cotton linen notes and the coins. The money factory (the US Bureau of Engraving and Printing), in keeping with the narrative of history, memory and nation, refers to the portraits on the cotton linen dollar bills as those of the "Founding Fathers." The notes are always designed and undersigned by the Treasury. The signatures (not the faces) of five African Americans who occupied prominent positions in the treasury have borne their traces on the currency.[3]

Given this national history of white male elites, in the exchange that ensued after Obama's performative enactment of the utterance "I don't look like the faces on dollar bills" during the 2008 primaries, he was able to draw on the transformative tension and potential of his "outsider" status. Some aggressively and blatantly have presented his outsiderness as a liability and a threat to the American nation as a *de-legitimizing* mechanism. Others, at least initially, drew suspicion from this unknown and difficult to categorize entity, wondering: "Who is Barack Obama?" (Remnick 2010: 3). Knowing this, Obama responded to the undercurrent of doubt that hung over him, by making his *outsiderness* into a political virtue: Turning what made him into a liability into a strength. He worked on his denigrated strangeness and foreignness into an asset through which he could tell through his story, a story of America that his contenders or previous presidents had not embodied. The constitutive properties of Obama as both an outsider with a racialized body and a uniquely multicultural American story, were activated in the theatrical grammar of rhetorical exchange; a cogently dialogic call-and-response between him and his diverse audiences. Obama was able to signal the historical repertoires of racial exclusion that have marked the making of democracy and U.S. presidential leadership, while at the same time calling on the desires to unleash the potential for liberation that was betrayed in America's founding dream of opportunity. His seemingly Svengali-like abilities to hail audiences was built on harnessing his capacities as a raced figure who reckons with the troubled U.S. racial past, and whose very im/possible arrival can deliver an alternative futurity; one that carries the productive forces of hope and change for audiences. Indeed, the very *im*possibility of what stood before audiences on podiums in 2008, a black figure running for the presidential office for the very first time, augmented his capacities. Obama is a figure who is racialized, yet, at the same time, euphorically imagined to be not exactly beyond "race" but at least more than race. It is the perceived historical im/possibility of Obama—especially on the global stage—that generates fervor among his supporters and critics.

His former Democratic Party opponent in 2008, Hilary Clinton, could not have riffed on the dollar bill to the same affect (even on the grounds of gender); she was clearly part of an earlier political dynasty. Barack Hussein Obama was a freshman senator with an "exotic" name and not the known Clinton brand name. While there was no way he could escape his heavily derided and amplified name—associated with being a Muslim, terrorist, "other," and close to Saddam Hussein—at the same time Obama captured the processes of de-legitimation to tell a different story of foreigners coming to and making America. He trumped this further by playing the candidate who was not part of the partisan wrangling in Washington and instead had a remit that was post-partisan *and* post-race (Ceaser, Busch, and Pitney 2009: 16).

Biographical Discord

To grasp the irreducible tension embodied by Obama, we can briefly turn to his biographical past. Obama is exemplary as a figure whose biography and history of social mobility are inextricably interwoven. His personal upbringing has been well documented, especially through the publication of his autobiography, *Dreams of my Father*. While he was raised by (white) grandparents of modest means, he also had the cultural capital of an intellectual and internationally minded (white) mother. Although he spent little time in the company of his biological father, his absence and often alienating presence was influential for instilling a worldly outlook in Barack Obama. His father (Barack Hussein Sr.), a Lou from western Kenya, is usually characterized as a goat herder, yet he was an economist who won scholarships to study in Nairobi and Hawaii (where he met Obama's mother at a Russian language class), as well as to Harvard. The Lou ethnic group is known for its diasporic travels to improve itself. The colonial and anticolonial framework inflected these travels. A developmental-based scholarship brought Obama's father to Hawaii. His own father was a cook in World War II in the British Army and a domestic servant.

Barack Obama had spent some of his early childhood in Indonesia with his stepfather, growing up among different languages, foods, and religions that were more than simply American, (the right-wing de-legitimizers used this to claim he was schooled in a madrassa in Indonesia). His international experience was further augmented in multicultural Hawaii where he spent his teenage years. The diverse experiences at a young age no doubt registered in the future imaginative possibilities of Obama. Besides, at the age of 10, in Hawaii he went to no run-of-the-mill school. Punahou was as stated by Obama started by missionaries in 1841 and had "grown into a prestigious prep school, an incubator for island elites" (2008: 58). Here, as he did not fully belong on the basis of class and "race," he was conscious of being part of the other "misfits" in the school. He was one of only two black children in his grade. His Kenyan background was a source of discomfort and shame, not least because of the racist taunts, despite the over exuberant efforts of his school teacher to publicly indulge in his Africanness.

Attending Columbia University and studying law at Harvard provided a training ground for both his intellect and oratory verve. It is not surprising that he was able to mix campaign stops in the lead-up to the Presidential elections with his book tours for *Audacity of Hope*, a title declaring the effrontery of his personal and political position. In order to comprehend his conditions of inclusion, while he was a freshman senator devoid of the Clinton brand, he accrued a respectable habitus through a series of social life trajectories in terms of class (Bourdieu 1998). The educational routes of Obama were generative of a bodily hexis; for example, when attempting to become a politician, he was mentored to drop the overly intellectual attention to detail in speeches, for a more engaged political performance. Without doubt, Obama's educational trajectories enabled him to operate with a degree of cadence in high-profile, public and elite spaces, inculcating him with an attire that made him acceptable and respectable to this constituency, which was critical for acquiring institutional and economic support. In terms of engaging with the wider populace, at times he was even charged with being too connected to the liberal elite circles of New York, and too aloof from ordinary Americans. As Remnick notes, during the early campaigning years:

> Obama was an awkward, if earnest, novice. He was pedantic, distant, a
> little condescending at times, a better fit for the University of Chicago

seminar room than for the stump or the pulpit of a black church in Englewood. In debates, he was in the habit of crossing his legs and holding his chin up at an imperious angle while an opponent spoke, as if his mind were elsewhere or the proceedings were beneath consideration.

(Remnick 2010: 323)

Added to this disposition was his earlier existential angst as a young man over his blackness—not least of all because he was bought up by white grandparents and away from the urban politics of mainland America. Nevertheless, Obama's community involvement and the informal education it gave him in the political field, especially in Chicago, also forged his formation; as did his marriage with Michelle Obama. Unlike her husband, Michelle Obama's racial legacy was a product of black Atlantic crossings of slavery, and according to some critics on the left, helped to stabilize Barack Obama's American racial identity (Bonilla-Silva 2009).

David Remnick, in his authoritative biography of Obama *The Bridge*, summarized the tension of Obama as a productive discord, "insinuating a disqualifying otherness about the man: his childhood in Hawaii and Indonesia; his Kenyan father; his Kansas-born, yet cosmopolitan mother" (2010: 3). He mentions how Obama productively harnessed his biography to America's past and potential future. Obama took the global routes of his family—used at times by both black and white to de-legitimize his Americaness—and deployed them to offer a multicultural mirror of America as a nation. For instance, he deployed this global mixture to indicate that his family was (as progressive and future orientated) as it looked and sounded, like a UN gathering at Thanksgiving, with the latter bringing the home/national/American reference in to the fold. Remnick further details how:

Obama would make his biracial ancestry as a metaphor for his ambition to create a broad coalition of support, to rally Americans behind a narrative of moral and political progress. He was not necessarily the hero of that narrative, but he just might be its culmination. In the months to come Obama borrowed brazenly from the language and imagery of an epochal American movement and applied it to a campaign for the Presidency.

(2010: 4).

Obama's background has been central to his ability to cultivate relationships with divergent groups, including blacks, whites, Latinos, Jews, gentiles, Arabs, conservatives and liberals (Hill 2009).

Obama has been an outsider to the specific history of slavery that has defined the U.S. black experience, and his alternative multidiasporic roots have been used to delegitimize his blackness. Conversely, his position as a leader of the nation operating beyond race has been continuously scrutinized. As a universal figure of leadership, Obama has had to persistently legitimize himself, often by means of aggrandizing performative enactments. This theatrical political choreography has included the harnessing of props around him. When he gives speeches the patriotic stars and stripes flank him. He can never be seen to be American enough, precisely because of the doubt placed on him as a racialized outsider with a Muslim middle name to boot. In his speeches he incessantly portrays his nationalism—accentuating "we" and "us" Americans—by offering an indubitable, positive self-image of the nation's standing on the world stage, one that has often indexed both the transformative potential in America's political forbearers as well a positive multicultural melting-pot mirror of the present. Over and above ethnic, racial, class, and political differences he asserts the *United* States of America; one people with a passionate allegiance to the stars and stripes of America, thus providing a futurity and an image of the past built on natio-nalistic narcissism (cf. Hage 2003). The invocation of America as having progressive histories including the evidence of his own remarkable journey to presidency has been one of the ways in which Obama made claims to being a universal national political leader, as opposed to a particularized black leader. He often referred to his very arrival as an incumbent in the Presidential elections—as a racialized body with his biography—as a uniquely American possibility, one that facilitates the immigrant dreams of aspiration and opportunities built on hard graft. For instance, early on in his public appearance he was greeted by loud affirming cheers in the vast amphitheatre at the 2004 Democratic Convention when he stated "My story is part of a larger American story. that in no other country on earth is my story even possible."[4] Once again, deploying a posture that he often used that at once both acknowledged and deployed his outsiderness (as noted with his dollar bill statement) as a rallying call to the populace, and one that simultaneously offers a national narcissistic mirroring of America.

Carole Pateman (1989) has insightfully remarked that in relation to gender, because the "political lion-skin" is male, when women don it, it is exceedingly ill fitting. With racialized figures, arguably it is even more ill fitting. When "outsiders," in terms of race and gender enter privileged posi-tions that have not been historically or conceptually reserved for them, there is a performative arsenal they call on to claim universality from a body that is seen to be overly determined by its particularity. Margaret Thatcher for instance—as the first and thus far only female British prime minister—pro-duced her political persona by grafting the scripts of the imperial political doyen Winston Churchill with the chariot fires of Queen Boadicea, as well as Joan de Arc (Nunn 2002). In turn, Obama's performative arsenal has called on the revered American "Founding Father," Abraham Lincoln, whom he has frequently invoked in campaign speeches.[5] Obama's legitimiz-ing strategies have skilfully allied himself to those canonized and memor-ialized in the American psyche. It is not difficult to discover in Obama's speeches references going even further back in time in European democracies, such as Greek mythology and Roman leadership figures. These references have continued in his speeches. In the Democratic Convention of 2012 he mentioned Lincoln and Franklin Roosevelt and called on the greatness of America in the world. Obama has been adept at advancing an assemblage of political grammar that is borne with authoritative power not only via speeches, but also physical bodily gestures, the designs of buildings, stages and backdrops (including fake Greek columns!).[6] With this political assemblage, Obama has managed to situate himself at the heart of elite spaces that are not historically or conceptually reserved for raced bodies.

Race Matters

As Obama fought to be re-elected for a second term in 2012, the spectre of race continued to haunt him. When elected in 2008, a persistent concern occupying commentators seeking to come to terms with the "enigma" of Obama was: "Is he the first Black President, or is he the first President who happens to be black?" (Kovel 2009: 2). The more commentators attempted to unravel the different logics of racial ascription and designation operating in this (rhetorical) question, the more they seem compelled to declare whether the significance of race remains formative of American life, or that it has been effectively overcome. Either way, Obama's position as the President has to be reckoned with his raciality, whether a determinant of his subjecthood or an anachronism that can no longer be countenanced. It is an understatement to point out that efforts to understand the phenomenon of Obama are deeply contested. Moreover, we contend that accounts of Obama as some kind of "Zelig" celebratory figure fall short of grasping how his racialized agency is critical to situating him as a post-/racial phenomenon.

Obama can be interrogated by examining both his supporters and critics in their reckoning of his raciality. One the one hand, race deeply matters for critics both on the American left and radical right. Leftist positions contend that a black man in the White House, built by slaves and working class labor, does not mark a post-racial overcoming of discrimination in the United States.[7] On the contrary, they maintain that any talk of a post-race Obama both obfuscates the terrors of history and the brutalizing inequalities that continue to structure the life chances of all racialized peoples (Hill 2009: 77). The plethora of groups on the right, from the rabid "birthers" to Tea Party activists continue to race bait Obama, and seek to de-legitimize his authority by invoking his outsider, miscegenated Muslim ethnoracial "origins." Notably, for very different reasons, both left and right standpoints remain preoccupied with race in their encounter with Obama.

While acknowledging his post-racial reach, it would be naive to claim that Obama has been able to escape the ascriptions of race. It remains incredulous that a nominee for president—a lawyer and Senator—was compelled to publicly display his identity cards (both birth certificate and passport) to prove he was who he claimed to be, an authentic American citizen. Obama's critics and detractors continue to fabricate his perceived biography as source of threat. Mitt Romney, his contender in the 2012 election campaign, at a rally in Michigan, proudly referenced the authenticity of his own birth in America, in contrast with his rival, as is implied by innuendo in the following joke he made, standing next to his wife and running mate, Republican Paul Ryan:

> Now I love being home in this place where Ann and I were raised, where both of us were born. Ann was born in Henry Ford Hospital. I was born in Harper Hospital. No one's ever asked to see my birth certificate. They know that this is the place that we were born and raised.
>
> (August 24, 2012, Commerce, Michigan)[8]

De-legitimizing forces continue to seek to exclude, by dressing up Obama to be Muslim, a terrorist sympathizer, a foreigner, a socialist and a "race" hater who cannot be trusted to lead America. Obama functions in a deeply racialized space that relentlessly attempts to capture and contain the potential of race becoming otherwise. The threat of essentializing Obama to his raced body is for ever present. For example, during the peak of battles over U.S. health care provision in July 2009, Obama was condemned by the mainstream media for his comments that the police had "acted stupidly" in their risible arrest of the respected (black) Harvard Professor Henry Louis Gates for breaking into his own house. And even within the Democratic Party, contestations over Obama's racialization during the 2008 primaries against Hillary Clinton were manifest. Clinton's own campaign volunteers resigned over a hoax email falsely declaring that Obama was "a Muslim intent on destroying the United States" (Associated Press 2008). Perhaps more damaging was the photograph, circulated by "Clinton staffers," of Obama donning a white turban and wrap-around robe during his visit to Wajir, Kenya in 2006. The accusations by Obama's team of Clinton's campaign being "offensive fear-mongering," was met by an exemplary liberal denial of the salience of race by Clinton's campaign manager, Maggie Williams:

> If Barack Obama's campaign wants to suggest that a photo of him wearing traditional Somali clothing is divisive, they should be ashamed. Hillary Clinton has worn the traditional clothing of countries she has visited and had those photos published widely.
>
> (Associated Press 2008)

Predictably, albeit no less shocking, has been the vitriolic racist response to Obama by the American right. The deluge of odious anti-Obama racist commentary and images circulating on- and offline has been stupefying. It is not uncommon to find ape-like pictures of Obama, or more recently depicting him in primitive African dress, "with a bone through his nose and the White House with a lawn full of water melons" being displayed at some

Tea Party rallies (Zengerle 2010). Neither has the First Lady, Michelle Obama, been immune from racist portrayal. During late 2009 an offensive picture of her with monkey features ranked at the top of Google image search results for the words "Michelle Obama." Undoubtedly, one of the most disturbing images of President Obama has been the "Rape of liberty" cartoon created in response to Obama's health care plans (by the conservative blogger Darleen Click 2010). The President is gratuitously depicted as a black (gang) rapist, walking away from a weeping, naked woman in the figure of the Statue of Liberty. He sneers: "Oh, shut up and stop your whining. You gave all the consent I'll ever need Nov. 2008. Get yourself cleaned up. I'll be back—CapNTrade, Immigration, whatever. And I'll bring 'friends'."

It is easy to morally dismiss the race-baiting hysteria of the American right as puerile and despicable. And focusing on right-wingers exclusively may occlude how the figure of Obama has continuously sought to disentangle himself from the traps set for him by way of the racial particularity that has been both assigned to him, and that he has himself activated via his postcolonial agency. Many "liberal" supporters celebrate Obama's racelessness, his ability to seemingly defy and overcome racial ascription. Obama represents a future America, unshackled from its troubled racist past. Obama unsettles any easy categorizations, be they ideological, geographical, or racial. And this is more than simply alluding to his miscegenated, diasaporic background. Rather, Obama's appeal to divergent populations, both nationally and globally appears to have been based on a capacity to "universalize" a persona to the point that his morphing identity becomes a screen for the projections and desires of his diverse supporters. It is tempting to follow Sean Redmond and conclude that Obama "exists as an avatar, with multiple identities not limited to a fixed corporeal self, ground in one nation state or narrow set of political circumstances" (2010: 92).

However, the problem is that constructing Obama as an ephemeral "liquid celebrity" too readily glosses over his embodied political meanings and neoliberal formations. Take for example the popular magazines Redmond highlights that Obama has been featured in, which either celebrated the "raced" or "not-raced" status of Obama. *Vanity Fair* (2007) and *Ebony* (2008) both foregrounded Obama's black heritage in relation to other successful African Americans. In contrast, *Time* magazine (2008/9) animated Obama in red, white, and blue, his body effectively becoming the American flag.[9] According to Redmond (2010: 92), it "is a spectacular celebratory image, mass-reproducible and therefore part of the Obama brand. [he] is all colors to all people." This kind of account presents an "Avatar Obama" that can be either racialized and/or deracialized: We do not need to choose or settle on his raced or non-raced status. Obama exceeds his identity, whatever it is—it appears that he can literally be anything to everyone. After all, does this line of reasoning not explain Obama's stunning U.S. election victory, and dazzling global appeal in 2008?

It needs to be stressed that Obama's auratic appeal has not been based on simply *surpassing* his racial ascription as a celebratory, "shape-shifting" avatar. What is unique, and unexpected, is that it is precisely Obama's deterritorializing "outsider" status—that which we have identified as his post-racial agency—which imbues him with ostensible transcendent qualities of global leadership. It is Obama's ability to lever race, and assemble its force towards rupturing the universal claim to authority and command of white (male) bodies. The global celebrity status of Obama has rested on an ability to reconfigure his racial ascription via the generation of a multiplicity of intensities and affects, which arguably vitiate the exclusive leadership capacities of white bodies.

In this chapter, we have argued that the legitimacy of Obama as a candidate in 2008 and 2012 as president has been one in which he has been compelled to negotiate the charged neoliberal arena of race. The im/possibility of Obama is not simply symptomatic of the contradictions of global politics and neoliberalism. Rather, it is his capacity to lever the de-legitimizing aspects of his biography, as well as the class capital he brings to the global stage, which has activated Obama's post-racial agency (especially during elections) that has given rise to the space of his im/possibility, including the initial thunder of global attachments. The dynamics of insider/outsider attributes—symbolically, socially, and politically—place him in a tenuous location. As a contradictory "post-racial" political figure, he has been able to wade through the challenges of the 2008 election, to arrive at the door of the White House as its master rather than servant. We are yet to see if his revitalized version of hope in the 2012 election slogan of "Forward" will generate enough emotive attachments or cold rational calculations between the parties to deliver votes that offer him another term in the house.

Notes

1 Obama, Barack. Democratic Convention, September 6, 2012,
2 www.guardian.co.uk/commentisfree/2012/jun/11/obama-drone-wars-normali sation-extrajudicial-killing
3 The 1869 US dollar featured a vignette of Christopher Columbus sighting land to the left, alongside a portrait of George Washington, who was himself Commander-in-Chief of the Colonial army in 1775, before he became the first U.S. President in 1789.
4 For a detailed analysis of how this speech reflects racial healing and post-race, see Frank and McPhail (2005).
5 Some de-legitimizers have even gone as far as asserting that Obama has a Muslim revisionist reading of Lincoln!
6 This is not surprising given that the prominent frontage of the White House features Palladian and neoclassical styles of architecture.
7 Obama referred to the "Joshua generation" in a speech he gave in Selma, Alabama on March 4, 2007. Using biblical references in the church he referred to the "Moses generation" as those who were the "giants" (parents, grandparents and great grandparents) who paved the way for change, took risks, and fought the struggles, without seeing the change in fruition. The Joshua generation,

who were perhaps not so well deserving, nevertheless bear the responsibility of realising the change that previous generations had fought and pioneered the way for. This generation has to fulfil the legacy by taking current generations to the Promised Land.

8 When called to task on this statement, Romney asserted that he was working the crowd with humor and that he had no doubt that Obama was born in the United States.

9 This illustration was created by *Time* magazine commissioning the graphic artist Shepard Fairey, who will be discussed later for his original iconic 'Hope' poster image of Obama.

Bibliography

Ali, T. *The Obama Syndrome: surrender at home, war abroad* (London: Verso, 2010).

Amin. A. "Remainders of race," *Theory, Culture & Society* 2010: 27, 1, 1–23.

Associated Press. "Photo of Obama causes stir on internet," msnbc, February 2, 2008, www.msnbc.msn.com/id/23337141/

Baker, P. "Whose president is he anyway?," *New York Times*, June 4, 2008, www.nytimes.com/2008/11/16/weekinreview/16baker.html

Battiston, G. "Anticipating Obama: an interview with Zygmunt Bauman," *Thesis Eleven* 2009: 98, 140–5.

BBC News. "Growing number in America believe Obama a Muslim poll," August 19, 2010, www.bbc.co.uk/news/world-us-canada-11027568

Berlant, L. "Cruel optimism: on Marx, loss and the senses," *New Formations* 2007: 63, 33–51.

Berlant, L. *Cruel Optimism* (Durham, NC, and London: Duke University Press, 2011).

Bonilla-Silva, E. "Is the USA post-racial? Towards an explanation of the Obama 'miracle'," *Darkmatter*, 2009, www.darkmatter101.org/site/2009/11/06/is-the-usa-post-racial-towards-an-explanation-of-the-obama-miracle-audio/

Bourdieu, P. *Practical Reason: on the theory of action* (Oxford: Polity Press, 1998).

Breen, W. *Walter Breen's Complete Encyclopedia of U.S. and Colonial Coins* (New York: Doubleday, 1987).

Buck-Morss, S. "Obama and the image," *Culture, Theory and Critique* 2008: 50, 2/3, 145–64.

Carotenuo, M. and Luongo, M. "Dala or diaspora? Obama and the Luo community of Kenya," *African Affairs* 2009: 108, 431, 197–219.

Ceaser, J.W., Busch, A., and Pitney, J.J. *Epic Journey: the 2008 elections and American politics* (Plymouth: Rowan & Littlefield, 2009).

Coleman, B. "Race as technology," *Camera Obscura* 2009: 24, 1, 177–207.

Connerton, P. *How Societies Remember* (Cambridge: Cambridge University Press, 1989).

Cupp, S.E. "Barack Obama—empty vessel," *FOXNews*, November 3, 2009, www.foxnews.com/opinion/2009/11/03/secupp-obama-vessel-politician-election/

Deleuze, G. and Guattari, F. *Anti-Oedipus: capitalism and schizophrenia* (London: Athlone Press, 1984).

Deleuze, G. and Guattari, F. *A Thousand Plateaus: capitalism and schizophrenia* (London: Athlone Press, 1987).

Doty, R. *America's Money, America's Story* (Sydney, OH: Amos Press, 2008).

Frank, D.A. and McPhail, M.L. "Barack Obama's address to the 2004 Democratic National Convention: trauma, compromise, consilience, and the (im)possibility of racial reconciliation," *Rhetoric and Public Affairs* 2005: 8, 4, 571–93.

Goldberg, D.T. *The Racial State* (Oxford: Blackwell, 2002).

Goldberg, D.T. *The Threat of Race* (Oxford: Blackwell, 2009).

Grosz, E. "Thinking the new: of futures yet unthought," in Grosz, E., ed. *Becomings: Explorations in time, memory and futures* (Ithaca, NY: Cornell University Press, 1999).

Hage, G. *Against Paranoid Nationalism* (London: Pluto, 2003).

Harris, H.E., Moffitt, K.R., and Squires, C.R., eds. *The Obama Effect: multidisciplinary renderings of the 2008 campaign* (Albany, NY: State University of New York, 2010).

Helleiner, E. "National currencies and national identities," *American Behavioural Scientist* 1998: 41, 10, 1409–36.

Hill, R. "The race problematic, the narrative of Martin Luther King Jr., and the election of Barack Obama," *Souls* 2009: 11, 1, 60–78.

Jacobs, L.R. and King, D.S. "Varieties of Obamaism: structure, agency, and the Obama presidency," *Reflections* 2010: 8, 3, 793–802.

Keetley, D. and Pettegrew, J. *Public Women, Public World: a documentary history of American feminism, Vol. 3, 1960 to the present* (Lanham, MD: Rowman & Littlefield, 2005).

Kellner, D. "Celebrity diplomacy, spectacle and Barack Obama," *Celebrity Studies* 2010: 1, 1, 121–3.

Kirchner, S. "Berlin awaits the 'next JFK'," *Time*, July 23, 2008, www.time.com/time/world/article/0,8599,1825855,00.html

Kovel, J. "The Obama phenomenon," *Capitalism Nature Socialism* 2009: 20, 1, 1–5.

McClintock, A. *Imperial Leather: race, gender, and sexuality in the colonial contest* (London: Routledge, 1995).

Madiega, A.P., Chantler, T., Jones, G. and Prince, R. "'Our son Obama': the US presidential election in Western Kenya," *Anthropology Today* 2008: 24, 6, 4–6.

Marable, M. "Racializing Obama: the enigma of post-black politics and leadership," *Souls* 2009: 11, 1, 1–15.

Michaels, A.W.B. "Against diversity," *New Left Review* 2008: 52.

Mills, C.W. *The Racial Contract* (Ithaca, NY: Cornell University Press, 1997).

Nunn, H. *Thatcher, Politics and Fantasy* (London: Lawrence & Wishart, 2002).

Obama, B. *Audacity of Hope* (Edinburgh: Canongate Books, 2006).

Obama, B. *Barack Obama: dreams from my father* (Edinburgh: Canongate Books, 2008).

Papadopoulos, D., Stephenson, N., and Tsianos, V. *Escape Routes: control and subversion in the 21st century* (London: Pluto Press, 2008).

Pateman, C. *The Sexual Contract* (Stanford, CA: Stanford University Press, 1988).

Pateman, C. *The Disorder of Women: democracy, feminism and political theory* (Stanford, CA: Stanford University Press, 1989).

Powers, N. "Shepard Fairey: purveyor of hope," *suicidegirls*, 2008, http://suicidegirls.com/interviews/Shepard+Fairey:+Purveyor+of+Hope/

Puwar, N. *Space Invaders* (Oxford: Berg, 2004).

Redmond, S. "Avatar Obama in the age of liquid celebrity," *Celebrity Studies* 2010: 1, 1, 81–95.

Remnick, D. *The Bridge: the life and rise of Barack Obama* (Basingstoke, UK and Oxford: Picador, 2010).

Sharma, S. and Sharma, A. "White paranoia: orientalism in the age of empire," *Fashion Theory* 2003: 7, 4, 301–18.

Smith, R. "Dollar ReDe$ign project," 2009, http://richardsmith.posterous.com/pri vate/nrAygGGnqB

Warner, M. *Monuments and Maidens: the allegory of the female form* (Stanford, CA: University of California Press, 2000).

West, C. *Hope on a Tight Rope* (Carlsbad, CA: Smiley Books, 2008).

Zengerle, P. "Analysis: race issues beset Obama's 'post-racial' presidency," *Reuters*, July 24, 2010, www.reuters.com/article/idUSTRE66K6JN20100721?pageN umber=2

Zweigenhaft, R.L. and Domhoff, G.W. *Blacks in the White elite: will the progress continue?* (New York: Rowman & Littlefield, 2003).

13 Mormonism and the 2012 Presidential Election

Lee Marsden

The 2012 elections held out the possibility, for a short time at least, of something that would have appeared impossible just a few years previously—a Mormon in the White House. The Republican nomination of Mitt Romney, after having been beaten to the nomination four years previously by John McCain, seemed unlikely in a Republican Party that had become increasingly dominated by the white evangelicals and conservative Catholics of the Christian Right and the Tea Party. Would the base of the Republican Party work and vote for a candidate many considered to be part of a cult? If they were prepared to do so how would the rest of the electorate respond? Would they, too, be willing to vote for a candidate who had served as bishop in a religious organization representing slightly less than 2 percent of the American population? This essay considers what has become known as the "Mormon moment," before considering Mormon beliefs and their impact on support for Romney within the Republican Party primaries and the extent to which this affected the election campaign. In the aftermath of the election, it examines how attitudes to Mormonism have changed among the key constituent parts of the Republican Party before concluding that Romney's faith was not a decisive issue in the election campaign and that the prospects of a future Mormon presidency have been enhanced.

The Mormon Moment

The candidacy of Mitt Romney coincided with what *Newsweek* magazine described as the "Mormon moment." Not only was Romney running again but fellow Mormon Jon Huntsman was one of the early declared candidates. The Senate was led by co-religionist Harry Reid, while popular culture appeared dominated by Mormonism including Stephanie Meyer, author of the best-selling Twilight vampire novels, Glenn Beck, the radio show and television personality, HBO's "Big Love" series, and the big-budget Broadway musical *Book of Mormon* (Applebome, 2011; *Newsweek* 2011). While Americans still knew little about the religion, or held misconceptions about Mormonism, the Church of Jesus Christ of Latter-Day Saints received unprecedented interest and publicity. Whether this would harm or benefit a

Romney candidacy was a question that clearly had to be addressed, particularly by Republican voters in the first instance and later by the electorate as a whole.

Mormon Beliefs and the Republican Party

White conservative evangelicals make up a significant proportion of the Republican base and have traditionally been concerned with social issues around abortion, same sex marriage, traditional family values, and abstinence outside marriage, opposition to homosexuality and stem cell research, support for Israel, small government, and school prayer. The main distinguishing feature of this grouping, however, is belief in the literal truth of the Bible and that the only way to salvation lies in repenting of your sin and accepting Jesus Christ as your personal saviour. Such a belief is prescriptive and exclusive and finds Mormonism theologically troublesome. However, not all conservative evangelicals are theologians or pastors and so many do accept Mormons as fellow believers. According to a Pew Forum survey undertaken in late 2011, 54 percent of Republican voters felt the Mormons were Christian while 33 percent felt that they were not. For white evangelicals, however, these statistics are reversed with 35 percent agreeing that Mormons were Christian while 53 percent felt they were not (Pew Forum 2011).

Of the 13 tenets of the Church of Jesus Christ of Latter-day Saints just two are problematic for evangelicals:

> 8 We believe the Bible to be the word of God as far as it is translated correctly; we also believe the Book of Mormon to be the word of God. [...]
> 10 We believe in the literal gathering of Israel and in the restoration of the Ten Tribes; that Zion (the New Jerusalem) will be built upon the American continent; that Christ will reign personally upon the earth; and, that the earth will be renewed and receive its paradisiacal glory.
> (Church of Jesus Christ of Latter-Day Saints 2013).

The suggestion that the Book of Mormon is equal to the Bible is decidedly problematic, as is the idea of Zion being built in America. Other tenets may contain elements that are critiqued by evangelicals but for Mormons themselves, there is little doubt of their bona fide Christian credentials. A Pew Forum survey examining Mormon beliefs conducted in late 2011 revealed that 97 percent of Mormons considered themselves to be Christian, with a slightly higher number believing in the resurrection of Jesus (Pew Forum 2011: 10). The similarity with conservative evangelicals is manifest with over three-quarters saying they attend church at least once a week, 7 percent claim to tithe to the church, and over 80 percent say they pray every day. Three-quarters of Mormons surveyed considered abortion morally wrong with only 4 percent saying that it was morally acceptable and nearly 80 percent felt that sex outside marriage between adults was morally wrong (Pew Forum 2011: 15). For some, this was not enough and a plethora of Christian right websites emerged or changed their emphasis to challenge the idea that Mormonism is Christian at all (see Christian Research and Counsel website).

The Republican Primaries

From announcing his candidacy Mitt Romney was the candidate to beat in the Republican primaries. The former Massachusetts governor brought to the campaign a considerable personal fortune and invaluable experience from the 2008 elections where he was eventually beaten to the nomination by John McCain. He had the additional advantage of the two preferred candidates of the Christian right, Sarah Palin and Mike Huckabee, declining to stand. The issue of his Mormonism had in large part been addressed in his speech "Faith in America," delivered for the previous campaign in December 2007. Hailed as his "Kennedy moment" from a similar speech delivered by John F. Kennedy to reassure critics about his Catholicism during the 1960 campaign, Romney sought to assuage people's fear of his religious beliefs. Unlike Kennedy, who cited the separation clause in the constitution and reinforced the division of civil and religious, Romney encouraged discussion of his faith and appealed to conservative evangelicals and Catholics in particular by tackling their doubts head on: "There is one fundamental question about which I often am asked. What do I believe about Jesus Christ? I believe that Jesus Christ is the Son of God and the Savior of mankind" (Romney 2007: para. 16). Again unlike Kennedy, Romney rather than appeal to the constitution invited his audience to pray (Kaylor 2011: 503).

Romney had a further advantage entering the primary season that even if the "Faith in America" speech had not convinced the Christian right in the base of the Republican Party the bigger rubicon of race had already been crossed with Obama's election victory. Obama had had to endure four years of prominent Republicans attempting to persuade the wider public that the new president was both a Muslim, and possibly not even an American citizen at all, and yet was favorite to be returned to office. In comparison, Romney's Mormonism was relatively insignificant. Far more problematic than his religion was his liberal record when governor. Opponents sought to juxtapose Obama's welfare reforms with similar reforms the former governor had introduced in Massachusetts and to question the veracity of his conversion from leaning towards pro-choice on abortion to the pro-life position he presented in the campaign. George W. Bush had demonstrated that in order to win the Republican Party nomination it is necessary to court the Christian right. Since leaving office the influence of these religious actors on Republican politics had grown further. Romney in order to secure the Republican nomination would be obliged to tack further to the right and espouse domestic policies that would appeal to this audience.

Romney was not the obvious choice of white evangelicals, despite Mormons being even more supportive of conservative positions in the U.S. culture wars than members of those churches. Michele Bachmann, a leading figure in the Tea Party movement and Rick Perry, Governor of Texas are both prominent conservative evangelicals, while Newt Gingrich, former speaker of the House, and Rick Santorum, former governor of Pennsylvania, are Catholics, and Ron Paul, serial election campaigner, is a mainstream Protestant. These five alternative candidates would fit the preferred presidential profile for white conservative evangelicals and Catholics if the only consideration were religious belief. However, the Christian right as a movement is not centrally organized or coordinated. Its most prominent figures had either died or were entering semi-retirement, including Jerry Falwell, Pat Robertson, and James Dobson by the 2012 elections. Tony Perkins of the Family Research Council played a highly vocal role in the campaign organizing Value Voters summits, and a tour bus to argue the social issues in local campaigning and even attempting to get rival candidates to pool their support behind one candidate who would campaign on a socially conservative agenda approved by the Christian right (Martin 2012). The preferred candidate for the assembled religious leaders was Rick Santorum after earlier surges by Herman Cain, Newt Gingrich, and Rick Perry as the stop-Romney candidate. However, grassroots conservative evangelicals and Catholics preferred to support the candidate with most prospect of defeating Barack Obama in the main event.

Presidential Elections 2012

The Republican nomination was secured for Romney when Rick Santorum withdrew, aware that the religious right vote was slipping away from him. During the primaries Romney was able to regularly secure between 25 and 35 percent of the white evangelical support despite the best efforts of Perkins and others to rally support behind non-Mormon candidates. Once the nomination was secure the religious right including its leadership backed Romney emphasizing what they had in common on social and international issues and their differences with their democratic opponents. In 2008 the Christian right had backed McCain because of the belief that he was the strong leader necessary to protect America's security in a volatile world and advance U.S. national interests. The financial crisis changed the nature of the election and ended prospects of a Republican victory. In 2012 while Romney's reputation among the Republican base was as someone suspect on social issues, he sought to promote a foreign policy position that accorded with the established republican position. To a large extent, he sought to mirror Obama's policies but promising to be tougher on Iran, Russia, and China, to re-engage with Latin America to counter the Bolivarian revolution, and to be more supportive of Israel (Romney 2011). Such language resonated with Republicans and in particular the base.

Romney's support from born-again/evangelicals who make up 23 percent of the electorate was even higher than Bush obtained—79 percent with 20 percent voting for Obama. McCain managed to secure just 73 percent support from this group with 26 percent voting for Obama. Among white Catholics, Romney improved by 7 percentage points on the 52 percent secured by McCain and reduced support to Obama from 47 percent down to 42 percent; 78 percent of Mormons voted for Romney compared to only 21 percent who voted for Obama, remarkably similar to the margins of preference shown by born-again/ evangelicals (Pew Forum 2012b).

Despite winning over the religious right, Romney still lost the elections, failing to persuade women and ethnic minorities to vote for him. In order to win the Republican Party nomination, a prospective candidate is obliged to court the religious right but in securing the nomination, loses the wider population who appear alienated by social policies that are considered divisive. The base of the Republican Party has become increasingly narrow and, as is observed elsewhere in this book, increasingly white. The demographic shift in America's population where more non-white people are born each year means the size of the white protestant population has shrunk from 45 to 39 percent and the white Catholic population from 21 to 18 percent (Pew Forum 2012b); 59 percent of white voters backed Romney but 55 percent of women voted for Obama and only 45 percent for Romney, black voters decided for Obama 93 percent against 6 percent, Hispanics 71 percent to 27 percent, and Asian 73 percent to 26 percent (Statista 2012). The issue in the 2012 election would appear to be not so much Romney's religion but his policies and the narrow base of support with a lack of appeal to key demographics including women, who make up a majority of the electorate, and ethnic minorities who will soon represent a majority of the electorate.

Changing Attitudes to Mormonism

The year 2012 was not to be the Mormon moment or indeed the Romney moment. Indeed, the candidate's faith ceased to be an issue after he had successfully secured the Republican nomination and born-again evangelical and white Catholics came out to support him in record numbers (in percentage terms). For the electorate, his faith was a non-issue; apart from the curiosity of thinking about the candidate's sacred undergarments and secret rituals in the temple, it was the issues and the electorate's perception of the sort of society they would like to live in that determined the outcome of the election. When questioned about how much they had learned about Mormonism in the 2012 election campaign, 82 percent of respondents claimed that they had learnt not very much or nothing at all (Pew Forum 2012b: 1). For white evangelicals, however, they had learned more about the Church of Jesus Christ of Latter-Day Saints. The Pew Forum survey asked religious groups whether they felt they were more different or had a lot in common with Mormons. In 2007 66 percent of white evangelicals, 56 percent of white mainline Protestants and 61 percent of white Catholics considered they had greater difference, with 24, 32, and 25 percent, respectively, believing that they had a lot in common. Interestingly, by the start of the presidential campaign in November 2011 the numbers, considering they had more differences with Mormonism, rose among white evangelicals to 70 percent and white Catholics to 68 percent, while mainline white Protestants remained the same. After the 2012 election the number of white evangelicals considering they had a lot in common with Mormons had risen to 27 percent, white mainline protestant to 42 percent and white Catholics to 27 percent. Now only 61 percent of white evangelicals felt that they were different from Mormons (Pew Forum 2012b: 2). These figures do not represent a seismic shift in Christian right perceptions of Mormonism but they do reflect that there has been some movement and acceptance of what they have in common.

Conclusion

The 2012 elections offered a fleeting glimpse of what it might be like to have a Mormon in the White House. This chapter has sought to demonstrate that such a scenario was conceivable and that it was policy and a dwindling Republican support base rather than antagonism to Romney's faith that handed the election to Obama. Although the white evangelical and Catholic base of the Republican Party remain unconvinced about the extent of similarities between their faiths and that of Latter-Day Saints these differences have not proved insurmountable. Indeed, greater awareness of Mormonism has brought an appreciation for the shared social, moral, and traditional family values they hold in common. Mitt Romney secured marginally greater support than that enjoyed by white evangelical President George W. Bush from Bush's natural demographic but it was insufficient to secure the election. In appealing to this powerful movement within the Republican Party, the candidate secured the party nomination but, in the process, ensured he would not win the presidency because of alienating independent voters and more moderate voices within his own party. The Christian right have showed considerable pragmatism in backing McCain in 2008 and Romney in 2012 as the more credible candidates rather than supporting a weaker white evangelical or Catholic candidate. The prospect of defeating Obama took precedence over religious belief. The Romney tilt at the presidency will have done Mormonism no harm in promoting itself as an all-American religion where most co-religionists share religious right values. Romney did not make the breakthrough for fellow Mormons in the same way J.F. Kennedy did for Catholics or Obama did for African Americans and, indeed, a Mormon might never occupy the White House unless the Republican party breaks free from being a party that mainly appeals to white males, conservative evangelicals, and conservative white Catholics.

Bibliography

Applebome, P. "A Mormon spectacle, way off Broadway," *New York Times*, July 13, 2011.

Christian Research and Counsel. "What Mormons don't tell," Christian Research and Counsel, 2011, http://crcmin.org/What_Mormons_Dont_Tell.html

Church of Jesus Christ of Latter-Day Saints. "The articles of faith of the Church of Jesus Christ of Latter-Day Saints," 2013, www.lds.org/scriptures/pgp/a-of-f/1?lang=eng

Kaylor, B. "No Jack Kennedy: Mitt Romney's 'faith in America' spech and the changing religious-political environment," *Communication Studies* 2011: 62, 5, 491–507.

Martin, J. "Social conservatives back Rick Santorum," *Politico*, January 14, 2012, http://www.politico.com/blogs/burns-haberman/2012/01/social-conservatives-back-santorum-110869.html

Newsweek. "Mormons rock!," *Newsweek*, June 5, 2011.

Pew Forum on Religion and Public Life. *Romney's Mormon faith likely a factor in primaries, not in a general election* (Washington, DC: Pew Forum on Religion and Public Life, 2011).

Pew Forum on Religion and Public Life. *Mormons in America: certain in their beliefs, uncertain of their place in society* (Washington, DC: Pew Forum on Religion and Public Life, 2012a).

Pew Forum on Religion and Public Life. "How the faithful voted: 2012 preliminary analysis," November 7, 2012b, www.pewforum.org/Politics-and-Elections/How-the-Faithful-Voted-2012-Preliminary-Exit-Poll-Analysis.aspx

Romney, M. "Faith in America," December 6, 2007, www.npr.org/templates/story/story.php?storyId = 16969460

Romney, M. *An American Century: a strategy to secure America's enduring interests and ideals* (Washington, DC: Romney for President, Inc., 2011).

Statista. "Statistics and facts on the 2012 US election," 2012, www.statista.com/topics/893/2012-election

Notes on Contributors

Lisa García Bedolla is an Associate Professor in Language and Literacy, Society and Culture at Berkeley Graduate School of Education, University of California.

Heidi Beirich is Director of Research at the Southern Poverty Law Center, Montgomery, Alabama.

Robert Busby is a Senior Lecturer in Politics, History, Media, and Communication at Liverpool Hope University.

Desmond S. King is Andrew W. Mellon Professor of American Government at the University of Oxford.

Michael L. Krenn is a Professor of History at Appalachian State University.

Mark Ledwidge, Senior Lecturer in the Department of History and American Studies, has been appointed Vacation Visiting Research Fellow at the prestigious Rothermere American Institute (RAI), University of Oxford. Dr Ledwidge, who is also a founding member of the Arts and Humanities Research Council Network on the Presidency of Barack Obama, his research focuses on the relationship and impact of African Americans on U.S. foreign policy. It provides a unique insight into the effect race and ethnicity has had upon U.S. foreign policy, as well as highlighting how race has been relatively excluded from mainstream theories in international relations.

Kevin J. McMahon is Associate Professor of Political Science at Trinity College, Connecticut.

Lee Marsden is a Senior Lecturer in International Relations in the School of Political, Social, and International Studies at the University of East Anglia.

Inderjeet Parmar currently teaches in the Department of International Politics at City University London, having for the previous 21 years taught at the University of Manchester. His latest book is *Foundations of the American Century: Ford, Carnegie, and Rockefeller Foundations in the Rise of American Power*. He is President of the British International Studies Association and Chair of the Obama Research Network.

Carl Pedersen is Adjunct Professor at the Copenhagen Business School.

Nirmal Puwar is a Senior Lecturer in the Department of Sociology at Goldsmiths, University of London.

Evelyn Schlatter is a researcher at the Southern Poverty Law Center, Montgomery, Alabama.

Sanjay Sharma is a Senior Lecturer in Sociology and Communications at Brunel University.

Rogers M. Smith is Christopher H. Browne Distinguished Professor of Political Science at the University of Pennsylvania.

Kevern Verney is a Professor in American History and Associate Dean in the Faculty of Arts and Sciences at Edge Hill University in the United Kingdom. Together with Professor Inderjeet Parmar and Dr Mark Ledwidge he is currently a co-organizer of the Barack Obama Research Network funded by the Arts and Humanities Research Council.

Index

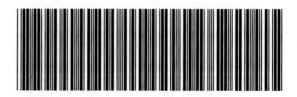